FOUR SYSTEMS

FOUR SYSTEMS

Carl Cohen
The University of Michigan

Random House New York

First Edition
98765
Copyright © 1982 by Random House, Inc.

Library of Congress Cataloging in Publication Data

Cohen, Carl, 1931-
    Four systems.

    Includes index.
    1. Democracy. 2. Fascism. 3. Communism.
4 . Socialism. I. Title.
JC348.C64   321   81-13949
ISBN 0-394-32531-1   AACR2

Manufactured in the United States of America

This book is dedicated to the memory of my sister, Bryna Graff.

"Justice, justice shalt thou pursue."

TO THE READER

Governments set the frames of our lives. They establish policies and make decisions that limit our freedoms, affect our economic well-being, and contribute greatly to our happiness and to our discontents. Which system of government is best—for each of us individually, or for all of us collectively—is therefore a question of great and universal concern. It is also a question around which bitter disagreements have long raged. The aim of this book is to present, concisely and fairly, the strongest case that can be made in support of four conflicting systems of government.

Each of these systems—socialist democracy, individualist democracy, fascism, and communism—is defended, in turn, in the authentic voice of its advocates. The best arguments for each are given their most forceful statements. I try to represent each with complete honesty, holding nothing back, distorting nothing to the advantage of one system or the disadvantage of another. I try to defend each so persuasively that its wise and earnest supporters would say, upon reading my account, "Yes, that's just what we mean—and that's just the way we would say it ourselves."

Each of these defenses is *serious* in that it makes a case for a system of government that is and has been widely and enthusiastically espoused. Fascism and communism, as well as the varieties of democracy, are not merely academic possibilities, but genuine systems that have won the loyalty and intellectual support of deep thinkers and ordinary citizens. It is a grave mistake to caricature any of these systems, to erect a straw man to serve as a foil for the system to which we have in fact committed ourselves in advance. That common mistake breeds superficiality. It results in failure to comprehend why statesmen, political scientists, philosophers, and whole nations have adopted world views conflicting with our own. We may be right—whichever view is ours —and they wrong, but we will remain puzzled by their conduct and by their enthusiasm until we have heard and understood the best case that can be made in their defense. To appreciate that best case we must—at least for a while—adopt their perspectives, feel their concerns, follow their reasoning. We must think and empathize with each serious spokesman in turn.

Each of these defenses is *deep* in that it makes the case for its system on the most solid foundation possible. Political systems rely not merely upon rhetoric, or tradition, or force—though all of these are used, of course—but also upon reasoned beliefs. Each system rests upon a different set of fundamental premises about the nature of human beings, their needs and capacities, their rights and obligations, their histories and aspirations. The best case for each will be firmly built upon these premises and will give evidence from history and from common life in their support. Each case, therefore, encompasses both abstract arguments and the application of these arguments to concrete circumstances. Details may be bypassed, but the roots and the realities of each must be exposed.

Each of these defenses is *passionate* in that it makes the case for its system not coldly, with a clinical treatment of argument and evidence, but with the warmth and enthusiasm that a loyal advocate will exhibit in real life. Rights and freedoms are much more than topics for academic discussion; they are so precious that people will fight and even die for them. Naturally, therefore, they argue in defense of what they think just—government by the many or by the few, the primacy of the individual or the state or the class, the centrality of economics or politics or morality—in words and tones that convey the intensity of their convictions. I try to capture that spirit, bringing the arguments to life with inflection and phrasing that reveal the feelings as well as the judgments of the human beings represented.

But isn't emotion out of place in rational argument? If right and wrong in matters of government can be objectively determined—as the advocates of all four systems believe—won't enthusiasm obscure the truth and mislead the unsophisticated? It may, but it need not. There is no incompatibility between a sound defense and its effective formulation; effectiveness involves much more than heat. In this John Stuart Mill gave good counsel. We ought to determine our verdict, he wrote, after considering both the substance and the manner of each advocate,

> . . . condemning everyone, on whichever side of the argument he places himself, in whose mode of advocacy either want of candor, or malignity, bigotry, or intolerance of feeling manifest themselves; but not inferring these vices from the side which a person takes, though it be the contrary side of the question to our own: and giving merited honor to everyone, whatever opinion he may hold, who has calmness to see and honesty to state what his opponents and their opinions really are, exaggerating nothing to their discredit, keeping nothing back which tells, or can be supposed to tell, in their favor. This is the real morality of public discussion: and if often violated, I am happy to think that there are many controversialists who to a great extent observe it, and a still greater number who conscientiously strive towards it" (*On Liberty,* Chapter 2).

The most effective advocate of each system of government will be one who combines the virtues of intellect and spirit, who is enthusiastic but honest, penetrating in argument, and personally convinced. The full force of each system is best exhibited in its most persuasive defense.

A delicate problem arises here. To be persuasive, earnest advocates tend to emphasize the strengths of their own case, the weaknesses of their opponents' cases. There is a temptation to color the true state of affairs, to gloss over failings in one's own system while exaggerating those in others. How, then, can we expect a balanced account of any one of these systems? From its own defenders we cannot. Just for that reason we should not be content to hear one case alone, especially that one toward which we may have some prejudicial leanings. The several cases contend with one another. In each case, flaws are better elucidated by incisive critics than by evasive or confusing advocates. Each defender will strike without reservation at the others; each will try to ward off attacks foreseen. What the fascist would soft-pedal, we can rely upon the democrat to underscore; what the democrat may omit, the fascist will spotlight. The faults of individualism, and of socialism, will each be grist for the mill of the other. The defense of each system, taken singly, should be understood as the best sets of arguments *from that point of view.* But the points of view differ vastly. True balance comes in the presentation of all four cases; it arises from the tension among competing advocates aware of their opposition.

Each advocate will present a defense of his own system in its *ideal* form. He will exhibit the benefits and extoll the justice of his system when it functions at its best, in the best of circumstances. Opposing systems he will criticize for their practical failures in the real world. We must therefore avoid a common mistake: comparing the ideals of one system with the realities of another. We must be careful to weigh ideals against ideals, and realities against realities. On both levels—as competing theoretical constructs, and as rival practical solutions to human problems —these four systems must be judged.

A word about the structure of the book is in order. The four systems—socialist democracy, individualist democracy, fascism, and communism—are not simply coordinate; they have complicated interrelations. Because two of them are varieties of democracy (socialist and individualist), the arguments that support both of these come before the arguments for each of them separately. This general defense of democracy I call the Prologue. Upon that foundation the special case for socialist democracy (System One) and then that for individualist democracy (System Two) are constructed. A short concluding note on democracy in general highlights the chief agreements and disagreements of the first two systems. Fascism (System Three) and communism (System Four) require no such combination and receive no such review.

The need to be scrupulously fair in allocating space to the competing advocates gives rise to an apparent—but unreal— inequity. The special case for socialist democracy receives (it will be seen) far fewer pages than that for individualist democracy. Later in the book, however, extensive arguments against capitalism and individualism—arguments that strengthen the case of the social democrat—are incorporated in the case for communism, which is sharply distinct from that for socialism in what it proposes, but related to that case in what it condemns. Equity in the apportionment of space is to be found—as is all balancing of the opposing arguments—not in any one section, or two, but in the structure of the whole.

No conclusions are drawn in this book. For the author to extract a political moral, or to score final points for one system against the others, would betray the entire enterprise. These arguments are not charades. If, when all is said, I have a rational preference for one among the systems presented, I earnestly hope that it cannot be detected within these pages.

It cannot be true, of course, that two (or more) of these systems are both (or all) right. It is conceivable that all of them are wrong, or that on such matters there is no right and wrong. And more than one system may share a given principle. But each denies much of what the others assert, and each asserts much that the others deny. Therefore, if one of these systems is sound, as a whole, the others are not sound. Which system we ought to adopt, and why, remains for each of us to decide.

I make two requests. I ask, first, that the reader join my enterprise by making up for deficiencies that may be encountered in each defense. All my efforts to be fair, to put the best case in the best way for each system, may neglect arguments thought to be important, or may give too much or not enough weight to some considerations. I urge the reader to fill gaps that may be found and, where there is imbalance, to reestablish the balance I had sought to achieve. Then, with a perfected view of the arguments in tension, each reader can more wisely make the needed judgments.

Finally, I ask the reader to approach the defense of each system with an unprejudiced spirit and a mind truly open. Bias and doctrine are embedded so deeply in us that impartiality is extremely difficult to sustain. But if there is truth to be found in these matters, we need to find it. Resolving such monumental issues wisely, in our own minds and for our communities, is so very important that it behooves us to use in judgment all the intelligence, experience, humanity, and good sense that we can muster.

CONTENTS

System Three: Fascism 117

System Four: Communism 173

FOUR
SYSTEMS

PROLOGUE
DEMOCRACY

1. Anarchism

By what right does government govern? Legislators, policemen, and judges tell us what we must do and what we may not do. Who or what gives them the authority to rule over us? What *justifies* any system of government?

Anarchists insist that *no* government can be justified. They reason as follows. All governments compel obedience to their laws. All compulsion is inconsistent with free, voluntary action by individual citizens. Free voluntary action is presupposed by true morality. Every state, therefore, in enforcing its laws, forces its citizens to forfeit their autonomy—and thus every state subverts morality. States and governments are intrinsically coercive; they can be powerful, but they cannot be moral.

By what right does government govern? By no right. The state is the enemy of morality (the anarchist concludes), and all right-thinking people are enemies of the state.

This conclusion is profoundly mistaken—and yet the argument seems plausible. If morality presupposes individual autonomy, and every government denies that autonomy, then no government can be morally justified. Where is the mistake?

2. Autonomy

Autonomy *is* the cornerstone of morality; the anarchist is not mistaken about that. For an act to be moral in the fullest sense, the actor must do it out of respect for a rule he imposes upon himself, not out of fear or habit. Two persons may act in ways that are on the surface indistinguishable, both (for example) returning lost property to its rightful owner. If one does so as an application of a self-imposed moral rule, while the other acts merely out of prudence, we do not need the help of moral philosophers to see that the former—the self-legislating, autonomous actor—is the more honorable.

Autonomy, although necessary for complete morality, is not sufficient for it. Autonomous actors, even if well-meaning, may do wrong, like Robin Hood and Pancho Villa. They may even be bad, like Stalin or Lady Macbeth. Autonomy is not itself a virtue, but the requisite condition of virtue. If we know only that an act is self-legislated, we know nothing about *what* was done, but a great deal about *how* it was done. With autonomy conduct might not be right; without autonomy it cannot be fully moral. Full moral approval of an agent requires not only that the acts performed be in accordance with good rules, but also that the rules obeyed be truly self-imposed. That, as Kant taught, is part of our common rational understanding of morality.

The anarchist confronts us with this problem: How can moral autonomy be maintained in the face of governmental authority? When the commands of the state coincide with those a citizen gives himself, no conflict arises. But governments *enforce* laws; they make people do what otherwise they would not do. Not just tyrannical government (says the anarchist), but every government imposes laws upon its citizens from without. I may be obliged to stop at a stop sign, or wear a seat belt, even when I am convinced that safety does not require it. I may be obliged to pay a tax I think unfair. Can *state*-legislation be consistent with *self*-legislation? Yes, it can.

3. Commitment and Democracy

Autonomy does not consist in doing whatever one pleases. Autonomous action is legislated, although that legislation issues from one's self. Rules for conduct, even if they are one's own rules, entail constraints. These restraints are sometimes hard-

ships. We are obliged, *because* we are self-legislating, to do sometimes what we might prefer not to do, or to refrain from doing
what would please us.

Can such obligations be morally justified? Of course they
can. They are justified by self-*commitment*. We are governed by
our own rules because of the self-imposed obligation to keep our
word.

That obligation is realized when we give our word to others.
If I agree to pay a man five hundred dollars to paint my barn, and
he does the job satisfactorily, I may not refuse to pay him because, after the agreement, I established a new rule for myself
never to buy or sell labor. I may adopt that rule for the future,
but doing so cannot cancel my debt to the man I hired. Part of
my self-government is the restriction upon my own conduct arising from commitments I make deliberately. The promises I give,
the contracts I entered upon, are among these.

In real life we make many commitments—to other people, to
ourselves, and sometimes to institutions. Some commitments are
made in writing, others orally or through our conduct; they differ
in strength and importance. The web of commitments that we
build provides the framework of our moral lives. Moral conflicts
result from tangles in this web.

Some strong commitments are made between individuals
and their governments; this explains the possibility of the moral
justification of government. Although we are autonomous moral
agents, we are constrained by our voluntary commitments to our
fellow citizens, our community. These constraints may be expressed in laws—and such laws we have an obligation to obey. In
obeying them we do not forfeit our autonomy. On the contrary,
we would be untrue to ourselves if we did not respect them.

The anarchist's mistake is the failure to appreciate the obligations that flow from a self-commitment to obey the law. These
obligations can arise under democratic governments only.
Democratic governments alone are based upon participation. By
participating in civic life, every citizen makes commitments to the
community. That participation renders the authority of government legitimate; only participation in making the laws can justify
the moral obligation to obey them.

In a democracy—but only in a democracy—each citizen has
a right to a voice in the lawmaking process. Enjoyment of this

right commits the citizen to respect the laws resulting from that process. The agreement to participate is not contingent upon getting one's own way. Each citizen knows, even before learning what issues will arise, that no one will always get his way. But believing the legislative process fair, each person is committed in advance to observe the rules that are its outcome. To that system, full consent is given. Governments derive their just powers from this consent of the governed.

Democracy alone—of all possible systems of government—can reconcile the autonomy of the citizen with the authority of the state. No aristocracy or despotism, however benevolent, can effect that reconciliation. Every authoritarian system must and will deny the moral autonomy of its citizens. Here lies the key to what democracy is, and why it alone is right: It is the way in which a group of people impose legislative restraints upon themselves.

Who gives democratic government the authority to rule over us? *We* do. Only we have that authority to give. The Preamble to the Constitution of the United States puts this crisply: "We the people of the United States . . . do ordain and establish this Constitution for the United States of America." When the laws of any government result from the deliberative participation of its citizens, all its citizens are rightly bound by them. Democracy is autonomy writ large.

4.   Moral Disobedience

Is the duty to obey the laws of a democratic government absolute? No. In rare circumstances our self-imposed commitment to obey the laws may be overridden by other, more powerful obligations. The conscientious citizen may then face an agonizing dilemma, being obliged to break the law, not for pleasure or convenience (indeed, the punishment may be severe), but out of respect for his own highest personal principles.

When two moral principles conflict and cannot be reconciled, one must overrule the other. But the principle overruled remains a genuine component of the moral situation, and continues to deserve respect. If I promise to meet you for tea, but the compelling need of an injured neighbor obliges me to miss the date without any opportunity beforehand to tell you how things stand, I certainly act rightly in helping my neighbor. Such an obligation overrides my obligation to you in this case, but it does not erase my promise. I have a *prima facie* obligation to keep my promises; that obligation is general and weighty. If exceptional circumstances compel me to break a serious promise, I must justify the decision to subordinate (in those circumstances) my general obligation to do what I had committed myself to do.

The obligation to obey the laws of a democratic state is, like the general obligation to keep promises, *prima facie* and very powerful. Only rarely may it be overruled justifiably. The participating citizen in a democracy commits himself, autonomously, to respect the laws in general. He does not make himself slave to the state; he may remain responsive to truly exceptional circumstances. But the rules of his own government he is under weighty obligation to obey.

5.   Participation

How can the citizens of a democracy genuinely participate in lawmaking? Can they really govern themselves? Critics of democracy commonly contend that self-government is a delusionary ideal. In tiny groups it may be realized, say they, but in communities of thousands, or millions, it is an impossibility. In every state a few powerful people make the laws and enforce them; the rest accept them and obey. The self-government of the masses is a dangerous myth. At most (these critics conclude) the masses may hope to influence the lawmakers; they cannot hope to govern.

Not so, we answer. National self-government is difficult, but it is entirely feasible and in many cases genuine. The criticism arises from a misunderstanding of what self-government entails. It does not entail most citizens' involvement in making most community decisions. The bulk of day-to-day governing consists of technical decision making, applying rules to cases. The technical issues are often sophisticated, the rules complex, and the cases numerous. To do such work, special bodies are appointed, special officers employed. They make the run of administrative decisions, and their specific powers are carefully delegated to them by the people.

The officeholders who temporarily exercise those powers are ultimately controlled by the citizens of a democratic community. In setting policy, in making *directive* (as opposed to *administrative*) decisions, the people may truly govern themselves. Democracy is genuine when every citizen has the equal right to participate in that steering of the whole.

That equal right is realized and protected in some countries —but certainly not in all. In Sweden, in Israel, in Holland, in Great Britain, in the United States, in Canada, and in many other lands, citizens enjoy the right to participate in setting the direction of the whole. Like all democracies, these named have flaws —but there remains all the difference in the world between countries in which the people have a genuine voice in their government and countries in which they do not. No one who has experienced the oppression of fascism, or of totalitarian communism, will call the right to participate in government a delusion. Self-government is precious just because, although sometimes real, it is very far from universal.

General participation is the essence of democratic government. It takes many forms, of which voting is but one. It is difficult to measure, and it is realized in varying degrees at different times and places. Democracy is always a matter of degree; some communities are more democratic, some less. Some states claim the name but do not deserve it. The critical question is easy to ask but not so easy to answer: Do the members of the community have, in practice, the protected right to participate in making directive decisions for the whole?

6.   Indirect Democracy

Direct participation by the citizen in policy making is feasible where the community is small. In clubs or committees, in villages run on the town-hall model, almost all may be heard, their participation being immediate and effective. In a very large community, a referendum may occasionally give the individual citizen direct voice on some issues. Direct democracy, where size and circumstances permit it, is ideal. But it is often not feasible.

Most democratic governments are indirect. The laws are made and policy issues deliberated upon and resolved by representatives of the people, elected by the citizens to make decisions in their name. In choosing representatives, therefore, popular participation becomes most lively and most concrete. By participating in the election of persons who will act for them, for limited terms and with limited powers, the people make, indirectly, the policy decisions and laws that govern all.

7. Voting

Voting is central to democracy. Although not the whole of citizen participation, it is its most evident and most decisive form. Fairness in the electoral process is therefore critical; it requires, at a minimum, respect for certain *operating principles,* and the protection of certain *procedural rights.* Among the essential rights, the most important are these:

—the right to run for office;
—the right to campaign freely, for one's self or another;
—the right of all to register to vote;
—the right to cast one's vote free of all coercion;
—the right to join with others to form parties, caucuses, movements;

and in general the right to do whatever fair competition for election may require.

Among the essential operating principles, the most important are these:

—that the apportionment of voting constituencies be periodically adjusted to insure all voting citizens equal weight in the outcome;
—that the method of election (whether by geographical district, proportional representation, or some combination of these) be fair, and be itself chosen by the electorate;

—that money, essential for a political campaign of any size, not be allowed to corrupt the electoral competition;

—that the system for counting, recording, and appealing the votes cast be scrupulously honest and impartial, and the results completely public.

These procedural aspects of the electoral process make participation effective; they constitute the skeleton of a working democratic system. Safeguarding these rights, and realizing these principles concretely, with voting lists and machines, offices and officers, regulations and appeals, and so on, is a complicated and expensive affair. Electoral methods and their mechanical details, of which there is an unlimited variety, must be adjusted to the needs of the particular democracy and the preferences of its citizens. Improving the voting system will be a never-ending business in a healthy democracy.

Electoral devices are the bones of democracy; its muscle is the spirit of the electors, always inspecting, activating, and safeguarding their instrument.

8.   Paper Democracy

No voting system, however technically perfect, can by itself insure democracy. Everyone is familiar with electoral systems that sound splendid on paper but are empty in practice. Paper democracy is of two kinds. The first results from fraud. Votes may be cast and representatives elected, all the forms given lip service—while the power to make important decisions remains in the hands of a few who really govern. The trappings of democracy are paraded and lauded, while the real will of the people is ignored. Much fuss is made about voting and the tabulation proudly announced, but there is no genuine opportunity for the citizens to choose their own representatives because nominations and elections are fully controlled by the powers that be—the land-owning oligarchies in some Latin American countries, the managers of the one dominant party in some Asian countries. The outcome is manipulated by permitting no serious opposition, or no opposition at all. Conflicting interests inevitably arise in large communities. Political parties reflect these conflicts of interest. Where there is but one party permitted, therefore, or where efforts to oppose established authority are punished, or where we learn that through some miracle a candidate has been elected by 99 percent of the vote, we may be sure that there is fraud afoot. Opposition and argument are essential in honest democratic politics; if they are missing, the rest is phony.

Paper democracy may also result from apathy. Self-government demands the energy of the selves concerned. The breadth and depth of interest will fluctuate with different issues and times, of course, but where the citizens do not bother to use the machinery of politics, the democracy rots from within. If the people are not interested enough to do what is necessary to govern themselves, there are always those who, with contempt and self-satisfaction, will gladly govern in their place. Either the people will direct themselves, or others will do the directing for them.

We democrats, therefore, have a heavy and continuing responsibility to make our government truly our own. We must serve as gadflies, evaluating skeptically the legislators and executives we elect—and the technicians they hire in our name. We must devote more time and energy to public matters than citizens under any other system of government, just because all that public business is our business, and we ignore it at our peril. What George Bernard Shaw said of socialism is certainly true of democracy: It consumes a great many evenings. Factual investigation, reflection upon public issues, expression of convictions to friends and representatives, political argument and lobbying—all that is involved in the laborious process of making policy—is our duty. Its fruits will be sour or luscious depending upon the vigor, the persistence, and the intelligence of our day-to-day political activity. That activity is the flesh of democracy. Without it, the rest is dry bones.

9. Democracy as Method

So democracy is a process, a kind of governing. It is not socialism, capitalism, or any other economic system. It is not to be identified with the forms or institutions of any country—the United States, or Great Britain, or any other—although such countries do try to realize democracy. It is not just majority rule, or the competition for leadership, or the protection of minority rights, or any of those good things normally associated with it. Democracy is the general name for a *way* of conducting our common business. It is that way in which the business is conducted according to the people's wishes. No one can know in advance what the people of any community will wish. It follows that democracy, in itself, entails no particular conclusions in resolving controversy. It is not itself a solution to any particular problem, but an instrument with which solutions to many problems may be sought. This explains its very general applicability. In distinction from every specific plan for the preservation of peace, or the elimination of unemployment, or the improvement of human beings, democracy is a method by which a community's objectives are established and advanced.

Democrats may therefore be advocates of any goal or plan they believe appropriate—so long as they are prepared to accept as legislative what the people choose, and to protect the procedural rights of all in choosing. A commitment to democracy is a commitment, in John Dewey's classic phrase, to the supremacy of method.

Even good methods cannot guarantee good results. Can democracy, honestly pursued, yield bad outcomes? Yes. Genuinely democratic governments may make serious errors in economic or educational policy; they may adopt unwise or inequitable laws; they may wage unjust wars. That the people choose their own course gives no guarantee that the right course will be chosen. Just as individuals acting autonomously may act unwisely or unjustly, societies in which autonomy is writ large may do the same. Intelligence and goodness in the behavior of self-governing communities must flow from the intelligence and goodness its citizens manifest.

The fact that democracies err does not condemn them; no system of government is perfect. But which system makes the most mistakes? And which makes the worst ones? If the mistakes of the people are not to be borne, whose mistakes are to be preferred?

10. Why Democracy?

There are only three basic forms of government, as Aristotle long ago explained: government by one person, autocracy; government by the few, oligarchy; and government by the many, democracy. These days almost everyone agrees that government by the many, democracy, is the fairest and the best. But *why* is this so?

Democracy (as we have seen) is the only form of government that can respect the moral autonomy of individual citizens; it is therefore the only form that could be morally justified. But *is* it justified in fact? Let us put emotional attachments aside, so that we may better see what reasons there are for defending government by the people, in which the directive decisions are reached through the participation of the citizens.

11. Democracy Works

Two families of reasons defend democracy. The first is complicated in detail but simple in outline: democracy works. It does for us—better than any of its alternatives, by far—what we want a government to do. What is that? To decide matters justly and wisely. To provide for the common defense, to promote the general welfare, and to provide the blessings of liberty for ourselves and our posterity—the Preamble to the U.S. Constitution again sums it up nicely. Does democracy achieve these objectives? Not perfectly; but no other system does nearly as well. And therefore no people that has won the opportunity to govern itself has ever given up this authority voluntarily; that by itself is compelling evidence. No nations have been more progressive than the democracies, nor have any been more productive, happier, or more free. The political history of the nineteenth and twentieth centuries is vivid testimony to the practical success of government through general participation.

Many governments that profess democracy do not really permit their citizens to practice it. Many peoples that aspire to democracy have not achieved it. But where it has been achieved, and practiced honestly—as, for example, in Switzerland, or Norway, or New Zealand—the people are reasonably secure, prosperous, and free. Democracy—truly broad and deep participation by the people in community decision making—really does what governments are supposed to do. What better defense of a system of government can there be?

Democracy succeeds as it does precisely because it is essentially participatory. The purpose of a government is to protect the *general* well-being and *universal* liberty; when the actual governors are the delegates of the people, "deputies" hold office only so long as the people themselves permit them to. The careers of the governors then depend upon how effectively they advance the interests of their constituents. And those constituents—the people—are the ultimate judges of their government's performance. Thus democracy alone ensures, by its nature, the honest and vigorous representation of the many diverse interests of the community in the corridors of power.

When the power of government lies in the hands of leaders who are insensitive to the people's needs, government invariably works badly. In a dictatorship, or an oligarchy, that insensitivity may flow from the sheer selfishness of the rulers. But even where the rulers are well-intentioned, even when despots seek to be benevolent, they cannot be sensitive to the great host of popular concerns in the way the people themselves can. Leaders are not supermen, and they are not likely to be saints. Those who occupy the seats of power have many opportunities to enrich themselves, and there are many ego satisfactions in the exercise of authority. The only way in which to ensure that such opportunities are not abused is to structure the government so that the governors are subject—not metaphorically, but literally—to the will of the people. Only in that way can insensitivity, and ultimately corruption, be reduced to a minimum.

An acute judge of the American democracy, himself an aristocrat, put this elegantly:

> Democratic laws generally tend to promote the welfare of the greatest possible number; for they emanate from the majority of the citizens, who are subject to error, but who cannot have an interest opposed to their own advantage. The laws of an aristocracy tend, on the contrary, to concentrate wealth and power in the hands of the minority; because an aristocracy, by its very nature, constitutes a minority. It may therefore be asserted, as a general proposition,

that the purpose of a democracy in its legislation is more useful to humanity than that of an aristocracy (A. de Tocqueville, *Democracy in America,* 1835).

Suppose—although it is not very likely—that the community is ruled by an altruistic prince who genuinely loves and cares for his people. Even so, he cannot govern best because he cannot know best what citizens' interests are. He may think he knows; dictators and oligarchies always claim to rule for the good of the people, and sometimes (not very often!) they really have tried to do so. But it cannot be done. The interests of the people are too many, too various, too tangled for any one person or small group to reconcile. Even if recognized, the interests of the many cannot be justly weighed by an elite. In the constant process of trade-off that government entails, only the traders can know what is worth what. The interests traded are those of the governed; *theirs* are the satisfactions of security, the pleasures of prosperity, the risks of enterprise, the resentments of inequity, the pains of restriction, and the joys of liberty. Is it better to be freer with greater risk, or to be safer with less liberty? Is it better for everyone to enjoy a little more of some good or service at the cost of greater inequality of wealth, or for all to enjoy more nearly the same amount at some cost in the absolute wealth of each?

Citizens can answer such questions for themselves, if given sufficient information about the alternatives, but no one has the right or the ability to answer for others. There is no way that a dictatorship or an aristocracy, however honorable, can surpass the wisdom of a people in resolving such issues. In tax policy, in welfare policy, in deciding upon levels of support for education, for the military, for public housing, or in framing labor legislation, or antitrust legislation—in any sphere where the direction of the community must be set—justice will require some complicated compromise of interests, a solution made possible only through the interaction of the people's representatives.

This process of interaction is indispensable in helping us to learn what we ourselves value most. As we trade our support for the interests of others in return for their later support for different interests of ours; as we push and pull in the legislative arena, victorious on some matters but beaten on others; as we compromise on virtually all important issues—we are obliged to order our own priorities. What we would like to protect, what we are desperate to protect, and what we will protect to the death, we ourselves may not know until the democratic process compels us to bargain. In this process we learn our real wants, our levels of tolerance and the relative priorities of our conflicting desires. In this process, too, we bring others to learn about themselves; we oblige them to hear us and be sensitive to us, as we are obliged to hear them and feel with them. Sometimes the process is harmonious; often it is tumultuous and leaves most participants less than fully satisfied. But it is the process with the best hope of good decision making, and the only process with any hope of reconciling the deepest wants and needs of all conflicting parties. If wisdom and justice are the ultimate aims of government, democracy is its proper form. The people who are threatened most must have the opportunity to make their voices heard in the decision-making process that governs all. The results may still be imperfect; democracy offers the best prospects, but no guarantees.

12.   Majority Rule

On every issue some decision must be reached, even if it be the decision not to decide now. Who wins and who loses must be formally determined by some procedural rule. Usually, but not always, that will be the rule of the majority, the rule of the greatest part. The greatest part may be only a *plurality,* as in many elections contested by several candidates. On some special matters a majority of at least two-thirds may be required. In rare cases we may seek virtually unanimous consent. The more sensitive the issue, the greater is the size of the majority appropriately required, as a protection for the minority against the acts of the majority. Where a *qualified majority* is required for positive action (two-thirds or three-quarters of those voting, or of the whole), change is likely to be slower, it being easier to mount the opposition needed to block that action. To amend the constitution of a community, for example, much more than a simple majority is likely to be required. For the general run of community ordinances, efficiency is essential, so the majority required will normally be *simple*—one-half plus one of the votes cast. Different rules will be suitable for different kinds of questions and different kinds of decision-making bodies.

13.   The Gyroscope of Justice

Whichever the rule, some citizens may get hurt by the action taken. That is true of all systems. Widespread oppression, however, is much less likely under democracy than under any alternative system because of the representative process essential to it. And if injustice be done, the likelihood of its correction through normal channels is greatest under democracy because those who are pinched by the act will be protected in their right to howl, to petition for redress, and to bargain with their voting strength for concrete remedy. Democracies do oppress some among their citizens sometimes. But we wash our linen in public. We are ashamed of the dirt, but we are proud of our capacity—and serious intention—to clean things up.

Our lawmaking system is time-consuming because so many parties demand an opportunity to be heard. Sometimes it is tedious, and sometimes maddening in its vaccillation. But it incorporates a self-correcting element, a gyroscope of justice, available to no other system. Every group may one day find itself the victim of injustice and will have then the same opportunity to argue its case that democracy preserves for all.

This is not merely theoretical but historically proved. Any group without a voice in making the laws has always been ripe for exploitation. When at last it comes to be represented in the legislature, that change in status is reflected very quickly in new laws protecting the group's interests. Blacks in the United States are a good example, although the changes are perhaps too recent to be appreciated fully. The case of the English laboring class is distant enough to be clearer. Ordinary workingmen without property had virtually no voice in British government until the reform legislation of 1867, when for the first time they won the right to vote. Having become members of the electorate, they could no longer be ignored. Very shortly thereafter came a stream of legislation protecting the interests of workers and trade unions. Group after group has had the same experience. Without the right to participate, they are "looked after" in a paternal spirit by others, who sooner or later exploit them. With the right to participate, they can look after themselves and may be relied upon to do so. The only reliable protection is self-protection through the political process; and only democracy ensures, by its constitution, the right to self-protection through participation.

Some groups, racial or economic, may still get less than they deserve from the elected legislature. But in a democracy every group is in a position to press for the remedies to which it believes it is entitled. If the inequity has been real, an oppressed group can expect a response from democratic government, because of its structure, as it could from no other system. In this very practical and very important sense, democracy really works.

14.　Democracy and Wisdom

More than justice is needed. We want our government to be smart as well as fair, to make wise decisions on complicated issues. We want economic policies that will encourage stability and reasonable growth, avoiding both inflation and depression. We want foreign policies that will protect our interests on the world scene, encourage international harmony, and keep us out of war; and so on. We want leaders with intelligence and foresight, people with balanced judgment who are really competent to manage the affairs of state. Can democracy give us that?

It can, and often it does. There are no guarantees here either, of course; elected legislators and executives are sometimes incompetent. But incompetence is everywhere. The real question is whether democracy, over the long run, will do better than its competitors. Is it more likely to provide wise leadership, less prone to catastrophic blunder? Experience answers yes.

Great leaders are uncommon under all systems. But democracies get more than their share. Lincoln, Roosevelt, Jefferson in the United States, Churchill in Britian, Brandt in West Germany, Benes in Czechoslovakia—these are only some of the names that come immediately to mind. There have been wise despots too—Frederick the Great of Prussia, Marcus Aurelius in ancient Rome—but they are rare and outnumbered a thousand times by selfish or power-hungry dictators. Authoritarianism rewards the shrewd and the ruthless. Glory for the flag and riches for the rulers are the chief attainments of despotism. If wisdom in the interest of the masses is our aim, we do far better to take our chances with leaders that the people choose for themselves.

That choice is the culmination of a competitive campaign for the support of the voters. The irrationality of the voters is the common complaint of our critics, who think the people a rabble. Undisciplined crowds may respond emotionally. But a people practiced in democracy is no rabble. The rules of a working democratic system channel participation and give it form; the discipline of argument promotes self-control. The entire system provides unending opportunities for the citizens to put their heads together, to profit from one another's insight and knowledge. Democracy relies upon the voice of the people in its most rational form, as the expression of men and women who may be ordinary, but who are strengthened by mutual understanding and enriched by discourse, sensitive to the tension between private and public considerations.

This faith in the capacities of ordinary citizens is the watershed between democracy and authoritarianism in all forms. We democrats have no illusions about humanity; we know well that people are often emotional, selfish, ignorant, and sometimes stupid. But often, too, they are generous, perceptive, and reasonably well-informed on matters that concern them. And they know better than anyone else where their own interests lie. Technical decision making is not what democracy commonly requires of citizens. We do not all have to set pollution standards, or decide on military procurement, or negotiate treaties. We hire experts to do such jobs for us. But on the larger questions of community policy—whether to provide more support for schools; whether to introduce military conscription; whether to support a weak but genuinely democratic ally, and so forth—we know what we want. Many of us are not very sophisticated; many of us cannot articulate our aims with refinement. Yet we understand clearly enough the alternatives our elected leaders (and would-be leaders) present. We can choose well enough the direction in which we want to go; and although we sometimes err, we generally get ourselves pretty close to our destination.

Sometimes we are for a while misled by smooth but hollow leaders, and occasionally (but not too often) by outright crooks and phonies. But we have the wits and the power to throw the rascals out, and we generally do, in time. We do hedge and procrastinate; we are sometimes appropriately chided for inefficiency. But most of the time we are not as dumb as our critics suppose. We watch what is going on; we learn from experience and are pretty good at judging character.

Sudden reversals and brilliant coups are not our ways. Important public issues, we think, should be argued patiently, wisdom not hurried. Alleged facts should be skeptically examined; alternative programs should be sifted, mulled over by the body politic while candidates for election defend and attack them. Comprehensive codes of law, neat and definitive, we find too rigid. We prefer to see legislation cautiously reworked, sometimes deliberately ambiguous or incomplete, with some details left unsettled, until widely satisfactory compromises are reached. Everything does not have to be done at once, and we do not suppose that what we do is permanent or perfect. This style of ours may yield untidy results, but tidiness in human relations is a virtue we have learned to live without. We want solutions that will avoid damage to ourselves who enact them; we are cautious in making great changes because we think ourselves to be doing not too badly as things are, and we are not ready to take romantic risks with our families' lives and fortunes for the sake of glory, or for the sake of principles of questionable worth. We do not lack courage; but for us it is peace and prosperity, not heroism, that government is designed to promote.

We have confidence in our own collective good sense over the long run. We hate being on the losing side of any political battle, but that is a risk we are prepared to take in order to run our own affairs. We prefer to trust ourselves to ourselves, the many, rather than trust "them" or "him," however smart or impressive they or he may be. The most durable wisdom, we have learned, arises from the deliberations of the whole community— ordinary citizens who know their own interests best and have the best reasons to strive to protect them. Vesting ultimate authority in ourselves, the *demos*, we proudly call ourselves democrats.

15. Elitism and Censorship

But (say our critics) statecraft is too complicated and subtle a business for ordinary folks. They treat us like milling sheep in need of shepherds. Isn't it odd that they never consider themselves to be as dumb as the rest of us? Oh, no; *they* understand; they will make the rules, for our sake. Thank you, but no thank you.

Who are they, anyway? Who anoints them, appoints them to govern over us? If they choose themselves, we certainly ought not to trust them. If they are chosen by others, who are the choosers and why should we trust them? If there is an elite so good and so wise that we should place our lives in their hands, let them prove themselves to us. If they cannot prove themselves to us, there is no good reason for us (or anyone else) to accept their claims to authority. If they can, let them do so! Let them run for election! When they persuade us, we will test their claims in office —for a limited term, of course.

Their arrogance is like the arrogance of those who would censor books or newspapers alleged to be "dangerous"—morally or politically—to us innocent folks. Who will be the censors? Isn't it interesting that those who are most anxious to protect us don't worry about the danger to themselves? Are they tougher and smarter than we? They may think so, but we don't. We can take care of ourselves; we condemn their condescending efforts to manage our affairs.

That goes for every form of elitism, in every sphere. The censor is just the crudest example. We are not so weak-minded or so servile a people as to need others to protect us from ourselves. Anyone with a bit of experience in the world knows that would-be revolutionaries are always running about, some crazy, some not, some sincere, some not; we tolerate them and sometimes learn from them. Every healthy human animal knows, too, that there are many forms of carnal pleasure, some perverted, some not, some commonly accepted, some not. We reject with contempt the notion that an elite may decide for us what we will read, see, think about. *We* will decide. It is one of the truly satisfying things about democracy that we citizens have the power to ensure that we do get to see and hear what we (and not anyone else) think we need to see and hear, in making our choices. We govern.

Elitism is just like censorship in another way. Forbidding adults certain books or pictures because they are obscene always supposes what is not true—that there is some objective category of "obscenity" independent of those who are constructing the categories and passing judgment. One person's debauchery is another's delight; one person's passion is another's prudery. That is not to say that objective judgments, in literature or in politics, cannot be made. It is to say that such judgments cannot fairly be made *for* some *by* others. We meddle as little as possible in the private affairs of our fellow citizens; we make laws affecting private conduct only when restrictive legislation is essential for community protection—since *we* will suffer the restrictions, and only we can say what interests can justify that burden.

16.   Compromise and Marksmanship

So it is with wisdom in all political matters. As a community we try to keep our hands off, giving private citizens the opportunity to reconcile their differences through mutual accommodation. Sometimes that method cannot work, and the whole body politic is drawn in. When that happens, how are conflicts best resolved? Not by recourse to some person or party claiming a special grasp of the Truth, not by superstition, not by dogma. We argue about it. We shake the matter around lengthily and repeatedly, considering every proposed alternative, reviewing our traditions, evaluating our goals, until a way is found, somehow, to work it out with reasonable harmony. The wise course is what we find best meets our needs (long-term as well as short) and best satisfies us as a community. There is no target set by some invisible target master in the sky, citizens having to match their marksmanship against a few trained sharpshooters. That is the elitist image, fascists and censors being convinced at heart that they know where the bull's-eye is, and know also, better than the rest of us *hoi polloi,* how to hit it. Hence democracy, to them, seems silly.

That conception of political wisdom as an antecedently set bull's-eye, clearly perceived only by the sharpest marksmen, is profoundly mistaken. Governments do not shoot at fixed targets; they *choose* the targets to be shot at. We argue about competing targets; we debate tirelessly the best means of hitting them. Since ends as well as means are under our control, we can change our direction as we learn more about the difficulties or disadvantages of pursuing the goals we had originally set for ourselves.

17. The Ship of State

Better than a shooting match is the image of the ship of state, sailing perpetually through perilous waters. Should we entrust that ponderous vessel (the critic asks) with its priceless cargo of human lives to the half-baked understanding of inexperienced and jittery passengers? The passage will be rough; sure hands and cool heads will be needed at the helm. Our chances of making port safely are slim if we do not have a wise captain in command, assisted by forceful lieutenants and sophisticated navigators. We would not dream of making a dangerous voyage on a real ship commanded and navigated by the majority vote of the passengers. It is equally unwise, the critic concludes, to risk our lives and fortunes in a ship of state run by ignorant amateurs.

But this criticism puts the issues wrongly; it seems plausible only because again it misconceives the role of the governors. Of course we want steady hands on the tiller and accurate calculations when charting the course, in real ships and in the ship of state. Complicated vessels require many special skills for their successful operation. We democrats insist, however, that we, the passengers, are the only ones entitled to decide where this great ship is to *go*. We need skilled navigators to help us get there, to advise us of the risks and advantages of alternative paths; we need brave officers to take us through the storms we will surely encounter. But the ports of call are for us to determine, in the light of their professional advice. This ship of state is ours; it has no other purpose than carrying us, meeting our needs. We—not the captain, or the navigator, or all the professional ship handlers—are the only ones who can evaluate those needs.

To this end we select our officers, weighing their character, experience, and previous record. If they prove competent we retain them; if they give notable service we honor them; if they bungle an important passage we replace them—providing the ship and its passengers remain afloat. The authority to determine destination remains ours. Government by the people is no more, or less, than self-chosen direction.

The enormous practical advantage of democracy over every other governmental system is revealed in this extended metaphor. Democracy gives ordinary citizens the right to help shape policy, choose direction. It does not suppose that amateurs will perform technical functions or administer details. We hire technicians and administrators for such tasks. But for the selection of destination there *are* no professionals. Experts can help us adjust means to our ends; they cannot tell us what our ends should be. To make these larger decisions wisely, human beings must reflect and decide upon their own values. No one can do that for us but ourselves.

18.   Democracy and Peace

Democracy works in other less obvious ways, too. It tends to keep the peace. Ordinary people hate war; they get no satisfaction from killing and destroying. War as policy we will not tolerate unless we are convinced that oppression by others has forced us to it. To defend ourselves and our families from oppression, to save our country and our ideals, we will fight; we are not cowards. But the so-called glories of war we can live very well without. We have little relish for conquest and triumph—and the bloodshed that goes with them. There is no glory in that for us; the price of victory is much too high—and *we* pay it. No, we are not warlike.

Kings and dictators thrive on victories in war, on threats and treaties and dominion. War has played so large a part in history because those holding absolute power—monarchs and autocrats —have commonly used international conflict to deflect the dissatisfactions of their own peoples. By focusing attention on alleged threats from without they obscure the injustices within. Increasing military strength, and celebrating it, have been central to their style of government. The game of empire is played in the spirit of ceaseless conflict.

That is not our spirit or our style. We have a living to make, children to rear, small pleasures to enjoy. Contentment in private life, we have learned, is more surely achieved without striving for national grandeur. Where the powers of government rest in the people, therefore, there will be continuing controversy over housing and the economy, schools and parks—but you may be confident that everything possible will be done to keep us out of war.

A few autocrats have been of peaceable spirit, and some democrats do get notions of martial glory. But how an autocrat behaves, what he does with his country, depends only on quirks of character or mood; the elected officeholders of a democracy answer to us. Where the people themselves rule, the citizens' longing for peace is reflected in the policies of their chosen representatives.

All experience confirms this. Armed conflict is widespread in the world, but very rarely does it break out *between* genuine democracies. Almost invariably democracies go to war only to defend themselves against the aggression of some authoritarian regime. Democracies seek peace not accidentally, but because of their essential nature—another demonstration that they do what governments are supposed to do.

When forced to war, however, we democracies enjoy an advantage that renders us, although not invincible, always dreaded enemies: we fight for ourselves. Our soldiers are not mercenaries. The corps of professional military men we retain for defense and training are kept strictly under civilian control. In battle we rely chiefly upon citizen-soldiers. The courage and tenacity of democratic forces have been proved repeatedly. We know how to defend ourselves and have shown our willingness to wage war when given no alternative. The nation and the government is ours; because we identify ourselves with it, there is no limit to our devotion. Democrats will fight when they must—and win.

Among ourselves, as well as among nations, peace is a natural product of our system. Battling with words and votes in the political arena, we have no need to take arms against one another. Subjects of oppressive regimes, knowing themselves to have no recourse, will sooner or later rise in rebellion against their oppressors. We have good reason to channel our energy and anger more constructively. The system is ours; most of us are clever enough to make it work at least tolerably well for us. We are not constant victors, of course; but we are not helpless either, even after a defeat, and we know that. We know how to bide our time, how to regroup our political forces, to win political supporters, and eventually to put our case with greater chances of success before the elected legislature. Long experience has taught us that the politics of argument, rough but fundamentally civil, are more successful and more productive than the politics of threats and guns.

Because we do not threaten armed rebellion, our elected leaders do not feel or act like beseiged conquerors. They do not need force to maintain order, because the citizens, even when dissident, accept the obligation to obey legitimate authority. Our obedience is to the offices, we say, and not to the persons who occupy them. The threat of arms (except from criminals) plays no part in the internal life of our national community; we go about our politics with high energy, but with intestine peace.

Our success in this is demonstrated by the orderly, constitutional succession of our leaders. We elect persons to office and reelect or remove them upon completion of their terms, without serious disruption. Political campaigns excite us, of course; but our tradition is one of civic decency, reinforced by carefully framed statutes, and ultimately backed by citizens who will not tolerate the abuse of powers they have delegated. In parliamentary democracies—Britain, for example—the prime minister resigns when the administration loses, in a vote, the confidence of the elected parliament. Although not liking it, the prime minister has no alternative in that constitutional tradition. In the United States, the transfer of power—that of congressmen and senators, and especially the enormous personal power of the presidency—is made by losers to winners with formality and grace. When a powerful leader dies or resigns, there is no cut-throat struggle for power; one duly elected as second-in-office serves until the next election. Political figures in a democracy maneuver constantly to advance their positions, true, but they are most successful in this when they win the trust and respect of the electorate. Purges and coups, hidden struggles for the royal sceptre, we despise. Our politics are mature.

19. Democracy and Good Order

Where power rests at the top of the hierarchy, good order can be preserved, under stress, only by fear, by threat, or by the use of force. But good order in a democracy—even in the face of temporary injustice—does not rely upon threat, because the law-making process is under our own control. An injustice done—to one or to many—is no less an injustice because we did it to ourselves, collectively. But we can tolerate more, and be more patient, when we know that the injustice we suffer results from a process to which we have committed ourselves, with the general understanding that all will comply with duly-enacted legislation. Our anger may be no less, but we channel it differently. It pays us, over the long run, to bear with injustice for a time, knowing that there will be continuing opportunity to plead the case, in legislatures and in courts. On other matters our own side has won the day; it may on this matter too, eventually. But win or lose, we have committed ourselves, have not been forced by others, to this system and to its laws. Does this implicit undertanding really make for deeper and more rational respect for the legal order? The actual conduct of democratic citizens proves the answer yes. The introspection of each thoughtful citizen will confirm that proof.

20. Democracy and Education

Only democracy—because of its reliance upon general participation—has intrinsic, structural reasons to educate *all* of its citizens to the limits of their abilities.

If policy makers are ignorant or narrow-minded, all of us are endangered. On the other hand, if we see to it that the whole of each generation receives the best possible preparation for active citizenry, all members of a democracy stand to benefit directly. Parents are anxious about the education of their children under all governments, of course. Democrats have special reason to be anxious about the education of everyone else's children as well as their own. As a practical result of this anxiety we support education, at all levels, with a generosity and universality no-where equalled or approached in authoritarian states.

This systematic contrast in attitudes toward education is deeply revealing. Authoritarian regimes select a few, who will be leaders, for high-powered schooling, leaving the rest to be trained to serve as functionaries at some lower level in the hierar-chy. Their elites will be well polished; culture and good manners will mark their ruling classes. Special schools will inculcate an aristocratic spirit. The mass of citizens will be much more nar-rowly trained, moving quickly from elementary grades to schools that prepare students for special roles—as nurses, accountants, technicians, and so on. Schooling there has a narrowly practical purpose. Literature and philosophy are cultivated chiefly by those destined to govern; for others such studies are luxuries going beyond the demands of the jobs to be filled. For those whose role in the state is menial service, even illiteracy may not be thought an inappropriate condition. The hierarchical spirit warps education as it does everything else. Common citizens are viewed as essentially subjects, to be prepared for subjection. It is counterproductive for an obedient servant to know too much.

A democracy, however, views the common citizens as the ultimate governors, all to be prepared to serve, one day, as legis-lators. High polish among the elite counts little for us. Our con-cern is that learning be universal and solid. It must be general in aim, broad in substance. We do not channel students into sub-missive roles; we set no limits in advance upon their achievement. Whatever a citizen's daily work may prove to be, we aim to pre-pare him for his role as participant in the political process. Who can say what any given citizen may learn to do or become? We permit no one's growth to be cramped by illiteracy; it is in our collective interest to develop everyone's capacities to contribute to the common weal. Every child and adult must be exposed to the full range and depth of the culture in order to function well as one of the ultimate governors.

In practice, therefore, we democrats have the most *open* edu-cational system, the best *public* schools, and universities serving the *largest proportion* of college-age youth. Our system of com-bined public and private education, most of it supported by self-imposed taxation, extends from nursery school to post-doctoral study and encourages the continuing education of all citizens.

Our enormous expenditures in doing this, our passion in arguing how it can be best accomplished, and our long-term overall success in education all serve as further proof of how well democracy works.

21. Democracy and Freedom

Democracy helps to keep us free; that is its most satisfying success. The terms "free" and "democratic" are often used as though interchangeable; in fact, they are importantly different and should not be confused. But they are closely related, and that relation is our pride.

Freedom is a *condition* in which citizens have the ability to choose and pursue real alternatives in conduct. We are free when we can act as we will, in our own way, without external restriction. Democracy is a *system* in which common affairs are governed through the participation of the citizens. The system and the condition, although distinct, are closely tied.

Democracy *requires* freedom. No nation can hope to govern itself unless its citizens are protected in their rights to do the things self-government entails. Hence we speak appropriately of "democratic rights"—the right to vote, to run for office, to criticize and campaign, to travel and organize, to read and publish. Democracy does not simply permit people to do these things; it posits their entitlement to do them. Such freedoms come to be thought of as part of the democracy they help make real. These freedoms are constitutional, not merely because they are honored in some document, but because they help to *constitute* the democratic system.

The constitution of an authoritarian system, in glaring contrast, cannot give those guarantees. Some freedoms it may allow; but what we call our democratic rights must be severely restricted by any single ruling party. Where power rests with the few, freedom will be enjoyed at the pleasure of those few and will be denied when they find denial convenient. Democracy, by its constitution, precludes such denial of freedom.

The bond between democracy and freedom is yet deeper, strengthened by custom and training. Freedom is infectious and knows no natural borders. Persons enjoying fundamental political freedoms will not be content unless also free in other spheres of their lives. Those accustomed to subjection may expect to be restricted and may fall naturally into the pattern of doing as they are told. Those accustomed to expressing and defending political judgments openly will tend to resent every restriction and will naturally develop the habit of self-determination in all activities. In work, recreation, and private conduct, democrats demand even those freedoms that the system of government does not require.

Freedom is thus not only a condition of democracy, but one of its pervasive and abiding ideals. Democrats insist upon their freedom to travel, to spend their money as they please, to choose their own private entertainments, being accountable to no one. Above all, democrats will demand the right to read, speak, and publish without censorship. Democrats tend to distrust interference by government and will vigorously oppose regulations denying their freedom to act, within reasonable bounds, as they think best.

To those who would compel us for our own good, democrats give an indignant response. "It's a free country," Americans like to say—and whatever its faults, no one can deny that America is that. No wonder we jealously guard our ultimate authority in government. Elsewhere freedom may depend upon the permission of rulers; among us freedom depends only upon ourselves.

Liberty is sweet. Because democracy is the system that best protects and promotes it, we say that democracy, of all systems, works best.

22. Democracy and Equality

To the question "Why choose democracy?" the first family of answers (as we have shown at length) is based on its good *results* in practice. Democracy works—if not perfectly, at least better than any alternative system of government. A second family of reasons for choosing democracy is based on *moral principles*. Democracy is right, as no other system of government can be. We turn now to its moral justification.

There are two principles only that we rely on; both are simple, profound, and almost universally acknowledged. They are: First, *that all human beings are equal* in a fundamental sense; and second, *that equals should be treated equally.*

The second of these needs no defense. Treating equals equally is part of what we mean by justice. Everyone understands that intuitively. If we treat people unequally—pay some more than others, punish or praise some more than others, tax some more heavily than others—we must believe that those differing treatments are justified by some differences among the people affected. More pay is justly given to those who do more work; punishment is meted out to those who break the rules, but not those who obey them; heavier taxes are imposed on those more able to bear them, and so on. If our fellow humans are not distinguishable in some respect, and yet we distinguish among them by treating some with preference, our conduct is unfair. We do not treat everyone alike, of course, because we recognize many differences among people that justify differential treatment. Disparities in our treatment of individuals, however, are justified by objective inequalities alone. That is a requirement of justice; to act otherwise would simply not be fair.

We err sometimes, of course. Differences that are not relevant we may take to be so, thus discriminating improperly. Differences of race, religion, or sex, not ordinarily relevant to employment or educational opportunity, are often unjustly used to favor some, disfavor others. Sometimes we fail to take account of differences that should matter, as when, in making awards, we fail to weigh properly the achievements or the needs of competing candidates. There will be much disagreement over what is, and what is not, rightly attended to in different contexts. But all will agree to this: If those persons in question are equal in the critical respects, they ought to be treated equally; justifiable inequality of treatment demands some relevant inequality in those treated. That is all our second principle asserts: to each his due; equals are due equal amounts. This is the heart of distributive justice.

The power of government must also be distributed in some fashion. Authority will be vested in one person, or in a few, or in all. What is the *rightful* distribution of that authority? We democrats answer: an *equal* distribution, a voice of equal weight to each adult citizen. Here enters the critical first premise: that all human beings are equal—not in every way, of course, but in those fundamental respects that are relevant to the distribution of power. The issues of policy upon which governments decide affect them all. What makes one a citizen of the state? Nothing more than humanity—being born there, or being naturalized as a permanent member of the body politic. A voice in the affairs of that body is rightly possessed by every member of it who has—no more and no less than any other—a life to lead. In this most fundamental respect all human beings are equal. This equality requires equal treatment in the distribution of ultimate governmental authority. That each citizen is entitled to one and only one vote follows as a *moral* demand. Thus democracy, unlike other systems of government, exhibits an essential moral element at its very core.

Between democracy and equality (as between democracy and freedom) the relations are deep and close. Yet again the concepts are distinct, and not to be confused. As democrats we are ardent advocates of human freedom, because without freedom we *cannot* govern ourselves. As democrats we are deeply committed to human equality, because without equality we could not prove that we *ought* to govern ourselves. Freedom is a *condition* for the success of democracy; equality *justifies* democracy.

Our understanding of human equality is not naïve. We know very well how human beings differ in strength, in intelligence, in character, and in a thousand other ways. We glory in the fact that every human being is different from every other. This uniqueness renders each person, with whatever special attributes, irreplaceable and beyond all ordinary value. If democracy places its faith in any one thing it is in humanity, collectively and distributively. We contend that every human, however poor or plain or weak, is a center of priceless being, a life deserving of respect and attention—and deserving that respect equally with all others.

Some persons accomplish more than others; some are more talented than others; some are morally superior to others. But all mature human beings have an equal *stake* in the fortunes of the political community: their lives, their well-being, and that of their loved ones.

In the makeup of the political community, all citizens have, also, equal *standing*. Their rights as citizens are not derived from any contribution they have made or may make to the common good, or from any property they own, or any rank they hold, or any achievement or other external attribute. Citizens derive their rights, *as citizens,* from their sheer humanity. All of them, from the most eminent to the most ordinary, are in that respect exactly equal. Hence one vote, and only one, to each. Democracy makes fundamental human equality operational.

This fundamental human equality must not be misunderstood or misapplied. In saying that all persons are equal, we do not mean that all are equally competent to perform various tasks, or equally qualified to serve in various offices. We certainly do not mean that all should receive exactly equal rewards, regardless of achievement, effort, or need. Any fair system of compensation must be very complicated; a just distribution of money, schooling, jobs and the rest will require the subtle weighing of many differing factors, in people and in their circumstances.

We do not ignore that complexity. But we say that before talent or schooling or any attribute is weighed, we must first decide who gets a voice in determining what factors should count in questions of distribution. At this primary level all are equal— equal in the kind of membership they hold in the political community. Whatever is the right of a member just because he or she *is* a member and for no other reason, is the right of every one, equally. This equality is consistent with all the varieties of talent and attainment that humans exhibit. Beneath all that variety lies the equality upon which democracy is grounded.

Some express this equality in religious terms, saying that all humans are "the children of God," or that all people are "created equal." Some take a pantheistic world view, regarding each human as a vital part of the living whole; others present an atheistic metaphysical account of this deep equality; still others reject every explanation of it, finding it simply the true and natural state of affairs. Democrats differ widely, perhaps irreconcilably, in their metaphysical beliefs. But we all agree upon the fundamental human equality to which all these views point. Democracy makes this equality concrete in political life; no other form of government can.

So profound is the link between democracy and equality that the words are sometimes interchanged. In dividing a pie, giving double shares to some is called "undemocratic"; when free tickets are distributed, giving the same number to each may be called the "democratic" way. Such usage is inaccurate, but understandable. An equal division of whatever is to be distributed is the likely outcome where the power to decide on the distribution is itself equally divided. The same principles that justify democracy apply even to mundane matters. Equals should be treated equally. All who have an equal claim on the pie deserve an equal share of it. That is, very deeply, the democratic way of doing things.

In some communities the members are truly not equal. There democracy is not justified. Democrats do not claim that theirs is the proper form of government for every community, whatever its character. If the community is one in which there are fundamental *in*equalities of standing among the members—as in the family there are fundamental differences between the roles of parents and young children—it is right to give the members unequal voices in the government of that community. Some communities (unlike the body politic) may have memberships of differing kinds—that of the teacher and the pupils in a classroom, for example. It is absurd to insist that every family and classroom, every community regardless of its character, must be governed by the equal participation of its members. Just as equals ought to be treated equally, unequals ought to be treated unequally.

Which communities are composed of members having genuinely unequal standing is no easy question and will be much argued. It is clear, however, that political communities are not like that. Citizens, as citizens, truly are equal. Democracy is therefore universally right in the political sphere; to understand why it is right in this context is to understand also why it may not be appropriate in some other contexts.

23. Varieties of Democracy

Democracy must not be identified with the institutions of any particular country—with a given electoral system, or party system. Differing patterns—parliamentary or presidential or other—may all be democratic. Differing traditions—separation of legislative, executive, and judicial powers; separation of church and state; symbolic monarchies or established churches—may all serve to implement democracy. Which institutions best support democracy depends on the circumstances and history of the community in question, and the character of its citizens.

A democracy may be very small—all participation direct and representation unnecessary. A democracy may be concerned solely with religious or with recreational affairs, resulting in no civic legislation, no judges, no punishments. A professional association may govern itself democratically, as may a chess club or any other group, large or small, whose members know themselves to be equals as constituents of that community.

Democracy, in sum, is a very general and widely applicable procedural idea. There are no limits upon the size or the nature of communities that may be democratically governed. States and nations come first to our minds when we look for democracy in practice. Partly that is because of the importance of these political communities; partly it is because, in them, democracy is not merely possible but morally obligatory.

24. On Appraising Democracy

Our defense of democracy applies, of course, only to *genuine* self-government, not to frauds. The good consequences that vindicate it can be expected only when the participation of the people in their common affairs is active and real. Maintaining a genuine democracy is not easy, we know; most efforts fall short in some ways. Still, the ideal can be approached; pursuing it in practice is politically healthy and morally right. For every community of equals, therefore—including those in which practical circumstances make the full realization of the ideal impossible—democracy is the standard of justice in government.

Each of us, naturally, will want to pass judgment on actually existing governments, including our own. When we do so—as we should—we must be careful to attend to essential characteristics, ignoring superficial features. What counts is not the constitution on paper, or what the leaders profess, but how the government really works, how decisions are actually made. Each would-be democracy must be judged by the degree to which the citizens of that community exercise ultimate authority *in fact,* and work their own will on matters of concrete importance to them. Do the citizens truly participate in their government? Do they, through that participation, truly call the tune?

No country is more closely associated with democracy—in history and theory—than the United States of America. Yet critics often say that the present American system does not deserve to be called democratic. They point to great inequalities of wealth and influence among its citizens, to the helplessness of individuals caught in the web of governmental bureaucracy, to the enormous power of corporations, and to the vast and systematic influence of the media of communication and publication. They point to the historical oppression of minorities in America, and to the pursuit of foreign policies with which many citizens are deeply unhappy. Similar complaints—perhaps more justifiable still—can be registered against every country calling itself self-governing. But for Americans such criticisms are especially troubling. We pride ourselves on democracy above all. Is that pride justified?

Philosophy cannot answer this question; only honest citizens, comparing American practice with the ideals of democracy, can be the final judges. In making that judgment, two things should be kept constantly in mind. First, democracy is always a matter of degree. No country—the United States or any other—can realize government through participation perfectly. Every democracy will fail in some ways, at some times. The question to be answered is whether, over the long run, on the great body of political issues, the people really get things their own way. In maintaining the schools and the courts, in managing the economy or controlling the military, and so on, are government policies generally those chosen by the people and their fairly elected representatives? Or are they imposed by an elite who govern in the name of the people, while in fact pursuing chiefly their own interests? It may be difficult to answer such questions confidently about another country of which one knows little; but few citizens, if alert and honest, will have difficulty in judging the democracy practiced in their own country.

Second, one must never forget that democracy is a way of seeking solutions to common problems, and not any particular set of policies or goals. Whether we think the United States (or any country) is substantially democratic, therefore, is not to be decided by whether we support the policies it adopts, or share its goals. In a nation of scores of millions of people, many will believe at any given moment that governmental policy is dreadfully unwise or unjust. The question must always be, not whether we as individuals approve of the decisions made, but whether those decisions are, indeed, made in accord with the wishes of a participating citizenry. When the people call the tune we may not think the melody a pretty one. Whether the tune is the people's own, however, is the paramount issue in appraising a democracy.

25. Autonomy Revisited

Why choose democracy? First, because it is vindicated in practice. Second, because it is required by the principles of distributive justice. Both reasons flow from the essential structure of democratic government and from its intrinsic connections with morality.

Democracy, we observed at the outset, is moral autonomy writ large. The power to choose freely and act out of respect for one's own rules is a condition of personal morality. The power of the people jointly to make their own choices and impose upon themselves their own rules is, in like manner, a condition of social morality.

Democracy is the only acceptable system of government, therefore, not only as a practical matter, and not only as a matter of justice, but as a presupposition of moral community life. We end as we began: The only system of government that could conceivably exercise legitimate authority over the people is one constituted by the people themselves.

Readings

(Other defenses of democracy as a general theory of government, arranged chronologically)

Ancient

Date of Origin

(11th cent. B.C.)   1 Samuel 8 *The Holy Bible.*

(430 B.C.)   **Pericles,** The Funeral Oration Honoring Athenian Democracy, in Thucydides, *History of the Peloponnesian War.* Crawley Translation. New York: Modern Library, 1951.

(51 B.C.)   **Cicero,** Marcus Tullius, *Republic,* in *The Basic Works.* Edited by Moses Hadas. New York: Modern Library, 1964.

Classical

(1690)   **John Locke,** *Second Treatise on Civil Government.* Oxford: Blackwell, 1966.

(1762)   **Jean-Jacques Rousseau,** *The Social Contract.* New York: Everyman, 1976.

(1776)   **Thomas Jefferson,** *The Declaration of Independence.* Edited by John Lind. New York: AMS Press, 1976.

(1787–1788)   **Alexander Hamilton, James Madison, et al.** *The Federalist Papers.* New York: Modern Library, 1964.

(1791)   **Thomas Paine,** *The Rights of Man.* New York: Pelican Classics Series, Penguin Books, 1976.

(1861)   **John Stuart Mill,** *Considerations on Representative Government.* Edited by Currin V. Shields. Indianapolis, In.: Bobbs-Merrill, 1958.

Twentieth Century

(1929)   **Alexander D. Lindsay,** *The Essentials of Democracy.* 2 ed., Westport, Conn.: Greenwood Press, 1980.

(1936)   **Jay W. Hudson,** *Why Democracy?* New York: Appleton Century, 1936.

(1939)   **John Dewey,** *Freedom and Culture.* New York: Capricorn Books, 1963.

(1941)   **Charles E. Merriam,** *What is Democracy?* Chicago: University of Chicago Press, 1941.

(1949)   **Cyril E. M. Joad,** *The Principles of Parliamentary Democracy.* London: Falcon Press, 1949.

(1951)   **Yves Simon,** *Philosophy of Democratic Government.* Chicago: Midway Reprint Series, University of Chicago Press, 1977.

(1954)   **John H. Hallowell,** *The Moral Foundation of Democracy.* Chicago: Midway Reprint Series, University of Chicago Press, 1973.

(1955)   **Walter Lippmann,** *The Public Philosophy.* New York: New American Library, 1955.

(1956)   **Robert A. Dahl,** *A Preface to Democratic Theory.* Chicago: University of Chicago Press, 1956.

(1957)   **Nathaniel Micklem,** *The Idea of Liberal Democracy.* London: C. Johnson, 1957.

(1958)   **Ernest Barker,** *Reflections on Government.* New York: Oxford University Press, 1958.

(1960)   **Henry B. Mayo,** *An Introduction to Democratic Theory.* New York: Oxford University Press, 1960.

(1962)   **Charles Frankel,** *The Democratic Prospect.* New York: Harper & Row, 1962.

(1962)   **Thomas L. Thorson,** *The Logic of Democracy.* New York: Holt, Rinehart, and Winston, 1962.

(1971)   **Carl Cohen,** *Democracy.* New York: Free Press, 1973.

ADVOCATE SYNOPSIS
Socialist Democracy

Socialist democracy is rooted in the nature of the human community. Problems facing an entire community can be solved democratically only when the community acts as a whole. Collective action, therefore, in the economy or elsewhere, is not a departure from democracy but its fulfillment.

Even in the United States, where the word "socialism" is suspect, many common concerns—national defense, law-enforcement, environmental protection —must be dealt with cooperatively. The same principle applies in other spheres: industrial production, health care, and social security. Democratic socialism enlarges the range of common control; it increases the power of the people by making their joint will effective where it counts most.

Capitalism, based on the private ownership of industry and the market economy, proves unjust and inhumane. Profit is its motivating principle and its only standard of success. This obliges cutthroat competition, encourages frivolous advertising, invites wasteful duplication. Human needs go unattended; poor service or no service is given where there is no profit to be made. The capitalist system is also irrational; it is unable to deal with unemployment, and unable to avoid the extremes of wealth and poverty. Relying upon a non-existent "invisible hand" to guide the economy, private enterprise is shaken by repeated disorders—inflation and recession—for which it has no remedies. Only social enterprise managed by elected representatives of the people, can rationalize the economy and ensure a fair distribution of society's benefits and burdens.

Democratic socialists defend two main principles: the public ownership of the means of production and distribution, and centralized economic planning. When public interests replace private ones, all community concerns—industry, agriculture, transport, energy production—are directed at the goal of general human well-being, rather than private profit. Mutual service replaces competitive greed. Long-range planning replaces the anarchy of the market.

Intelligence, rather than selfishness, governs wages and prices. The people, democratically, set their own standards for production, distribution, and service.

All this is feasible. The public ownership of industry, combined with democratic social planning, prove highly successful in practice. Socialism eliminates poverty, supports the growth of the economy, and in doing so provides a solid material foundation for the liberties of private citizens.

In sum: Cooperative socialism is the spirit of democracy, made concrete on the farms and in the factories and offices where common people work, and where their deepest interests are at stake. Self-government expanded to deal with all aspects of community life is both wise and humane; it is democracy socialized.

SYSTEM ONE
SOCIALIST DEMOCRACY

1. Democracy Fulfilled

We socialists agree that democracy is necessary and absolutely right. But it is not enough. Democracy is completed, fulfilled, by socialism—which is simply the democratic control of *all* resources in the community by society *as a whole.*

Socialism makes democratic ideals concrete. In it the collective will of the people is put to the service of the people in their daily lives. Through socialism the common interests of all the citizens are protected, their common needs met.

The name "socialism" has—at least to many American ears —a negative, even a threatening, connotation. Yet most ordinary people warmly support—under a different name—many activities that are truly socialist in nature. We all know that some things must be done for the community as a whole. And some things can be undertaken *for* the community only *by* the community, acting *as* a community. Constructive collective action in this spirit is socialism.

How, for example, do we "provide for the common defense"? Why, through social action, of course. Armies and warships cannot be maintained by private groups or individuals. National defense, undertaken jointly with democratic consent, is only one of many socialist enterprises that no one seriously questions.

How do we make and enforce the criminal law? Collectively, of course. Citizens can neither establish criminal codes and courts as individuals, nor punish as individuals. That would be the war of each against all, in which the lives of people would indeed prove nasty, poor, brutish, and short. The adoption of laws, and their enforcement, is an essentially *social* activity. Nothing else would be feasible or sane. Everyone grants that; to this extent we are all socialists.

Is not the same true of national foreign policy? We may differ as individuals, but do we not agree upon the need for one community position? And of health regulations? Do we allow the meat packers or the drug manufacturers to decide for themselves what is fit to eat or prescribe? And everyone now agrees on the need for community policies, collective undertakings to protect the environment, our forests and fish, animals and birds. Shall we not have public parks or seashores? Shall we not join to protect our historical treasures and the beauties of our land? Absurd even to ask. To do these things we must, of course, act as a society, because as individuals we are relatively helpless and ineffective. We will succeed, if we succeed at all, cooperatively, because there is absolutely no other way to have successful armies, just courts, or beautiful parks. All democratic experience teaches the need for collective action. Real democracy *is* social democracy, democratic socialism.

While we all practice socialism in many spheres, its applicability to other spheres in which it is equally necessary is widely denied. Sometimes manipulated by the rich and powerful, sometimes blinded by our own slogans, sometimes dreading unreal philosophical ghosts, we fear to take social action where we ought. We fail to complete our democracy.

How can we complete it? Where would collective action have greatest impact on daily life? In the economy, of course. Action as a society is needed most of all in producing and distributing the necessities and comforts of ordinary human life. Socialism is democracy extended to the world of work and money.

2. Socialism and Popular Will

All the wealth of the world—the houses and food, the land and lumber and luxuries—is somehow divided and distributed. How is that done? And how should it be done? We socialists try to rethink such fundamental questions: Who gets what? And why?

Satisfactory answers to these questions must, of course, prove acceptable to the masses. Being democrats above all, we trust the judgment of the people. Their choices, when fully informed, will be rational and fair. We lay it down as a restriction upon ourselves, therefore, that the great changes socialism requires must come only as the honest expression of the will of the citizens, through action by their freely elected representatives. An organic transformation of society can succeed only when genuinely willed by its members. True socialists—unlike some who falsely parade under that banner—never have and never will force their solutions on an unwilling community. Democracies around the world, from India to Sweden, have enthusiastically applied socialist theory to their problems, devising socialist solutions specially suitable to their circumstances. The same basic theory can be applied successfully, with American ingenuity, to American circumstances. Confident that we can prove this to the satisfaction of the citizens concerned, we commit ourselves without reservations to abide by the judgment of the people after the case has been put fairly before them. We compel no one; our socialism is democratic, through and through.

3. Rich and Poor

How the wealth of most of the world is now divided is very plain to see. A few people get a great deal, and most people get just barely enough, or a little less than enough, to live decently. Rich and poor are the great classes of society, and everyone knows it well. Early democracies accepted these stark inequities as natural and inevitable. We do not. Some democrats still accept them. Material success (they say) is open to everyone in a system of private enterprise, and rewards properly go to the industrious and the able, those ambitious enough to pull themselves out of poverty by effort and wit. Some succeed, some do not, and most (they conclude) receive their just deserts.

It isn't so. That picture of "free enterprise" is a myth and always has been. In fact, by putting control of industry and

finance into private hands, free enterprise results in the ownership of more and more by fewer and fewer, making economic
justice unattainable for most. For centuries, wherever capitalism
has prevailed, the great body of wealth has rested in the pockets
of a tiny fraction of the citizens, while the masses are divided
between those who just get by on their wages, and those who are
unemployed and poor, inadequately housed, and often hungry.
That great division, between those who have and those who have
not, is the leading feature of a private enterprise economy, even
when democratic. Those who have get more, because money and
property are instruments for the accumulation of more money
and more property. Economic freedom in such a system, for the
vast majority, is only the freedom to work for another. Working
men and women are free to sweat for paychecks, free to look for
another job, and maybe—if their needs are desperate—free to go
on welfare. These are false freedoms, not deserving the name.

Why does it work out that way? Will the poor always be with
us? Ought each person to look out only for himself or herself and
devil take the hindmost? We deny that this is the spirit of a decent
society. We do not accept the inevitability of poverty; we do not
think a democracy need be a cutthroat enterprise, and we know
that cooperative action by the members of a society in their joint
interests can protect both the essential freedoms of each individual and the economic well-being of all. That rational cooperation
is called socialism.

4. Parks and Industries

Consider this vivid contrast. No one questions the appropriate-
ness of public parks—places for play and the enjoyment of nature, owned by the people, and operated by their elected
representatives (and those they hire) in everyone's interest. Our
parks (national, state, and municipal) are among our proudest
possessions. Yes, possessions; we own them, each of us, and
though some abuse them thoughtlessly, most of us love them and
take satisfaction in their beauty. We do not begrudge the need
to tax ourselves to maintain them. We could sell the forests and
the land, reduce our tax burden thereby, and leave all citizens to

take care of their own recreational needs as well as they can. If unable to pay for access to private parks or clubs, or to afford a private lake or a canyon—well, that would be their lookout. Simply to formulate this attitude is to exhibit its absurdity. Natural beauty and opportunity for relaxation and play for ourselves and our children are deep human needs; we fully understand how vital it is that the limited resources of nature, the lakes and forests, streams and wildlife, be preserved, in part at least, for our common and perpetual enjoyment.

Compare with this the condition of the steel industry. Virtually all of the steel in the United States is produced by three companies: U.S. Steel, Republic Steel, Inland Steel. The private owners of these three companies—a tiny fraction of our citizens —literally possess, own as their private property, the foundries, mills, and other facilities that constitute the literal foundation of almost all other industry. Virtually nothing works without steel. Steel mills are not as pretty as parks, true, but are they any less necessary to the well-being of a people? Can any of us do without steel? Not for a day. Cars, trucks, ships, and trains are made of it. Housing and communication depend utterly upon it. Kitchens and radios, elevators and pens—practically all tools and all conveniences require it. Hardly any activity, public or private, goes on without some use of iron or steel. Then why not exhibit the same community concern for steel that we exhibit for our parks? Why let a few capitalists charge us as they please (since we cannot control them) for what we must have? Why suppose that a fair price for steel includes an enormous profit—over and above all the costs of making and shipping the steel—for the private owners of the mills?

What explains so blind an infatuation with "private enterprise"? Under its spell we allow ourselves to be manipulated by the private owners of the steel foundries, gouged (even in our own homes!) by the private owners of the telephone wires. Oil wells and forests, precious resources from our common earth, are exploited by giant corporations whose ultimate object is profit alone. We must wake to see that productive industry, vital to the life of a society, is properly the possession of that society as a whole, not of private individuals or companies. The principles we apply unhesitatingly to parks apply with equal force to factories. Production as well as recreation can be a source of public pride and satisfaction—when socialized. Socialism is nothing more than the *general* application of collective intelligence.

Every democracy, socialist or not, will seek to protect citizens' political rights—but only socialist democracies protect citizens' *economic* rights. Freedom of speech and assembly are priceless; are not freedom from unemployment and hunger equally so? We think so. The same collective action needed to defend the citizens against aggression from without is needed to organize production rationally and to distribute wealth justly within our own borders. In the economic sphere as much as any other, cooperation and foresight are central. The public ownership of industry is the only way to achieve them.

5.   The Unfairness of Private Ownership

History confirms this. The private ownership of productive industry has always resulted in deprivation for most, luxury for a few. The owners of factories and mines are forced, by competition, to exploit both workers and resources. Where private interests have been the foundation of the system, they have always been advanced at the expense of public interests. Why not build a power project in the heart of the Hudson River valley or on the seashores of Maine? It is not a concern for beauty but for bookkeeping that pays off. Drill for oil wherever it can be found—in the last of the forests, on the beaches, on the lawn of the state capitol. Business is business. The great redwoods of California, each hundreds of years old and a monument to nature's grandeur, fall by the thousands; the forests are clear-cut, left as ugly, muddy hillsides. The drive for profit is the sharpest of all saws.

The system of private ownership encourages, even demands, selfishness at every turn. Let buyers, employees, the general public beware! Cornering the market in computing equipment, controlling access to the telephone system, delaying the marketing of steers in order to raise the price of beef, steadily increasing the price of gasoline when petroleum is in short supply—all such maneuvers are within the rules of the capitalist game. Sharp play and toughness yield riches; generosity yields bankruptcy; and no one may refuse to play.

To limit the injustices done in the name of private enterprise, some have tried to adjust the rules of the game. It does not work. Fair business practice codes, antitrust legislation, minimum-wage laws, and the like, do restrain some of the excesses of the capitalists. But such changes are no more than cosmetics, mitigating but not eliminating the real evil. Injustice flows not merely from the excesses of capitalism but from the essence of the system of private ownership itself.

Changing the rules cannot eliminate exploitation and gross inequality; only changing the entire game can. If everyone is to be free from economic need, everyone must have the right to participate in planning production and controlling distribution. That can be only when industrial production and distribution is entirely in public hands. Just as those who are not represented in parliament will suffer politically, those not represented in economic decision making will surely suffer in the market. The very argument that justifies democracy in the political sphere justifies democracy in the economic sphere as well. Economic injustice in a private enterprise system is not an accident but a necessary outcome. To eliminate that injustice we must end the disproportion in the powers of its elements, just as the disproportionate powers of political elements were finally ended by giving the vote to all citizens. The case for socialism is the case for economic democracy.

6. The Inhumanity of the Market

Socialism is simply economic good sense. The long-term fruits of capitalism have become too bitter: cycles of boom and bust, unemployment and welfare, personal dissatisfaction and business failure. Inflation steals from everyone (except those who can raise prices and rents quickly); depression demoralizes everyone. Disorder and distress are widespread. Our land itself is abused, our water poisoned, and our air fouled. When everything is left "up for grabs," the grabbing will be vicious and the outcome chaotic. There can be no intelligent planning for future needs, no rational distribution of products or materials in short supply, no reasonable deployment of human energies, in an economy in which the fundamental rule is dog-eat-dog. Legislation designed to blunt the fangs can do no more than reduce the depth of a serious wound.

Capitalism relies upon the so-called "market economy." The prices asked or offered for raw materials and finished products it leaves entirely to private parties, individuals or business firms, who enter a supposedly open market. This free market, it is argued, will be self-regulating; supply and demand will rationalize prices, fairness and productivity will be ensured by competition, enterprise encouraged by the hope of profit.

None of this actually works in the way capitalist mythology depicts it. The system relies upon the wisdom and power of economic fairies that never did exist. Nothing in the market is dependable, since everything within it fluctuates in response to unpredictable and uncontrollable factors: the tastes of buyers, the moods of sellers, the special circumstances of either, accidents causing short supply, or fashions transforming reasonable supply into glut.

Rationality and fairness through competition? No claim could be more fraudulent. In a capitalist market prices depend largely upon the relative strengths (or weaknesses) of the traders. If I own all the orchards, and am therefore the seller of all the cherries in the market, you, dear buyer, will pay my price or eat no cherries. Steel, timber, farm machinery are for sale in the market. Go, dear friend, and bargain with the sellers. Anyone tempted to believe capitalist propaganda about the give and take in the market should put it to the test. Reflect upon your own recent experiences as a shopper: You were told the price of the item you looked at—a TV set or a can of beans—and you paid that price or left without. That is how the market works for ordinary folks. Giant firms, manufacturers or chain retailers, may bargain with suppliers on occasion—but even then the stronger get the better deals. Those who control resources and money control the market, manipulating it in their own interests. Those who enter the market (either as buyer or seller) with great needs but little power are squeezed and exploited. The weak get twisted, the strong do the twisting. That's free enterprise.

Fairness? Markets do not know the meaning of the word. All's fair in war—and market competition is perpetual war, through guile and threat, on a thousand fronts. Rewards go to the aggressive; the keys to victory are accumulation, possession, control. And rules for fair dealing? They will be evaded, broken surreptitiously, even ignored—just like the rules of war—when it profits the combatants.

Private enterprise is worse than unfair. It is no-fair; it does not recognize justice as any concern for *homo economicus.* The only things that count, for it, are the things that can be counted. Such a system is by its nature, explicitly *inhumane.* To render it humane it is necessary to transform it into an instrument for humans. Socialism makes human concerns the fundamental concerns in the design, manufacture, and distribution of material goods. Only thus can an economic system achieve justice. What should appear in that holiest of capitalist places, "the bottom line"? A record of increased human satisfactions? Or a record of profit?

7. The Cruelty of Capitalism

"Ah, but that callous system you attack," replies the capitalist, "is the most wonderfully productive in all the world. We do not, it is true, share everything and share alike—but by rewarding personal ambition and intellect, we encourage and tap the productivity of all. Capitalist societies may not be perfectly equitable, but they are rich—and that, in the end, is what we all want."

The true colors of the beast begin to show. Riches, material acquisition, is for it—but not for us—the paramount objective. Socialists think of human life in broader and deeper terms. For us money and goods are servants, not masters. General human well-being, we say, is the mark of a good society. Material wealth is only our tool.

Even on their own ground, however—measuring everything by prosperity—the case for capitalism fails. That private ownership leads to greater productivity is also myth. Enormous growth there has been, of course, in all modern economies; but that growth came with invention and discovery, with technological advance, with mass production and automation. It comes in capitalist countries *and* socialist countries, when relatively primitive methods of production are replaced by more efficient systems.

Human intelligence, not capitalism, should get credit for that. There is no reason to believe that human intelligence must be less energetic, or less inventive, when put to common service than when serving private ends.

The ironic consequence of that private service is *deprivation,* the hidden *lack* of that very prosperity capitalism claims. In a system of private ownership the factories and mines must produce at a profit or not at all. Most steel foundries—under capitalism—operate well below capacity most of the time. Produce too much steel and the price will drop; what profit, after all, is there in that? Houses and apartments are needed by tens of millions of Americans; we have the capacity to build that housing, but it goes largely unused. Carpenters and masons wait impatiently in union halls for work; lumber yards and designers lay off workers; contracters and salesmen search desperately for buyers who can afford loans at high interest rates; banks wait cautiously for safe borrowers. The entire system permits even needed construction only when a profit is to be made. If there is no money in it, those in need of housing will simply wait. You cannot make a buck by being a nice guy. What does get built is outrageously expensive, affordable only by the rich. Building slows to a crawl while housing needs soar. The human need for housing plays second fiddle to the demand for profit, and the building industry floats like a chip on the waves of a capricious economic ocean.

So it is with every industry. Production within the plant may be organized and efficient in the highest degree—but the "free market" to which skills and products are brought is madness itself. Again and again capitalism carries itself, now with unbridled enthusiasm, now with unrelieved desperation, to the brink of dissolution. "Business cycles"—the euphemistic name for the manic booms and depressing busts of the capitalist market—are the inevitable consequence of stupid inaction, leaving to pure chance and private avarice the control of our essential common business. The resulting human misery has been incalculable. After a chain of depressions through the nineteenth and early twentieth centuries, capitalism produced the super depression of the 1930s—a slough of despair, fathomless in depth and a decade in length. It was cut short, at last, only by the productive impetus of a terrible war.

In that great depression the true face of capitalism showed itself. Hunger was rampant in the midst of plenty. While humiliated citizens waited in soup lines for a dole, food in warehouses could find no profitable market! Food there was, in great quantities, but because it could not be sold profitably it had to be destroyed. Destroyed! To hold up prices for the rest! We Americans actually burnt huge stores of wheat; we killed and buried great numbers of pigs; we milked the cows and literally poured out the milk onto the ground—because, in the free market, it yielded no profit.

Madness, you say? Yes, the madness of the market economy. A sane economy is a human economy, directed by human intelligence, to serve humans. It will not leave the fate of citizens to chance, or the supply of industrial goods to unpredictable market forces, or the control of essential foodstuffs to private greed. The market cannot be sane, because sanity is a human quality and the market has no humanity whatever.

8. Disorder

"That chaos you rail against," the capitalist retorts, "is ancient history. You fight the battles of the 1930s while the twenty-first century approaches. We learn. We have devised sophisticated new tools to limit the fluctuations of the market. We protect individuals with Social Security; we use fiscal and monetary policy to compensate for excessive economic fluctuations. By correcting malfunctions we can maintain a market that is both free and healthy, enjoy its benefits, and protect ourselves against its collapse."

Pretty story, but untrue. After World War II the pattern of ups and downs returned—intermittent smaller wars obscuring the irrationality of the market in peacetime. Not the handsomest feature of capitalism is the fact that the unreason of the market thrives on the unreason of war. But even wars have not been enough to keep our economy functioning smoothly; as the century unrolls, new depressions, new excesses of unforeseen severity and character afflict us. Today, decades after the great depression, we are still destroying oranges and cherries, beef and grain, to keep prices high!

The one thing upon which capitalist economists agree with virtual unanimity is that they do not really understand the fluctuations of the market, cannot predict its movement, and do not know how to maintain its health. A thousand schemes are presented, backed by statistical pseudo-arguments and dire threats: increase taxes to cool the economy and dampen inflation; decrease taxes to stimulate the economy, encourage business investment, and create jobs; hold down the money supply to discourage borrowing and the devaluation of the dollar; increase the money supply to prime the pump of consumer spending and reduce interest rates—and on, and on. But it is all worthless speculation. There are no rational cures for a reason the capitalist cannot admit, even to himself: The system is itself disorder, and it spawns further disorder. Scientific remedies may be hoped for where the underlying system is sound, however complicated the illness. In the capitalist market there is no real system at all. It is, *in essence,* disordered.

9. Unemployment

Two consequences of capitalist disorder deserve special attention.

The first is unemployment. Capitalists speak of unemployment as though it were inevitable, arguing chiefly about what level of unemployment is "acceptable." No level of unemployment is acceptable; it is an intolerable cruelty for which no economic system may be excused. It is entirely possible to eliminate all unemployment—to assure productive work to every one—if only we will use our collective intelligence. There are socialist economies in the world, *now,* where unemployment is virtually *nil*—and these are not the communist dictatorships, but socialist democracies. In New Zealand, for example, the number of unemployed workers is reported in the hundreds—in a population of several million—and even those few could probably find some kind of work. Americans tolerate a dreadful unemployment rate in spite of our ability to put an end to it. We can end it promptly

—but not in a capitalist system. Capitalists employ workers only when it is profitable to do so. Socialism provides work for all so long as there is beneficial work to be done.

Is there work to be done? There is work unending, here in America and everywhere. Our cities need rebuilding; our vast railway system is decrepit; the majority of our factories are obsolete and in need of replacement; health care is in short supply; our parks deteriorate from over-use and under-care; many of our people hunger for houses not yet built, and so on and on. There is no limit to the work to be done. In the midst of this universal need, with vast resources of human skill and energy, the rate of unemployment remains absurdly large—rising among some groups to 15 percent and 20 percent, and even higher. What clearer exhibition of irrationality can there be than this?

We talk here abstractly about millions of men and women. Each of them is a flesh-and-blood human being, sensitive, anxious to be productive. Without work to do, human beings languish and are warped. Families wrangle and break up. Drug use increases, crime rates rise. Deteriorating cities, dirt, vandalism, and civic neglect are evidence of the underlying economic disorder. Capitalism traps its citizens—though they have the right to self government!—in a web of economic unreason. At work they are exploited; in unemployment, wasted.

10.   Inflation

If unemployment is the cruelest consequence of capitalism, inflation is the most insidious. It is funny, too, but the humor is sick. The joke is on all of us, busy making money and hoarding money and cherishing money in a system so uncontrolled that the money itself, the blood of the system, steadily declines in value, stealing from all the very essence of their accumulation—their power to buy! To keep the system operative when it falters, the currency that is its idol must be debased. Money is printed recklessly, and achievements measured in earnings turn to ashes. One might think it a fitting punishment, by a vengeful demon, for private greed. But, alas, the masters of the system do not suffer. Owning their property in the form of land and factories (productive wealth that should belong to us all), they endure comfortably. Indeed, they profit both coming *and* going because they operate largely on borrowed money. Their vast loans (from banks, insurance companies, and pension funds) are eventually repaid with inflated dollars worth only a fraction of the useful dollars originally borrowed. The little people (whose amassed savings had been used) discover too late that their nest eggs are shrunken, their retirements insecure. The rich get richer and the poor get children.

11. Public Ownership

Reasonable human beings can end all this. Production and distribution can be designed for human service. Cooperation is the key. Society must be organized with mutual service and mutual benefit as its fundamental theme. That theme is not alien to us; it lies at the core of our highest moral and religious ideals. We must realize these ideals in practice.

Economic cooperation entails two practical principles: (1) productive property must be publicly owned; and (2) production and distribution must be planned for the common good. *Public ownership* and *planning*—acting upon both we can readily achieve the substance of democratic socialism.

Public ownership is the base. Public ownership of what? Of the means by which goods are produced and work is carried on. Private persons are not entitled to own the instruments of our common good. A system enabling some to exact profit from the work of others, to wax rich while the glaring needs of others go unmet, is fundamentally corrupt. We would end that corruption by bringing all the elements of the productive economy—the electric utilities and the mines, agriculture and transport, the production of metals and paper and drugs, the airlines and the food chains and the telephone system—under public ownership.

We do not propose to confiscate anything. The capital now held by private owners we would have the community pay for, at a fair price. But we would end the surreptitious confiscation by a few of the common wealth. The people have a right to advance their own general welfare through state action. They have that right in the economic sphere as in every other. Individuals will not be deprived of their personal effects, their houses or cars, their books or boots. Indeed, we seek the enlargement of such private goods for individual satisfaction. Individual human beings, after all, are what government is created to serve. But productive property is our common good, our collective concern. We will move it—justly—from private to public hands.

12.   The Elimination of Private Profit

The nationalization of all industry will have two consequences. First, *profit* for some from the work of others will be no more. If there is surplus produced by the operation of the utility companies, or the design of computers, or the distribution of any manufactured goods, let that surplus return to the treasury of the entire community. Let all productive systems be used, we say, not for private enrichment but for public benefit, and for continuing investment in the components of public production themselves. Workers should know that they labor each for all, and that any value they produce beyond what they receive in wages will not be taken from them but returned to them in some form of general benefit. One of those benefits will be the reduction of prices; when profits do not need to be squeezed from an enterprise, the consumer need only be charged the actual cost of that product or service. Goods and services will at last be fairly priced.

Telephone networks, natural gas distribution, and electric power supply are good illustrations of the increase in efficiency. These are all virtual monopolies. It makes no sense to have two telephone systems, or two sets of electric power lines, in the same community. Such essential utilities properly belong to all the members of the community served, all of whom need and use them, and must pay for them. That public agencies, even in a capitalist economy, now regulate the utilities is an explicit recognition of our common interest. Why then should *private* parties be permitted to own the lines and generators of a *public* utility? Why should any small group be permitted to *profit* from the necessary use of these instruments by everyone? Of course they should not. In many democracies the public utilities are already completely owned and operated by the public; actual operations change only little; ownership changes entirely. The result is invariably better service at lower cost. Nothing else is fair.

13. The Return to Public Service

By eliminating the need for private profit, the public ownership of industry proves itself not only cheaper but more satisfying for all. A nationalized economy can be guided by one overriding purpose—the *general* welfare. The need for service overrules the need for a good return. Some services yield little profit, or none; yet the self-governed community can nevertheless provide such service widely to its own members.

Take the railroads as an example. The American public is poorly served, when served at all, by privately owned railroads. They would discontinue every service, passenger or freight, that does not maximize financial return on capital investment. While socialist democracies in Western Europe and elsewhere are perfecting their passenger rail services, rebuilding the roadbeds, introducing high-speed, comfortable, and dependable intercity services, the passenger rail network in the United States, because unprofitable, is allowed to rot. Many American cities—even including former great rail centers—no longer have any rail passenger service at all! The private railroads maintain passenger services only where clearly profitable (as between New York and Washington) or where forced to do so by regulatory agencies—and then they do so grudgingly and poorly. Does the public suffer? "Not our concern," reply the private railroads. "This is a business. A line that loses money regularly must be cut; our primary responsibility is to our stockholders." It is; they are right about that. If the owners of the railroads run them only to make money, they will not run them at all where there is no money to be made. But the fundamental aim of the railroads ought not be to make money; it ought to be to serve the people. It will become that when—but only when—all the people served are stockholders.

When the railroads (and all other vital industries) are nationalized, the task of striking a balance between wide service and reasonable economy will remain. Public ownership does not provide something for nothing; it distributes essential burdens more fairly. The decisions then to be made about what services are worth what burdens will be made by all of us, through elected representatives. Decisions affecting us all will not be reached in closed board rooms by capitalist magnates motivated by selfish interests. All productive enterprise—the railroads are but one illustration—will be conducted for people, and not for profit.

14. Competitive Waste

The competitive market—contrary to the capitalist mythology—is incredibly wasteful. Costly and needless practices in advertising and in packaging, which function only to lure the buyer and beat out the other fellow, can be eliminated. A host of different gadgets and machines, much more expensive to produce because of their variety, yet differing only minutely, can be consolidated into a few basic lines needed to meet genuine consumer needs. Old products need not be dressed in new garments solely to attract attention in a cutthroat market. Simple drugs, for example, costing pennies to manufacture, need not be given fancy trade names and elaborate packages to be sold at hundreds of times their real cost.

Built-in obsolescence, a curse of the capitalist market, will be eliminated too. When products are engineered for *use*, rather than for profitable *sale*, they may be built to last, to work well, rather than to break or deteriorate after brief usage so as to sustain next year's replacement market. Products will need to be attractive, yes, but not flashy. An annual model change (as in the American automobile industry) will not be needed to whet consumers' appetites. Durable quality will replace rapidly changing fashion.

Even advertising will be transformed. Under capitalism it demeans its practitioners, often appealing even to perverted desires. Under socialism it can serve the public, informing them of available goods and services, guiding reliably instead of misleading through flagrant exaggeration and the seductive uses of sexual suggestion.

In sum, putting the productive powers of human beings to common service is only possible through, because only motivated by, the public ownership of the entire economy.

15. Social Planning

Two practical principles, we said earlier, comprise the substance of democratic socialism. Public ownership is the first, the foundation of socialism. Planning production and distribution for the common good is the second, and the fruit of socialism. When all members of the community have equal voice in the management of the economy, the elected representatives of those voices will naturally seek to deploy productive powers rationally. The community, then fully in command of its own affairs, will deliberate carefully in choosing its economic goals and in devising the means to attain them. It will make plans.

All intelligent humans plan. Preparing for the future is the mark of rational beings. Capitalists plan thoughtfully for their own advancement, plan cautiously for the security of their families, plan assiduously for the growth of their businesses. Yet they bitterly attack us for advocating the same foresight in the larger community! In matters close to them they do not cease to think ahead. But they insist that the community as a whole should entrust its future to an "invisible hand" that is somehow to ensure social health and prosperity. Sophisticated in private affairs, their handling of public affairs is simply immature, primitive.

Critics of socialism (it should be noted in fairness) often do recognize the need to plan in some particular sphere of the economy. Doing so, of course, such critics implicitly abandon their devotion to "free" markets. They plan the supplies of oil or gas, the road system, the storage of grain, and the money supply. But if the use of careful planning is appropriate in any single sphere of the economy, it is no less appropriate for the economy as a whole. Capitalists who plan, but are infuriated by planning, are blinded by an ideology from which they cannot free their own minds.

A few wealthy critics of socialism, on the other hand, are more perceptive but less forthright. They recognize the inconsistencies of capitalism, but they reject large-scale planning in their own interests. They know that in a system without rational direction, the private owners of productive capacity are in the best position when stormy times come. They will be able to capitalize on every fortuitous turn of events. That is how they got rich and will get richer. Economic planning will equalize opportunities in ways they do not like. It will deprive them of opportunities to exploit. Planning—from their selfish perspective—is a threat.

16.   Planning Works

Two great objections to economic planning must be dealt with. The first is the claim that it does not work. This has been repeatedly proved false.

Every individual, and every community, has experienced successful planning. When we construct a budget for our school or business, for our family or our town, we plan. Ought we to cease budgeting? Bad budgets are sometimes devised, true; our aim then is to improve them, not to discard budgeting altogether. The same process of improvement through self-correction can take place on a national scale. Community planning need not be always partial, or short-run. What is clearly in our interest to keep under control we need not leave to chance. Department heads who do not plan for their departments, generals who do not adequately plan their battles, we censure and replace. We have learned how essential it is to plan, through zoning, for the growth of our cities, and how we suffer when we fail to do so. The redevelopment of Western Europe, after World War II, was carefully and very successfully planned under American leadership. Military preparedness would be impossible without planning of the most detailed sort. Thorough planning can bring humankind even to the moon. Good planning is the heart of intelligent policy in every sphere, and it always will be. Without a plan there can hardly be any policy at all.

The effectiveness of rational economic planning has been demonstrated again and again. Many socialist countries, maintaining five- and seven-year economic plans under continual adjustment, have met with phenomenal success. Their rates of economic growth have been markedly greater than that of the unplanned American economy over recent decades. True, percentage growth for the American economy is harder than for some others because of our great size. But other economies, almost the size of our own, have been rapidly overtaking us through planning. Economic planning in Japan, for example, has brought stability, full employment, and security for all citizens. The quality of Japanese goods is high, often higher than our own. The quality of their services is very high, often more complete than our own. We cannot hope to compete successfully with them unless we too are prepared to plan thoughtfully for the future.

Planning doomed to failure? Nothing could be further from the truth. The continuing growth of world population absolutely demands the wisest forethought in the use of agricultural resources. Allocation of food supplies will be planned or millions of human beings will starve. Rapidly advancing technology—in the production of energy, in automated manufacture, in the processing of information—will greatly change the appropriate distribution of labor. If we do not plan for that, and develop an economic system that *can* plan for that, we may soon be utterly unable to cope. As a community we must calculate our coming needs—for housing, transport, health care, energy, and food. We must design the capacities to meet these common needs collectively with our collective efforts and intelligence.

Our horizons expand without known limit. With production and distribution jointly owned and jointly managed, there is little we cannot accomplish. But we must use our heads—together.

17. Planning and Democracy

The second major objection to economic planning is the claim that it will cost us our freedom. This is as false as the claim that it does not work, and more pernicious.

Here lies the nub of the conflict between democratic socialists and our private enterprise critics. Freedom, says the critic, is the paramount social value. The freedom of each individual as an economic agent must be curtailed, they argue, by any large-scale economic plan. Once the goals are set, and the role of each economic element fixed, every private person must be sharply restricted in the use of his own resources. What can be bought and what can be sold or invested will be determined by the plan. The individual will be forced to work where, and when, and as the socialist bureaucrats have decided. Economic planning, they conclude, is but a pretty name for economic slavery.

The complaint is entirely unfounded. It is plausible only because it supposes, falsely, that economic planning under socialism will be imposed from above, by arbitrary authorities over whom we will have no control. Not so. Democratic socialism brings *democratic* planning. In an economy that is publicly owned and managed, *we* are the planners. Long-range designs for the allocation of resources, decisions about what is to be produced and how it is to be distributed, will come not from a secret, all-powerful elite but from *public* bodies, publicly selected, acting publicly, and answerable to the general public.

This genuine public accountability is absent, we agree, in some countries calling themselves "socialist." We despise that economic czarism as bitterly as do our capitalist friends. That is a false socialism which betrays the democratic spirit to which we are committed. Free citizens, accustomed to governing their own affairs, jealous of their own ultimate authority, will not be fooled by deceitful talk. They—we!—will know when our most important business is truly under our own control, and we will not stand for any other state of affairs. We will give up none of our freedom to do our own planning for our own needs. To the contrary, real freedom of action will be magnified in a truly *democratic* socialism by its increase of economic security for individuals and economic rationality in the whole society.

The critics' picture of socialist planning is a caricature of the real thing. They picture each citizen as a mindless cog in a great machine that grinds on unfeelingly, insensitive to mistakes or changing conditions. But the truly insensitive economy is the *un*-planned one, the economy that cannot respond to human needs because it responds to nothing human at all. In that disordered economy the individual is indeed helpless, a bobbing cork on uncontrolled currents. Those currents are brought under control only by giving each citizen a voice in the control of economic as well as political affairs. Democratic planning ensures that voice. The plans will be ours. We can adjust them as we make errors and learn from them; we can refine them as circumstances change. We can scrap bad plans and devise new ones as we develop new needs or new capacities. A planned economy, *honestly* socialized, will not be our master but our servant. Let our critics not forget that our first principle throughout is *self*-government, democracy.

18.   Planning and Liberty

For self-governed citizens liberty is, indeed, a paramount concern. And what is liberty, after all? It consists of the ability and the right of individuals to make choices in determining their own conduct. The greater the range of their choices, the greater their freedom. No one supposes that liberty is absolute, that individuals can be free to do entirely as they please without restriction. Even the best of our laws limit each person's freedom to do some sorts of things in order that all of us may be genuinely free to do many other, more valuable sorts of things. The more complex a society, the more essential are some kinds of self-restriction for the extension of real freedom within it.

We witness this rational trade-off everywhere. Primary education is made compulsory in order that all may enjoy the freedom possible only for those who can read and write. Social security taxation ensures freedom from want in old age. We may resort to a military draft, reluctantly, to keep the country free. And so on. Having to send our children to school, being deprived of some of our income by taxation—these and other sound policies clearly limit us. We accept such limitations in the interest of the greater liberties they promote.

In the economic sphere such trade-offs are essential. Even advocates of "free enterprise" readily admit the necessity of legislation that hinders private monopolies, obliges honest business reports, forbids the sale of untested drugs or spoiled foods, and so on. Such restrictions are justified by their benefits in safeguarding other more essential economic goods.

Limits on the absolute freedom of private economic agents will be entailed by socialized planning; we make no bones about that. Some of these limits—on the freedom to own, buy, and sell productive resources like factories and farms—will be painful to some, just as universal taxation or compulsory schooling are burdensome now to many. The freedoms gained, from economic insecurity and injustice, will be vastly greater than those given up, and vastly more important.

Socialist restrictions will be felt most keenly by a relatively small number of persons who now enjoy luxury and great economic power. Those who never had investment capital at their disposal, who never were the owners of profit-making wealth, are deprived of nothing in losing economic license. Socialist gains, on the other hand, will be felt directly by every citizen, experiencing steady improvement in the quality of his or her own life, and satisfaction in the increased well-being of others. Never was a wiser bargain struck.

19. Democracy in the Work Place

Democracy calls for participation in the important affairs of one's community. One's community is not only his town, or nation, but also his place of work—the factory or office, the restaurant or construction project. Can we make democracy genuine in such places, in the day-to-day lives of ordinary citizens?

Yes, we can, but only under socialism. Where the ownership of the enterprise is private, and profit-oriented, there must be bosses on the job to represent the owners and protect their profits. The workers are hired, whether by the hour or the month, in the owners' interests; they take orders from the bosses or they are fired. Capitalism inevitably produces authoritarianism in labor-management relations. Collective bargaining, of which capitalists make much, does no more than mitigate the severity of worker subordination.

This authoritarianism can be eliminated, however, if the enterprise is itself community-owned and-operated. We the people then make the procedural rules, and we can decide to institute democratic processes in the places of work themselves. This dramatic change is not merely utopian; it has already been widely introduced in socialist democracies—in Sweden for example, and even in a few isolated places in the United States. Where it has been thoughtfully designed, work-place democracy has usually proven very successful. It makes for a happier, healthier, and more productive work force. Men and women on the job regain the sense of personal autonomy that traditional hierarchies do not foster and cannot respect. Through collaboration and cooperation, the workers protect one another from abuse, whether deliberate or inadvertent. And everyone is served because day-to-day participation instills pride in the work force, and provides immediate incentives for energetic work of high quality.

Democracy in the work place does not mean disorder. It does not mean that everyone works when and where and how he or she pleases. It means simply that the members of the work force—knowing themselves as owners as well as consumers and workers—participate with community management in setting work rules, production quotas, hours, and procedures. Of all the ways in which democratic ideals can be realized, this is the most concrete, the most immediate, and the most satisfying. It can be achieved under socialism; on a large scale it can be achieved only under socialism. This by itself is a compelling argument for socialist democracy.

20. The Spirit of Socialism

Between the good of individuals and the common good there is no ultimate conflict. Tensions between the individual and society are sometimes real, of course, but they can be overcome in a healthy democracy. In this process we socialists emphasize the community side—our common interests and collective powers—because it is this aspect of our lives that has been widely neglected and impoverished.

Human beings are often selfish and greedy; we are much lower than the angels. Yet most of us do harbor good will for our fellows; we have a deep and natural inclination to help, to work cooperatively with others. We want to be of mutual service one to another.

This spirit we are not embarrassed to call the spirit of love —the love of one another that has been urged upon us by our wisest and most revered teachers. We think humans are capable of realizing, imperfectly no doubt, this spirit of mutual concern, even in the rough-and-tumble world of political economy. In bringing that spirit to life—as each will testify from personal experience—we are enlarged and enriched.

Private life we hold as sacred as any. But individuality flowers only in a social world. Human fulfillment, happiness, depend utterly upon the community by which we are molded and from which we draw life. The human condition is one of both loneliness and fellowship. Government must forever deal with that tension, somehow reconciling what is unique in each person with what is common to all. Believing that this reconciliation can be rationally achieved, we are socialists. Believing it cannot be achieved singly, and cannot be achieved by others for us, but only by us for ourselves, our socialism is democratic in form and in substance.

Readings

(Other defenses of socialist democracy, arranged chronologically)

Before World War II

Date of Origin

(1888)   **Frank Fairman,** *The Principles of Socialism Made Plain.* London: W. Reeves, 1888.

(1904)   **Thorstein Veblen,** *The Theory of Business Enterprise.* New York: Augustus M. Kelly, 1904.

(1920)   **George D. H. Cole,** *Guild Socialism Re-Stated.* Social Science Classics Series, New Brunswick, N. J.: Transaction Books, 1980.

(1920)   **J. Ramsay MacDonald,** *Parliament and Democracy.* London: L. Parsons, 1920.

(1920)   **J. Bruce Glasier,** *The Meaning of Socialism.* New York: T. Selter, 1920.

(1923)   **Sidney and Beatrice Webb,** *The Decay of Capitalist Civilization.* Mercersburg, Pa.: Irwinton, 1969.

(1928)   **George Bernard Shaw,** *The Intelligent Woman's Guide to Socialism and Capitalism.* London: Constable, 1949.

(1933)   **Harold J. Laski,** *Democracy in Crisis.* New York: AMS Press, 1969.

(1940)   **Evan F. M. Durbin,** *The Politics of Democratic Socialism.* New York: Augustus M. Kelly, 1940.

After World War II

(1944)   **Herbert Morrison** *et al., Can Planning Be Democratic?* London: The Labor Book Service, 1944.

(1945)   **Leon Blum,** *For All Mankind.* Translated by W. Pickles. Magnolia, Mass.: Peter Smith, 1940.

(1948)   **George W. Hartmann and Roger Payne,** *Democratic Socialism.* New York: Three Arrow Press, 1948.

(1951)   **William A. Lewis,** *The Principles of Economic Planning.* Winchester, Mass.: Allen & Unwin, 1969.

(1951)   **Kingsley Martin,** *Socialism and the Welfare State,* Fabian Tract No. 291. London: Fabian Publications, 1952.

(1952)   **Richard H. S. Crossman et al.,** *New Fabian Essays.* New York: Prager, 1952.

(1953)   **Norman Thomas,** *Democratic Socialism: A New Appraisal.* New York: League for Industrial Democracy, 1953.

(1956)   **Charles A. R. Crosland,** *The Future of Socialism.* Westport, Conn.: Greenwood Press, 1964.

(1957)   **George D. H. Cole,** *The Case for Industrial Partnership.* New York: St. Martin's Press, 1957.

(1958)   *Socialism: A New Statement of Principles.* (by Socialist Union). London: Lincoln-Prager, 1958.

(1966)   **Crawford B. Macpherson,** *The Real World of Democracy.* New York: Oxford University Press, 1966.

(1972)   **Daniel R. Fusfeld,** *The Rise of the Corporate State.* Andover, Mass.: Warner Modular Publications, 1973.

ADVOCATE SYNOPSIS
Individualist Democracy

Individualist democracy is rooted in the primacy of the individual human being. Democracy protects the right of each citizen to participate in making the laws that govern all and maintain social order. The larger purpose of these laws is to enhance the lives of the private citizens they serve. The freedom of individuals to live as they think best is the highest democratic ideal.

In every important activity—in the arts and sciences, in work and play—it is personal achievement that human beings value most. This respect for private enterprise is applied by individualism to all affairs, including economic affairs. Cooperative decision making is not rejected. But individualism is skeptical of state control, noting that threats to personal freedom arise most commonly from government itself. Collective action, and a single rule for all, should be resorted to only when clearly required for the general well-being.

Individualism therefore seeks to minimize government interference, in the economy as in all spheres. Citizens should enjoy the liberty to set their own goals, to work and earn, to spend and invest, to play and enjoy in their own ways, with the least possible direction from the state. The individual ownership of property and its enjoyment, the private management of business and industry, and the universal protection of economic freedom proves to be the truest form of liberalism.

Individuals work most industriously and happily for themselves, their families and their friends. An economy based on intelligent self-interest is not evil. It encourages thrift and foresight. It avoids the notorious inefficiency and corruption of collectivized economies. It protects open and competitive markets, thus rewarding energetic and efficient producers. It gives effective power to ordinary people by making their choices, as consumers, genuinely sovereign. Private enterprise is the surest path to prosperity, for individuals and for nations.

Capitalism goes hand in hand with democracy. The strongest bulwark of self-government has always been the middle class, and it flourishes best where private economic enterprise is encouraged. As freedom of enterprise is restricted, democracy is to that extent undermined.

Socialism gives authority to persons who are not individually accountable for its exercise. Economic policy without the discipline of personal responsibility is invariably insensitive and blundering. Waste and complacency are unavoidable. The powers of distant authorities grow; private freedoms are gradually sacrificed for alleged collective interests. In the end, centralized planning becomes inconsistent with democracy itself.

Individualist democracy keeps decision making authority as close as possible to the point at which the impact of the decisions will be felt. By dispersing powers throughout the community, it avoids a bloated bureaucracy. Competing interests check and balance one another. Individualism guarantees not economic equality (which is impossible as well as undesirable) but equality of opportunity, which justice demands. It does not presume to impose the utopian ideals of one party upon all citizens; it permits each private citizen to pursue his or her own goals, within a common framework of law.

In sum: Individualism is the true realization of democracy. It lives up to the principle, well-confirmed by long human experience, that that government is best which governs least.

SYSTEM TWO
INDIVIDUALIST
DEMOCRACY

1. Individualism

We begin with individuals. We think first and last of the distinct human beings who join as equal citizens in self-government. Democracy is nothing more or less than their instrument, our instrument. We use it to perform certain functions that cannot be performed by citizens acting separately. Where collective action is needed—as in national defense, or in setting the limits of individual conduct—we delegate limited authority to a representative legislature that acts for us. The members of that legislature are elected by the votes of many individuals, each having many separate interests. Government is created by and for private citizens.

Democratic government is by far the best, precisely because, built upon the participation of individual citizens, it best responds to their interests and best protects their rights. We therefore honor democracy, and prize it, but we do not romanticize it or worship it. We realize that representative assemblies, even when fairly elected, inevitably restrict some freedoms, injure some persons. Collective action that binds everyone is thus tolerable only where it is absolutely essential—and it can be shown essential only if the needs of the individual persons who constitute the community cannot otherwise be met. We are very wary of talk about "society." "Society" is not of flesh and blood; it has no rights; only human beings have rights. "Society" is a fiction, and often a dangerous one. There are only people, ourselves, to be served. The governors are our hired servants; let them never forget it.

We are *private* citizens. We have our own lives to lead, our own goals to pursue, our own values and tastes. The worth of our goals and the wisdom of our values are for the most part not the business of any legislature. They become its business only when (and only to the extent) we, the citizens, so choose.

We are not enemies of the state. We are proud of our country and its institutions. But we are not blind admirers of the state either. We have no illusions about the foibles of collective agencies, about the waste of dreary bureaucracy, about the insensitivity and occasional brutality of a faceless majority. We are democrats who have learned from experience to rely upon government with caution. We see clearly what our socialist friends seem not to see at all—that democratic government is a splendid instrument in some spheres, a poor substitute for private action in other spheres, and a serious threat to individual freedom when not kept strictly within its proper domain. We do not quarrel with democratic socialists about the basic principles of citizen participation. We do quarrel with them about the domains in which it is right (or wrong) and wise (or unwise) to take decision making from the hands of private citizens and put it in the hands of a collective body. Humans do not become smarter when they act collectively, but they often do then become more callous. We are troubled by the inescapable tendency of government to trespass upon the individual rights and freedoms it was created to safeguard.

But what is trespass? This is a question that honest democrats are forever disputing; there is no easy answer. In reconciling the separate rights of individuals and their common interests as a community, we apply certain well-established principles which, combined with those of self-government, yield what we call individualist democracy—private-enterprise democracy. Our defense of private-enterprise democracy, which follows, rests on compelling evidence and argument. We ask only that the reader's judgment be realistic, guided by practical experience and by calm reason.

2. Private Enterprise

Democracy and privacy go hand in hand—but the individuals whose business is being done must keep the upper hand. Collective action on common concerns is only one way to meet the needs of private parties who *have* concerns. Purpose, direction, does not come from governments, but from people. The interests of a government are always derivative; the original locus of all human rights and human achievements is private human lives.

In our private lives we engage in many varied activities, enterprises great and small. Private enterprise, properly understood, encompasses all these personal affairs. The chief business of democratic government is to safeguard the opportunities of its citizens to conduct their own business without interference, to pursue their private activities in peace and safety.

A private-enterprise system is thus one in which the undertakings of individual persons are respected and protected. Economic undertakings are among these, of course. Private freedom in the world of work and trade—capitalism—is part of private enterprise. Honest capitalism, intelligently pursued, we support proudly. But capitalism is not the whole of private enterprise, and should not be simply identified with it. Every artist, painting or writing with personal insight, is engaged in a classically private enterprise, as important as trade. Scholars and scientists are private enterprisers *par excellence.* Philosophical and mathematical investigations are deeply private pursuits. The explorer, the inventor, the musical performer, and the long-distance runner—all who pursue personal goals—are engaged in private enterprise. They may or may not cooperate with others in their pursuits; they may or may not aim to serve the community. The enterprise of most fundamental importance to every one is his or her private enterprise, which it is the duty of government not to direct but to protect.

Socialism encourages, and often requires, the collective support and collective direction of such activities. The socialist mistakenly supposes that the high points of human achievement are reached *en masse;* in fact, true human accomplishment is a solitary affair. In most socialist countries the government controls not just the economy, but scientific research, the arts, even philosophy and sports. They admit this with a mixture of embarrassment and pride: embarrassment because the absence of personal freedom is there so painfully evident, pride because collective enterprises (it is claimed) belong to everyone—"our" socialist realism in art, "our" gymnastic excellence, and so on. But a truly beautiful painting cannot be produced by a committee; artistic talent is very private and does not belong to everyone. The gymnastic competition is won not by the crowd, but by individual athletes whose long hours of solitary, disciplined training lie behind public efforts. The socialist's pride is misplaced; his embarrassment is well justified.

3.   Laissez Faire

What human activities should be protected from interference by others? All that can be. We seek the *widest possible range of private freedom that is compatible with the freedoms of others.* We want liberty in every sphere. Restriction or regulation is justifiable only where proved essential for the exercise of other freedoms. To understand why government interference so quickly becomes excessive, we must understand freedom itself.

Freedom is the ability to choose among alternative courses of action. We are free when we can do what we please. Many things in the world may interfere with the fulfillment of our desires, but the demand for freedom has always been a demand that, at the very least, others do not hinder us. Especially it has been the demand that governments—tax collectors, armies, secret police, bureaucrats of every kind—cease to interfere in our lives. *Laissez faire,* let do, the lovers of liberty have traditionally insisted; *laissez aller,* let go. This old motto, of which we are proud, has been unfairly ridiculed, as though it were a call for private rapacity. But it is not callous to want release from the choking grip of government; it is not unreasonable to want to be left alone.

We do not deny the need for the mutual accommodation of conflicting freedoms; being free does not entail being irresponsible. Precisely to achieve that accommodation we act cooperatively through government when we must. But only when we must. That understood, we do indeed defend a *laissez faire* society, in which private citizens are free, within the limits of essential laws and common human civility, to do what they please.

4.   "Negative" and "Positive" Freedom

This is too simple for socialists, who distinguish two kinds of freedom. Negative freedom (on their account) is freedom of the traditional sort—absence of restriction. Positive freedom is the freedom *to*, as contrasted with the negative freedom *from*. We are not positively free (say they) unless the achievement of our desired ends is concretely possible for us; we must be *able* to do it, as well as *not kept from doing it*. Such positive ability requires, in addition to the absence of restriction, developed personal capacities, and often tax-supported community assistance as well.

There, for example, stands a public library of which all are proud. It's open without charge to anyone; all are free to use it. "No," says the advocate of positive freedom: "one is not free to use the public library unless he knows how to read. If the only way we can get people to learn to read is by compelling them, then that compulsion will be part of their larger freedom. Similarly, the freedom to enjoy retirement entails the compulsion to save for it through taxation; the freedom to use automobiles safely entails the compulsion to wear seat belts, and so on. These compulsions," concludes the socialist, "do not restrict us; they enlarge our real power to do what is worth doing, and so they are the positive part of our freedoms."

This is intellectual fraud. When we are compelled by the government to act in one way and forbidden to act in another, that is plainly an infringement of our freedom and not an enlargement of it. I ought indeed to be sure my children learn to read, but if they are obliged by law to attend school for twelve years, and I am forced by law to see that they do, it is doublespeak to say that such comprehensive restrictions upon their lives and mine are parts of our "freedom." Nonsense. Some restrictions of their freedom may be in their interest and justifiable; but let us be honest with ourselves and call restriction by its proper name.

Every restriction must be thoroughly justified before it is imposed. No restriction can be justified by the paternalistic claim that it is for an individual's own good. It is very much in my interest to wear seat belts in my automobile, to be sure. But the legal compulsion to wear them is not an enlargement of my freedom; it is a clear infringement upon my freedom, by others. My own good, however much I may or may not understand it, is not the business of an elected legislature to determine. Nor is it its business to decide what freedoms I must give up to advance that good. We must never cease to remind ourselves: Freedom is one thing; compulsion, however well-intended, is another. I am free when I may choose. When I may not choose (because it is not good for me to be able to choose, they will say) but must do as ordered, I am insulted and cheated when also told that my "positive freedom" is being protected. Horsefeathers.

5. True Liberalism

Giving up some freedoms to advance others is, of course, an unavoidable necessity at times. Let us do it with our eyes open, however, and only when we must. We place limits on the conduct of everyone—and enforce these limits by law—so that everyone may live securely and in peace. Of course we are not free to assault others, or steal their property. But the joint decision to forbid everyone from acting in certain ways should be made only when, as in the criminal law, acting in those ways would be gravely injurious to others. Extending public law beyond this domain to any others is dangerous. "Every law," as Jeremy Bentham said, "is an infraction of my freedom." In the interest of freedom we must get along with the smallest reasonable number of laws and regulations. Careless collectivism will sacrifice—in an honest effort to do good—the very liberty whose protection was the object of our joining in government in the first place.

Here is the essence of genuine liberalism. Power may be rightfully exercised over any member of a civilized community, against his will, only—as John Stuart Mill argued powerfully—to prevent harm to others.

His own good, either physical or moral, is not a sufficient warrant. He cannot rightfully be compelled to do or forbear because it will be better for him to do so, because it will make him happier, because, in the opinions of others, to do so would be wise, or even right. These are good reasons for remonstrating with him, reasoning with him, or persuading him, or entreating him, but not for compelling him, or visiting him with any evil in case he do otherwise. To justify that, the conduct from which it is desired to deter him must be calculated to produce evil to someone else.

Mill was a true liberal, not in the peculiar modern usage of that term, but in the plain sense that he defended the liberty of ordinary citizens against their "benevolent" government.

6.   False Liberalism

There are not two kinds of freedom, "negative" and "positive." That pseudodistinction is the tool of those who think they know what is good for us and would force their will upon us. In the name of "positive freedom" we are told what we "really" want. If we honestly say that we prefer to do otherwise—that we do not wish to be taxed to save, that precautions for our safety are our own business, or whatever—we are told that such preferences, though we may think we have them, are not in accord with our "real will." The next step, in the name of positive freedom, is to "protect" us against ourselves; we are hedged by laws and regulations on every side so that we may be "truly" free. If our private will should conflict with the dictates of the authorities, we are likely to be told (or to be treated as if) the will of the community or the state is our own higher will which we haven't fully recognized. Since that will is "really" our own, we can't rationally object to the compulsion to obey it. On that theory—as Rousseau came to contend quite frankly—we must be "forced to be free."

This descent into totalitarianism is not mere theorizing. It has been, and is, common experience under socialist governments. Even in the United States there have been grave steps taken in this direction, tendencies needing to be perpetually combatted. When freedom is gone, the knowledge that we ourselves evicted it will be scant satisfaction. Whether on the political right or left, whether to "protect the revolution," "reestablish old values," or "create the new socialist man"—whenever a government has taken unto itself the power to abridge freedom for the good of those restricted but against their wills, the results are literally dreadful.

7. The Threat of Government

The horrors perpetuated in the name of "positive freedom" and its cousins are many. Yet there is a positive insight to be gained from it. In a society that protects the freedom of its citizens—to publish, to do business, to travel, to do what they please—the capacities of those citizens to take advantage of their freedoms are also matters of great importance. If citizens are illiterate or impoverished, some of their freedoms may be of little use to them. To take advantage of our opportunities, our abilities must be developed; we are all well-advised to look to our own education and health, and that of our children. In doing this we may take collective action: support public schools, museums, libraries. We may tax ourselves to support better the institutions needed to develop individual capacities. But we ought not to fool ourselves into thinking that such taxation is freedom. Freedom is the absence of restraint. It is always endangered by collective action. The single most serious threat to freedom comes from laws enacted by well-meaning but intrusive zealots.

Aware of this threat, the founders of the American republic laid down, in our Constitution, strict limits upon the government itself. The first ten amendments to the Constitution specify forcefully the things that government and its agents *shall not* do. "Congress shall make no law . . ." the first amendment begins. In that fence-building spirit, the rights of citizens, *against government,* were laid down as absolutely fundamental. Respect for this Bill of Rights is not mere sentiment; it is a continuing struggle whose successful pursuit has been the proudest achievement of the American body politic. If America stands for any single idea, it stands for this: that democratic governments are instituted only to protect individual human rights.

8. Property

Among those fundamental rights is the right of each person to possess and enjoy his own property. "Life, liberty, and property" was long the summary of basic rights. In the Declaration of Independence the word "property" was replaced in this summary by the phrase "pursuit of happiness"—which was certainly intended to include all rights of property. To make them, along with life and liberty, secure, "governments are instituted among men, deriving their just powers from the consent of the governed."

The American founders were learned men with good sense and much practical experience. They understood how essential the ownership of property is for human satisfaction. Without it there is neither social stability nor individual contentment. Arms and legs are the organic instruments through which we act in the world. Properties—houses, land, tools—are our inorganic instruments. Without property we lack the material capacity to advance our aims. Humans without their own property are diminished, helpless in a perilous world.

The point is metaphysical but not mysterious. Physical property (and the money or papers which represent it) is the external counterpart of our internal being. Our concept of our *selves* supposes that each of us has some personal aims and desires. But all talk of personal purpose is empty if we are forbidden the concrete instruments through which alone those aims may be pursued. Because aims differ so greatly, personal fulfillment requires the freedom of all of us to use our own instruments—our property —in our own ways. We must be free to save the products of our work or to spend them, to exchange our belongings with others as we freely determine among ourselves. Human "happiness" is not any single thing; it is but a word encompassing the unlimited variety of human ends. The right to own, exchange, and enjoy physical things is the practical side of the pursuit of happiness.

One person's happiness is another's hell. The general pursuit of happiness, therefore, is possible only if each is free to do it for himself. That is possible, in turn, only if each is entitled to own his own tools and use them in his own way.

9.   Economic Freedom

This boils down to economic freedom. "Economy" is from the Greek word "*oeconomous,*" meaning housekeeping. Freedom to keep our own house in our own way entails the freedom to enjoy, and deploy in our own fashion, the things to which our own efforts entitle us. It is the freedom to produce and sell, to buy and use, to save and invest.

The successful pursuit of this private enterprise results in the gradually increasing wealth of individuals, the accumulation of money and other forms of property. The name for such accumulation is *capital.* Capitalism is no more than the name of that system of national housekeeping which permits and encourages private accumulation and its productive use. From this system anyone may benefit, and most do. It is by no means for the wealthy alone, but for all of us who would make our own plans, save for our own purposes, control our own energies, and—in a phrase—pursue happiness in our own way. The freedoms a good government protects are not only economic, but they surely include the economic. If we are not free to keep our own house, all other freedoms are meaningless.

Recognizing this dimly, some socialists allow that nonproductive property may be privately owned, but they insist that productive property may not be. This distinction between "productive" and "nonproductive" property is illusory. Any two things of value to two parties may be exchanged, and that exchange may contribute to the accumulation of capital. What is mine is mine to use, within reasonable bounds, productively or in any other way. To forbid the private ownership of productive property is to forbid the private ownership of what may become productive, which is to forbid the private ownership of anything. A consistent socialism, it has been observed, must forbid all capitalist acts, even between two consenting adults.

Even if we could distinguish between productive and nonproductive property, we ought not to forbid the private ownership of either. Property used productively is no shame to its owner, but rather a credit to him. One who labors industriously, makes and sells intelligently, and comes thereby to possess land or a factory or a truck is as fully entitled to these as one with less energy or wit is to simpler accumulated goods. That some physical thing is used productively does not justify its appropriation by the state. On the contrary, it ought to be our collective concern to encourage private persons to use their property productively, thus maximizing their own usefulness to the community and advancing general prosperity.

"General prosperity," the socialist is likely to reply, "is what we are after. Hence ownership must be general. That is why we would nationalize—i.e., take for the nation—all productive industry." We will show that nationalization is *counter*productive. Calling its object "public ownership" is also deceptive. Under every system, socialism included, some persons will control the material resources of the community. We would have those powers distributed widely in private hands. The socialist tells us that when ownership of industry is "in common" we will all be the owners. This is simply not true. What everyone owns, no one owns. To own something is to have private rights to its use and enjoyment that others do not have. To claim that although no one has such rights, all are "owners in common" is to play deceitfully with words. In fact, the possessors of economic power under socialism are those members of the hidden oligarchy who exercise effective control of production and distribution. Under the guise of common ownership, not having to face the discipline of an open market, they feather their own nests. This consequence of socialism, after decades of experience, cannot be doubted.

The freedom to use private property, in an individualist democracy, is not absolute, of course; no freedom can be. Each person's rights to enjoy his or her own goods are bounded by the rights of others to do likewise. The health and safety of all calls for some regulation of what may be sold and how it may be used. Free enterprise depicted as without balance or discipline is a caricature. Nothing in our system precludes democratically-enacted regulation when such regulation—of monopolies, for example, or of the stock market—proves essential for the protection of freedom for all. We blend private enterprise and common restraint. But we begin with individual freedom to act, demanding justification for every collective restraint.

10.   Democracy and the Middle Class

The historical case for individualist democracy is overwhelming. Modern democracy and private enterprise have always been inseparable in practice. They are two aspects of the same historical process. Against aristocratic profiteers who owned virtually everything and ruled in their own interests, common citizens had to struggle to defend their rights. That struggle took political form in some contexts, economic form in others. As authority in the modern world shifted from the few to the many, the centers of power were broken up, and power itself diffused. That decentralization was first successfully achieved in the world of production and trade. So great were its benefits there, so intense its satisfactions, that the decentralization of power spread like prairie fire into every sphere of life.

The middle classes, fighting for economic freedoms, were the architects of modern democracy. The burghers of Europe insisted upon deciding for themselves what to make and with whom to trade. They demanded, and ultimately won, economic self-management. Having won it, they would not rest content without its political counterpart. But political self-management is democracy. Democratic government is the child of a free market; its parents are the self-directed employers and employees of a robust bourgeois society.

Socialists contend that working people are in essential conflict with the bourgeosie. The destruction of the middle class, by revolution or by evolution, then becomes the chief object of the so-called "proletariat." But their fundamental premise is false. There are recurring tensions between workers and employers, of course, when they bargain with one another. There are also tensions between competing producers and between competing consumers. The intricate and self-adjusting relations of all of these parties give balance to the whole. Together they constitute the threads of a vast economic fabric in which all may preserve independence. That economic independence provides the base for the distribution of political power—for democracy.

The same spiral may be travelled in reverse. The centralization of economic authority goes hand in hand with the centralization of political authority. An effective autocracy must control the barons who control the economy. In some hierarchies the barons are barons literally; in some they are called commissioners or agency heads. What counts is not the name but the fusion of power.

To protect against abuse of that power, decision-making authority has to be diffused. That diffusion is complete only when

the right to vote is universal. Voting rights were extended gradually, first to the bourgeoisie, then to workingmen, then to women.
That spread of political participation was only possible with the
spread of economic participation. Politics and economics are but
two aspects of the same social world. The decentralization of
authority in each was both cause and effect of decentralization in
the other. The impetus they give one another has democracy as
its result.

11. Socialist Centralization

One characteristic error of modern socialism is to suppose that
political authority can remain decentralized while the economic
authority that is part of its bone has been centralized. All experience shows that this cannot be. Countries in which socialism has
been adopted cannot maintain a genuine diffusion of political
power. The democratic convictions of their leaders may be sincere. Whatever the intent, however, the outcome of centralization is hierarchy.

In a free country, real differences among parties are in substantial measure economic differences. When production, distribution, the deployment of labor, and the control of money all
coalesce in a central presidium, real differences are squeezed out.
If they linger, they cannot surface but must boil underground.
Political parties wither; there is no "need" for parties in opposition to central authority. Where all planning for growth, saving,
consumer services, and the like, is made at the top, there is no
room below for political debate that is consequential. One party
is enough. If one plan for all is to be formulated and executed,
two parties are one too many. Opposition undermines hierarchical discipline; it becomes treason. What may have begun as
one political party among many becomes "the Party"—the central directive authority.

Party leaders then become, in effect, aristocrats, even dictators. To refuse to cooperate with them is disloyalty. To act independently of their plans is sedition. To contradict them publicly
is heresy. Socialism in every variety lays down a single, authoritative "party line."

Where the freedom of economic enterprise is restricted, political freedom is reduced proportionately; when all private economic freedom is gone, all political freedom disappears with it. Real power then is concentrated in the hands of the economic czars. In the U.S.S.R., for example, where there is the loudest profession of public ownership and economic democracy, there is no effective elected legislature. It is not the president or other nominally elected officers who govern, but the self-selecting leaders of the Communist Party. Centralized planning leads inexorably to monolithic rule.

Solidarity is often the pride of systems centrally organized and planned. But solidarity, fully understood, is precisely what genuine democrats do not want. A solid system is rigid; we want one that is flexible and changing. In a solid system the parts are tightly bound; we want one in which the parts act and interact loosely. Not homogeneity and dutifulness, but heterogeneity and self-reliance are our ideals. A healthy democracy will be open-textured, not solid, leaving spaces for individuals to move and grow as they see fit. We individualists take pride in variety and idiosyncrasy; we cultivate invention; we look for progress, offering incentives for imagination and creative enterprise. Some will take no advantage of this freedom, we know. Others among us will use it fruitfully, to the profit of all.

12.   Self-Interest and Profit

Profit is not a bad word. Some critics, Herbert Marcuse, for example, call the profit motive obscene. Does that stand the test of reason? Nasty accusations promote feelings of guilt on the part of those who seek their own profit. Of what are they guilty?

"Profit" is the general term for the benefits of self-interested investment. I invest time in study, energy in the care of my garden, money in the shares of a business. In each case, if I have invested wisely, I may hope to profit thereby—and why should I not? The time and energy are mine to spend as I will. The money is no less so. Suppose that I have earned, by honest work, enough to pay the bills and put a little money aside each month. May I not do with those savings what I please? If I spend my savings on a vacation in the mountains, no one will find me morally at fault. Am I any more blameworthy if, instead of consuming that surplus I came by honestly, I put it to productive use by lending it to a company that drills for oil? Or if I buy shares in a company that makes fertilizer? Surely there is no wrong in this. That is precisely what we do when we invest in corporate bonds or common stocks.

If I am careful in my loan or purchase, my savings may return an agreeable profit. Such profitable investments are entirely honorable. Every person must decide individually how to use the rewards that labor brings—whether to enrich present moments or to prepare for future pleasure or security. Each will judge, in the light of personal values, the variety of possible investments. It would be arrogant to presume to commend the expenditure that yields immediate gratification, while condemning the thrift that yields a future profit. Savings must be accumulated if we are to live more thoughtfully than from hand to mouth. Those savings—if they are not hidden under the mattress—will be invested in one way or another. Investing them profitably is wrong only for those soft-headed moralists who think it always wrong to act for one's own benefit.

Those who condemn profit are likely to argue in one of two ways. They may contend that the quest for profit is intrinsically base and demeaning—that profit is an immoral *motive*. Or they may contend that profit is obtainable only through exploitation —that profit is the mark of an immoral *system*. Consider these objections carefully.

13. The Profit Motive

Why is the profit motive base? Because (the socialist contends) it is heartless, inhumane. Is that so? Those who seek profit from their enterprise surely act out of self-interest. Is rational self-interest, as the reason for our conduct, necessarily inhumane? Spinoza—among the wisest and sweetest of moral philosophers —explained why intelligent self-regard is humaneness itself. Our own interests include, to some degree, the interests of others— our fellows and our families. We cannot care for them, or serve them, unless we care well and thoughtfully for ourselves. We must feed and clothe our bodies sensibly; we must train and cultivate our own minds; we must strengthen our own characters; we must work with discipline to acquire the material goods essential for the attainment of other ends. Much that we ought to do is rightly done with self-interest as its motive—rightly done for profit, if that concept is well understood.

"Selfish" we call those who allow immediate personal gain to override all other concerns. The quest for profit certainly need not have that character. Indeed, it is doubtful if narrow selfishness is profitable in the long run. It is a confused morality that identifies the intelligent pursuit of self-interest with heartless greed.

For any given act we usually have several consistent motives. Our own profit may be in view, as well as the interest of our associates, loved ones, and fellow citizens, in differing ways and degrees. Differing motives may not be equally apparent, even to ourselves. One of our motives often will be, and should be, our own self-interest. We seek a system in which, ideally, the mass of individual self-interests—yours, mine, and everyone's—will support one another, or at least fit together with reasonable harmony. The effort to achieve that harmony of selves is not in any way demeaning.

Self-interest—as Adam Smith wisely taught—is the great engine of human accomplishment. The work of the world is hard; often it is not pleasant. Yet it must be done; corn must be grown, steel forged. How shall men and women be brought to do it? They may be forced by the master's whip. They may sacrifice themselves purely for the love of others. Fear and altruism do often motivate us—but neither can serve as the foundation of a great and complicated economy. The underlying motivation for most productive work is and will be, as Adam Smith said, "the uniform, constant, and uninterrupted effort of every man to better his condition." It is this drive to advance one's own well-being, plain self-interest, that alone can cause people to make and do the things that must be made and done. In a famous passage Adam Smith wrote:

> It is not from the benevolence of the butcher, the brewer, or the baker that we expect our dinner, but from their regard to their own interest.

How serviceable will a political or economic theory be that denies the reality of this aspect of human nature? Socialists write with dreamy visions of a world in which all work is done with pleasure, and without the thought of profit or the "taint" of self-regard. Those pretty words are truly inhumane; their blindness to the real condition of humanity is dangerous. A system allowing no place for self-interest does not work. It never has; it never will.

Whenever socialist or communist revolutions have sought to eliminate the role of profit from the economy, the results have been catastrophic. Russian communists, enthused by the success of their revolution in 1917, collectivized farms and factories on a grand scale. Self-interest was to be forever put away. The results were predictably disastrous; production dropped sharply, distribution collapsed, millions starved. In a very short time Lenin himself found it absolutely necessary to reintroduce private trading and the opportunity for individual economic gain—under the name of the New Economic Policy! To bring the Soviet economy back to life, nothing worked but personal economic incentives. Even under Communism the economy proves efficient only where individual producers have the opportunity to wangle a profit from their labors—though the word "profit" will be avoided.

Communist China had to learn the same lesson in the same hard way. After years of Marxist collectivization, rigorously imposed and intensively propagandized, the facts of economic failure pressed themselves home. Chinese communes, it was admitted at last, had simply not been supporting themselves. As motive for production, altruism proved a flop. Decades of agricultural and industrial inefficiency and breakdown led the official Communist Party newspaper, *Jenmin Jih Pao,* to demand that factories begin to show *a profit!* A new slogan was proclaimed for the Chinese working classes: "It is honorable to make a profit, it is shameful to be in debt."

Socialist theorists are not usually so candid. Intoxicated by ideology, they are, as Mandeville put it,

> Unwilling to be short or plain
> On anything concerning gain.

So profit is condemned in doctrinaire fashion, while self-interest is promoted when it proves economically necessary or politically expedient. Dogmatic insistence upon unworkable theory leads to hypocrisy and cant.

For some, the objection to the profit motive is not hypocritical but the result of a logical mistake—an instance of the fallacy of composition. From the attributes of the parts, they reason incorrectly to the attributes of the whole. If those engaged in any interpersonal enterprise do their work for private gain, it is supposed, the larger institution in which they function must serve only private ends. This is clearly false. Hospitals, charities, labor unions, universities—corporate bodies of all kinds—may have public purposes and be generally successful in achieving them, while their employees do what they do within the corporate structure for reasons of private interest. Self-interested workers may serve themselves, the corporate body, and all of society, better than they know. Conversely, institutions aiming at profit are likely to have among their workers many who seek much more than monetary gain from their labors. Socialists who believe that the pursuit of private profit yields no social benefits are plainly mistaken. Socialists who believe that the pursuit of private profit must corrupt public institutions exhibit their unwillingness to test their doctrine in the real world.

14. The Profit System

Some critics of private enterprise complain not about self-interest as a *motive* for action, but about an economic *system* dependent upon profit making. Their objection is not to the (alleged) evil of persons, but to the (alleged) evil of institutions. For them also a dose of realism will prove helpful.

Democrats—socialists and capitalists—agree that a major goal of our system is and ought to be the prosperity of all citizens. We differ about the means to achieve it; surely the choice among alternative means should be based on demonstrated results. Which economic system will bring us the things and services we want, as good as we want, and as widely distributed as we want? Practical experience, as long as human history itself, gives reliable answers. Prosperity is greatest, and widest, in an economic system based on open markets. By coming to the market—the fruit market, the labor market, or the stock market—as independent and competing sellers and buyers, we will in fact be most likely to achieve our aims most fully.

What are the alternatives open to us? There are essentially only two: the market and the commune. They can be blended, of course; no one is likely to choose one to the total exclusion of the other. Goods may be produced collectively, brought to a publicly-owned storehouse, and distributed in accordance with principles politically determined—the whole system financed by general taxation. Or goods may be produced privately, brought to any one of many private markets, and distributed by a system of trade in which buyers and sellers compete by adjusting their asking or offering prices—each product of the system paid for by its eventual consumer.

Neither system in practice is quite so simple as described, of course. Both have many variations and are subject to a host of imperfections. But in the end our choice of fundamental path is between these two. Shall we buy from the noncompetitive public store, with taxes? Or shall we buy from the competitive private store, with earnings? If we combine them, which should be the dominant element in the mixture?

The competitive system we urge has this enormous and fundamental advantage: goods and services can be successfully sold only by meeting real needs—needs concretely manifested by the buyers' willingness to buy. A market is no more than a system (or place) of *trade,* in which parties enter and leave freely. Each offers voluntarily what he thinks is a fair price (in goods or money or services) for what he wants. The offer is accepted and the trade made only if the trading partner also believes the exchange is fair. The seller would like to get more for his goods; the buyer would like to pay less. They are in tension—but it is just that tension which tends to eliminate unfairness and waste. Buyers and sellers are always in the process of bargaining—directly or indirectly. Transactions will be consummated only when the bargain is agreeable to both.

Competition is the only principle that will ensure that customers get what they really want. To make a profit, the competitive producer must bring to market what will sell. Inferior goods or unneeded services are quickly and *naturally* discouraged in a free market by the simplest of all devices: no one buys them.

Buyers may be attracted by reducing prices. If producers bring an excess of goods of one kind to market—corn or used cars or what have you—the price of those goods is forced down as sellers compete for the business of the available buyers. Where goods or services are in short supply, competitive demand by the buyers drives the price and profit on those items up. The prospect of a ready market and substantial profit draws new producers and greater supply. Producers are strongly encouraged to exercise their ingenuity in devising products—new or improved drugs, toys, or machines—that will be valued enough to find a wide market, thus bringing profit to inventor and seller. Markets are nothing but the places in which the vast networks of human wants and needs are sorted, and human interests satisfied. The pushing and pulling of those interests tend inevitably toward an equilibrium in each sphere between what is offered and what is asked for. The larger equilibrium of the whole is the natural product of the host of smaller equilibria that the market system promotes.

Equilibrium is always short-lived. Desires are constantly changing, skills grow scarcer or more common, products become obsolete, discoveries revolutionize a market. Changes in demand and supply are natural features of the human condition. Socialist planners hope to direct these changes, encouraging some, discouraging others. But any such direction supposes a wisdom no planners can possess.

Consider, for example, the central decisions that would have to be made if we sought to plan the long-term pattern of energy production and consumption. Shall we base our plans upon the existing supplies of petroleum? Who will control those resources, and how? Do we really know how large the earth's petroleum reserves are? Perhaps we should return to coal as the primary energy source. What are the consequences, to human health and to the environment, of such a reversal? Is nuclear fission a safe source of power? Can it be made safe? Is nuclear fusion a practical alternative? Can it be made practical? And what of solar power in all its varieties? There are no easy answers to such questions. Which fuels or methods are to be chosen, and in what combination, depends utterly upon the price of each, in money or safety, and upon what we and others are willing to pay for what. The feasibility of large-scale uses of solar power increases, for example, as the cost of crude oil escalates. The mix of power sources will be forever changing, and it will be optimally determined at any given time if there is opportunity for the producers of each to compete with one another for the business of energy users. We cannot fix the outcome. Every socialist plan that seeks to do so will eventually collapse. The world market for energy will be the ultimate forum in which these economic decisions are made.

The task is not to manage human wants with artifical constraints, but to accommodate their fluctuation and growth. Resiliency is a paramount need; it is obtained only in a system designed so that its elements are self-adjusting. Markets have precisely that feature; from earliest human history the open market has proved the fairest and the most efficient device for accommodating change and growth. No system of distribution has ever succeeded without introducing—or reintroducing—the basic elements of a market economy.

15.   Is the Market Free?

"A pretty picture," replies the socialist critic, "but a fraudulent one. The market economy, in reality, is a snare and a delusion." His complaints boil down to three, bearing upon: (1) the questionable freedom of the market; (2) the questionable wisdom of the buyers; and (3) the questionable decency of the sellers.

(1) "The market is never genuinely free. It is distorted by the wholly unequal powers of seller and buyer. It is manipulated by private producers (or jobbers) who control essential technology or raw materials. Powerful sellers charge what the traffic will bear. Hungry buyers, utterly dependent upon products so controlled, function more like stooges in the market than like equal traders. Or the stooge may be the helpless seller, perhaps a small farmer, who has no choice but to accept the prices offered for his crops by the big buyers. Shrewd and powerful buyers or sellers can squeeze the market for exorbitant profits.

"The appearance of competition among buyers or sellers is usually deceptive. Producers collude in fixing prices or in determining the quantities of goods to be brought to market. The powers in the market will somehow ensure their control and exclude others who threaten to interfere with a good thing. Similar manipulation is widespread in the labor market, where those with skills in demand unite to set the price of their services. Professional guilds and trade unions sharply restrict entry into the 'free labor market,' ensuring employment and high wages for the ins, and keeping the outs out.

"When price fixing and collusion are forbidden by law, a hundred ways will be devised to achieve the same result. Sometimes the laws are defied. More often collusion and manipulation go on through informal understanding. Republic Steel and U.S. Steel, Ford and General Motors, the teamsters and the long-shoremen—all seem to fix their prices with amazing coordination.

"The market turns out to be anything but free. Often it is a mask for outright monopoly. More commonly it is simply a tool for private interests with the power to manipulate it. Its regular outcome, in any event, is crass exploitation."

These charges, if true, would amount to a serious objection to free enterprise. In fact, though markets are sometimes defective, the complaint as a whole is exaggerated and grossly unbalanced.

Monopoly and collusion, for example, are real threats to a free market. The advantages of a competitive system cannot be expected where genuine competition is absent. But the conditions needed to maintain a genuinely competitive market are known, and we can act, democratically, to ensure these conditions. Our critics allege that we trust an "invisible hand" and believe all will go right without intelligent attention. Not so. We think the open market is *fundamentally* self-correcting, but also in need of thoughtful regulation to maintain its openness. We set legal limits on business practices. We forbid fraud, monopoly, restraint of trade, and punish such crimes firmly. We, the buyers and sellers in the market, are the citizens who establish this legal framework democratically.

Our system has flaws; we respond to them by seeking remedies. If the open market is sometimes thrown off kilter by unscrupulous persons or uncontrollable natural events, we do not abolish the market but act to safeguard its stability. No economic system operates flawlessly. Because our system is essentially sound, it is within our power to protect it from most manipulation, so that it can yield its expected benefits.

The normal human body is beset with flaws. We intervene medically or surgically to correct malfunctions. Should we conclude from the need for intervention that we would be healthier if we eliminated the natural equilibria of the body and replaced them by external controls? Regulation of the body from without is sometimes medically essential. The good physician will rely upon it, however, only when he must; the aim will always be to restore natural function. The case is not essentially different for the body politic.

Markets, too, require supervision and occasional intervention to reestablish equilibrium. By calling attention to these needs, the socialist critic properly cautions us to expect occasional malfunctions in a competitive system. Such cautions cannot serve, however, as serious objections to the competitive principle. On the contrary, the socialist complaints of market manipulation rest upon an underlying recognition of the value of open competition. The objection tacitly affirms what ostensibly it would deny—that economic stability and growth depend upon *un*manipulated, i.e., free-flowing, supply and demand.

Ironically, socialist practice introduces the very evil socialism condemns in theory: monopolistic power. Centralized planning and direction of the economy does not eliminate monopoly; it *is* monopoly. Monopoly is characterized by the absence of mechanisms that can restrain the abuses of economic power. Public ownership, and with it the political control of all industry, crushes all such mechanisms. Nothing then prevents any abuse that may serve the purpose of some controlling political bloc. Any featherbedding that may win trade-union support in a labor government, any distortion in the location of industry that may win votes, any sloth in production or obsolescence in design that may "make jobs" or curry favor, even outrageous pricing that ignores costs in order to redistribute income in accord with political objectives—all this and more is unstoppable when the economy has been socialized. Political parties then exercise precisely that unrestrained control of supply and demand the socialist condemns when the free market is distorted.

Such distortion under our system is occasional and correctable; under theirs it is permanent and uncorrectable. Monopoly is a threat to the open market against which we can protect by regulatory agencies and legal measures. It is more than a threat when everything is monopolized politically, with no possibility of restraining that monopoly from without. Socialism provides no without; all is within. There, deleterious economic policies may be adopted by public officials who either do not understand the ultimate catastrophic costs (in inflation, waste, or stagnation) or who understand the costs but never have to bear them.

The forces of supply and demand are not the figments of a capitalist imagination; they are inescapable realities. Markets bring those forces into reasonable balance. By distorting the market, socialism inevitably sacrifices economic balance. Who pays for it in the end? We all do, painfully.

16. Should Consumers Be Sovereign?

(2) "Not only the power of monopoly," the socialist critic continues, "but the power of advertising corrupts the market. Capitalists laud consumer sovereignty. But when consumers are the dupes of professional deceivers, it is no blessing that they are sovereign. Unhealthy foods, unsafe automobiles, inferior goods of every description are pawned off 'freely' on gullible consumers by rapacious profit-seekers. The public is saturated with advertising propaganda; it permeates newspapers and television. Private enterprise—supported by little children humming the advertising jingles—drowns us in drivel. Can such a market be the foundation of a healthy economy?"

Caution is again the lesson. Where competition to sell is fierce, the buyer must beware. Buyers will sometimes be misled or disappointed. Advertising that is false or deceptive we forbid by law. Still, consumers must be free to purchase the goods and services they want—not just those others think best for them. Wisdom in spending is a matter to be judged, in the end, by those who do the spending and get what they pay for—by consumers.

What sells over the long haul? Which producers thrive? Superior electronic equipment beats out the shoddy; firms with a reputation for making rugged and efficient farm machinery grow from generation to generation; attractive and durable furniture wins for its makers a secure place in the market. Everyone makes mistakes in buying, but most consumers know very well what they want, and from whom they are likely to get it. The last place we look for good products, or good service, is from a state monopoly.

Our socialist friends object to popular tastes. So unrefined the entertainment! So gaudy the clothes! But who shall judge taste for those whose money is to be spent? Fads and cheap ornaments always attract some. Does that justify some planners in deciding what may be bought? In exchange for the loss of consumer freedom, we notice no elegance of taste in socialist housing or socialist clothing. In the real world, ironically, it is they who copy us.

In socialist societies even the arts are politicized. Often the only novels or plays permitted are those that teach "correct" doctrine, only that painting or music is distributed that has been governmentally "approved." "Let a hundred flowers blossom," wrote Chairman Mao at one point in his career—but the resulting partial freedom was so threatening to the established socialist regime that it was very quickly withdrawn. And what explains the constant defection of Soviet artists to Britain or the United States? Publication—even of fiction!—is carefully restricted in socialist countries; the publication of works written in Russian but forbidden in Russia is a profitable small industry in the United States! But the manuscripts have to be smuggled out of the writers' own country. Democratic capitalists find all this terribly offensive. In our system, true, bad novels as well as good ones are widely produced and enjoyed, as is music of every description. But aesthetic merit is not, in our view, for the government to determine. Our citizens read and hear what *they* want to read and hear, not what others think good for them. That's what freedom means.

A society that will be free must protect the opportunities of consumers in all spheres to control the expenditure of their own resources. The dictates of an economic czar are no more tolerable than those of a political czar. For some functions—military defense is one example—there simply is no alternative to collective action requiring taxation. For most functions, private choice is a real alternative, and where this is true the replacement of such choice by taxation for "public service" amounts to a command, to everyone, that certain things be done in certain ways at a fixed price. What each consumer pays in taxes will have little or no relation to the benefits he or she may (or may not!) receive.

Some choices made by consumers in a free market may prove unwise. This does not at all justify depriving them of their right to make choices. Democracy, nothing more, requires the diffusion of decision-making power in the economic as in every other sphere. Arrogance, nothing less, gives some persons the notion that they may choose what interests the economy shall serve, what aesthetic standards shall be invoked. No persons or agencies (however good their intentions) are capable of managing our private affairs, economic or other. We block such interferences only by protecting the open market in which private choices can be made.

Socialists contend that consumers are "exploited" in a free-market economy. The truth of that claim can be determined only by consumers themselves, who—in a democracy—will register their judgments in elections. Let those who advocate the abolition of a free economy and those who advocate its retention compete for office through election by secret ballot. What fairer test of alleged exploitation could be proposed? What does happen in such elections? When the competition is open and honest, those who would scrap the free market almost invariably lose, and lose overwhelmingly. Private citizens accustomed to directing their own lives, choosing their own jobs, and spending their own money, are not likely to yield those freedoms to the state.*

17.　Can a Profit System Do the Job?

(3) The socialist critic now withdraws to a final line of defense. "Surely there are some spheres in which cooperative public inter-

_____

*One form of voting is with the feet. Socialist countries often forbid the departure of their citizens, even building walls of brick and barbed wire to prevent escape. From the United States, noted for its free enterprise system, emigration is uncommon, although absolutely unrestricted. Those moving in the other direction, who risk punishment by entering the United States illegally, number in the millions; those awaiting formal permission to enter the United States as immigrants number many millions more. How could judgment be clearer?

est must replace competing private interests. If the economy is based on profit, any essential service that does not yield a profit will not be offered. There are many such services and they are important. The inability of a profit system to provide them at a decent level is evidence of its inadequacy."

This argument is confused, its conclusion false. Self-interest and cooperative public spirit need not be at odds. It is sometimes in our private interest to engage in joint action; we would not deny that for a moment. But the fact that private enterprise is wisely supplemented by some cooperative enterprise does not entail that it should be everywhere replaced by collectivization.

Adam Smith himself put this forcibly. Some services, "though they be in the highest degree advantageous to a great society, are, however, of such a nature, that the profit could never repay the expense to any individual or small number of individuals." To institute such services, reasonable citizens may act jointly and bear expenses jointly. Police and fire protection are among these. Park services and most schools are also appropriately public.

In every case it is for the people to decide whether they can best obtain the wanted services from private or from public institutions. They may err, or change their minds in view of costs or the quality of services provided. Garbage collection has shifted from public to private enterprise in many communities, while health services shift more and more from private to public hands. Whether, for a given service, the free market is the best instrument is always open to test; the claim that it is must be empirically defended. But the same is true of claims about public instruments. No economic arrangements are inscribed in heaven. We are not dogmatic about economics. We welcome fair and practical tests of alternative institutions. Our claim is simply this: Where the conditions of an open market can be maintained, free enterprise with competition for profit will generally prove more efficient and more satisfying for the entire community.*

---

*The founders of the London School of Economics, Sidney and Beatrice Webb, appointed a Board of Governors consisting largely of nonsocialists. They personally favored socialism but were prepared to put that belief to the test of scientific study. In that honorable spirit the argument between socialist democrats and individualist democrats ought always to be conducted.

18. The Capitalist Record

Socialist critics repeatedly claim to find private enterprise economies in their death throes; but the plain facts show that for the
provision of goods and services of high quality in virtually every
sphere, free market economies have proved ever more successful. Enormous benefits are reaped by the mass of workers and
private savers, and by the great body of citizens served. The
distinguished economist, Paul Samuelson, wrote in 1976:

> For the world as a whole, the third quarter of the twentieth century
> outshone any epoch in the annals of economic history. As far as
> growth of total world output is concerned, we did not see its like
> before.

Much of that growth took place in capitalist North America,
whose economic health and resiliency have been almost universally admired. The past few decades have also witnessed great
vigor in the free economies of Japan, West Germany, and Israel.
Not far behind them, in rates of growth, have been France, the
Low Countries, Italy, and Austria. Not only the developed nations have prospered. Some former colonies remain economically backward, but those developing countries in which private
enterprise has been given fullest opportunity—Singapore, Hong
Kong, Taiwan, Thailand, Mexico, and South Korea—have enjoyed rapidly growing economic prosperity. To a substantial degree, even such countries as Iran, Venezuela, and Brazil have
enlarged their industrial base and raised their standards of living
in a competitive environment. Even where the political system is
not fully democratic, economic freedom brings economic
growth.

19. Collectivization

Socialism stultifies. Public agencies providing goods or services
collectively must be governed *politically*. The agencies' income
must be got from taxes. Taxes are imposed on the basis of the
ability of the taxpayer to pay, not on the basis of what he or she
receives in return from that agency. Subsidized by the public

treasury, public agencies commonly distribute services at very low charge. But there is no such thing as a free lunch. Some beneficiaries of the services—especially big users—get a bargain they do not deserve; the rest of us, including nonusers, foot the bill. All taxpayers fall into one of two classes: those who get back more than they pay in, and those who get back less than they pay in. The more the economy relies upon taxes for its operation, the greater the percentage of the citizens who fall into the second class.

When the kinds of services to be generally provided, and the principles for funding and allocating them, are all determined centrally, political considerations rule. Complicated economic interactions cannot be respected. The public store almost invariably runs at a loss—our loss. In some spheres—national defense, public recreation—this mode of operation is unavoidable. Extended to other spheres, the socialized method imposes upon us all great costs of three kinds: (1) the costs of no discipline; (2) the costs of bureaucracy; (3) the costs of centralized planning.

20. Decisions Without Discipline

A socialized economy is without discipline because it does not link benefits to payments. It can be munificent in providing welfare treats only because it operates at a constant deficit. The public spenders—unlike responsible private citizens—are not restrained by the fear of loss, because there is no limit to the amounts government can borrow. The debts are paid, sooner or later, by printing cheap paper money, debasing the currency, and encouraging a repetition of the process. Socialists lose their economic senses. A public park may be run appropriately without fees for use, the public treasury making up the loss. But the same system cannot be applied throughout the economy, because there is then no outside profitable segment that can cover the deficits. The only way to pay for them then is to print still more paper money. Inflation—as we say in the United States—is made in Washington.

Moreover, the distribution of goods and services under such a system is sure to be unfair because, cut loose from the discipline of the market, it responds primarily to the clamor of political pressure groups. Electoral success requires quick results, swift gratification. Patient planning for the future is sacrificed to immediate desire; the redistribution of investment capital and the long-term deterioration of productivity and services are the inevitable drift. Insensitivity to the requirements of fairness in setting prices for goods and services is the universal mark of such systems.

Profligacy is the inevitable result of political decision making on economic questions. Legislatures respond to pressures from narrowly concerned minorities. Politicians want most of all to be reelected. Electoral support is more surely to be gained by the expenditure of tax monies to provide services badly wanted by a few than by prudent restraint in the provision of services that many do not want at all. Thus pressure groups—such as veterans and farmers in the United States—win massive subsidy from the public treasury. It is always easier to expand services than to contract them; it is practically impossible to eliminate public services, even though they may be shockingly wasteful. The economist Henry Wallich writes:

> If a monument were built in Washington in memory of each major federal program that has been discontinued, the appearance of the city would not be greatly altered. In contrast, when the Edsel doesn't sell, production stops. But the government is still reclaiming land to raise more farm surpluses and training fishermen to enter an occupation that needs subsidies to keep alive. Old federal programs never die, they don't even fade away—they just go on.

Political factions inevitably trade economic favors as they trade votes. It is part of the profession. To buy support for some juicy government program, support is given to another program to be juiced by another faction. You get more highways if we get more hospitals; you get more missiles if we get the aircraft carrier; if you support this dam here, we will support that one there —and so on. To increase a budget in one direction only is as difficult as letting out one's belt on one side only. Decreasing a budget is well nigh impossible until catastrophe strikes. And even then the brokerage of political forces obliges "even-handed" reductions—across-the-board cuts when economic realities call for selective pruning.

Neither stupidity nor crookedness is to blame for such blundering. The problem is *systematic*. Wastefulness is inevitable where decisions that should be made on the basis of fluctuating supply and demand are made instead on political grounds. The costs are buried in a tangle of taxation. Citizens feel the burden of their taxes, certainly, but are unable to trace their uses or control their growth. The more public expenditure spreads, like a cancer, the less it is possible to restrain it.

Worse yet, the socialized economy gives each participating taxpayer reason to behave irresponsibly. When costs are covered by general taxation, each person's benefits from every public service will be cheap to him, because so many nonusers are also paying. The system strongly encourages perfectly needless expenditures. Wallich again:

> When it comes to accepting benefits, the citizen taxpayers act like a group of men who sit down at a restaurant table knowing that they will split the check evenly. In this situation, everybody orders generously; it adds little to one's own share of the bill and for the extravagance of his friends he will have to pay anyhow. What happens at the restaurant table explains—though it does not excuse—what happens at the public trough.

21. Bureaucracy

Other ugly features inevitably characterize a state-run economy. Government agencies proliferate, overlap, bicker over their jurisdictional authority. Many people in different agencies will be employed to do essentially the same job—which none can do effectively while each is in the other's way. Civil-service employment practices make it virtually impossible to dismiss anyone, even the incompetent, except in cases of the most blatant malfeasance.

Internal convolution becomes the mark of government organization. Intrigue, appropriately called Byzantine, permeates all units and levels. Regulations grow more lengthy and more complicated until they are intelligible only to insiders. Minor injustices are common, but the procedures for appeal are cumbersome and ineffective. Too many share in the decision-making process, and no one is accountable; nowhere does the buck stop; authority becomes faceless. The operating principle of every bureaucrat becomes not the accomplishment of some specific objective, but the avoidance of any error for which he may be blamed. Gray incompetence is rewarded, bold energy punished, and all remind themselves not to blot their copybooks.

The inefficiency of a collectivized economy boggles the mind. The socialized dollar must pass through untold hands from the time of its collection as tax, during its travels within the labyrinth of government, to its ultimate expenditure on public welfare. At each way station, a slice of that dollar is cut off. By the time it reaches its destination, it will have shrunk so greatly that it will buy only a fraction of what it would have bought had it been spent by a citizen directly. And it is likely to be spent carelessly at that. Processing dollars through the public treasury has only one sure result: waste.

22. Unity and Freedom

Finally, government agencies differ from private ones in having the power to compel. Some functions—those of police, courts, regulatory agencies—depend upon that power and could not be performed by private parties. The use of that coercive power where it is not essential, however, is very dangerous.

Governments make laws. Through taxation and threat of punishment they tell us what we must do and may not do. That power has no proper place in day-to-day economic decision making. A modern economy is complicated beyond the power of any single rule-making authority to simplify. Wants and needs differ endlessly for different people in different circumstances. Problems of production and service are infinitely varied in different industries at different times. No institution, no matter how thick its rule book, can plan for all. The movements of a healthy economy cannot be directed by any single source. Centralized planning is the rock upon which the ship of socialism—however democratic its original intention—invariably founders.*

---

*The quality and quantity of consumer goods invariably declines when planning is centralized—for which reason (the saying goes) socialism founders on two rocks: roast beef and ice cream.

Socialism hungers for unity. It seeks to integrate the resources of the whole community to achieve common objectives. This tendency is tolerable only so long as the common objectives are expressed in terms so general that all may share them: "providing for the common defense," or "promoting the general welfare." The moment common objectives require concretely unified plans, serious tensions must arise. All agree readily that the general welfare should be promoted. We are sure to disagree about what plan will have that result. Any single scheme for the whole community is certain to ride roughshod over those who do not share the particular values that underlie it.

When all citizens may go their own way and are not obliged to justify their values to others, deep differences need not lead to conflict. X gives money to the church; Y spends money on travel; Z invests for retirement. They may argue, but they need not fight, because their differing budgets do not have to be reconciled. Once it is decided, however, that there will be *a plan* for the community, harmony with difference comes to an end. When some central authority establishes a master budget for the disposition of most community resources, through general taxation, all citizens are coerced. All must abide by the plan, be governed by its quotas, serve its objectives.

It does not matter how good the plan is. *Any* plan so devised and executed will impose uniformity. It will suppress the individuality and freedom that democratic government is instituted to protect. Centralized planning presupposes substantial agreement about values—about work and recreation, about saving and spending, about what is worth what. Such widespread systematic agreement is not natural—it can be achieved only by threat or force. Since centralized planning is impossible without that agreement, it must resort to coercion. If there is one comprehensive budget for production and distribution, therefore, those of us who do not like it will—for our own good, of course!—be forced to be free.

23. Centralized Planning Subverts Democracy

The same corrosive effects ensue no matter who is responsible for the central plan—even a representative legislature. Legislatures enact laws that restrict some freedoms in the interest of public order. That is unavoidable. In the economy, where legislative action is avoidable, the representative assembly is a wholly unsuitable decision-making authority.

If charged with the task of constructing a unified economic plan, legislators quickly learn that they cannot possibly cope with the overwhelming variety, detail, and conflict involved. On whom can their failures be blamed? The legislators themselves appear to be stupid and incompetent. Very soon socialists urge that central planning authority be delegated by the legislature to the "experts." Parliament is too confused and divided; let the job be done by an autonomous planning agency with a permanent professional staff. They understand economic complexities; they can be entrusted to lay down the rules for all.

Harold Laski, foremost British exponent of democratic socialism, makes the typical proposal:

> It is common ground that the present parliamentary machine is quite unsuited to pass rapidly a great body of complicated legislation. . . . A Labour [Socialist] Government would confine the House of Commons to the two functions it can properly perform: the ventilation of grievances and the discussion of general principles of its measures. Its Bills would take the form of general formulae conferring wide powers on the appropriate government departments. . . . The extension [of such delegated legislation] is inevitable if the process of socialisation is not to be wrecked by the normal methods of obstruction which existing parliamentary procedures sanction.

Revealing passage! Parliamentary processes are "methods of obstruction" only for those whose plan for the society cannot survive on its own merits—as no plan can—and who therefore would impose a plan through an agency given extraordinary authority. The plan must cohere, its parts must interrelate. It applies to all, so all must work for its common end. Representative legislatures, never in such full accord, are hence a terrible nuisance to the socialist planner. Leave them as a forum in which common folks can "ventilate their grievances"—and leave the decisions that really count to us experts. That is the fate of democracy collectivized.

Many of our socialist friends have genuinely humane ends in view. So do we. So do others, who disagree with their plans, and with us. Economic goals in a modern society are always in conflict. Machinery that ensures the central implementation of any single plan for society must prove incompatible with democratic process. Socialist governments once in power therefore commonly find it necessary to "suspend" democracy. An economic plan—for a whole country, for five years, say—cannot be amended on the floor of the legislature, or voted upon by parts. It requires centralized conception, universal allegiance, unified execution. Compromise, the essence of democratic process, is then not tolerable. Laski puts the matter bluntly. A socialist government, he says (in his book *Democracy in Crisis*), should "suspend the classic formulae of normal opposition" and "take vast powers and legislate under them by ordinance and decree."

Substance and procedure here conflict. Democracy is a kind of procedure; socialism is a substantive goal. When the goal comes to have overriding importance, any procedures, even democratic ones, that do not advance it will be discarded. Coercion, even ruthlessness, may be "justified" as the price of the objective.

In war, a general knows that his battle plans are likely to yield dreadful casualties. But he knows also that victory must be won *at any cost.* Just for that reason we do not expect armies to be run democratically. Our lives are at stake in the battle; the objective is everything, the methods used are strictly subordinate.

Democracy cannot survive where that is the pervading spirit. In political life, and in the economy, no particular result can be optimal for all. Agreement about desired results are usually shaky. Even shared objectives will have different priorities for different groups. For some, defense is primary; for some, environmental protection; for some, economic growth; for some, social equality. All aims cannot be in first place. Any institution that forces general agreement upon one ordering of community priorities cannot be democratic. Socialism forces this agreement. Its impact upon democracy may be readily inferred.

In practice, socialism lives up to this unhappy promise. Decade after decade its advocates insist that inefficiency and unfairness in its operations are but temporary failures. More complete plans, wider "cooperation" are demanded. More centralization is introduced, more uniformity sought, more coercion applied. Again and again, the "classic formulae of normal opposition" are suspended—and once sacrificed they are almost impossible to reestablish. But never is the dream fulfilled.

Frederick Hayek writes:

> Democratic government has worked successfully where, and so long as, the functions of government were, by a widely accepted creed, restricted to fields where agreement among a majority could be achieved by free discussion; and it is the great merit of the liberal creed that it reduced the range of subjects on which agreement was necessary to one on which it was likely to exist in a society of free men. It is now often said that democracy will not tolerate 'capitalism.' If 'capitalism' means here a competitive system based on free disposal over private property, it is far more important to realize that only within this system is democracy possible. When it becomes dominated by a collectivist creed, democracy will invariably destroy itself.

24.   Utopia for Whom?

Socialists think they know what is good for the rest of us. Their unified schemes for social or economic well-being fail because there can be no single successful scheme. One person's utopia is another's hell.

Individual interests—inclinations, drives, desires—vary enormously. Some of us seek satisfaction in groups, others privately. Some seek material wealth, others learning, or fame, or fun, or peace of mind. In matters of sex, for one example, nothing is clearer than that standards are not uniform. The imposition of uniformity has been a leading cause of human unhappiness. Simple and sophisticated, material and spiritual, the only general characteristic of aims in a healthy society is *variety* without limit. Socialists, no matter how learned or wise, cannot tell us what we want from our lives. We all want different things.

Democracy protects variety. It defends the rights of citizens to pursue their own ends, whatever those may be. It is attractive partly because it is designed to honor individuality; it does not force individuals to fit a common mold. Self-fulfillment is possible only when each person retains the authority to dispose privately of time and energy, skills and earnings. Take that from us, and, though the resulting scheme be ever so attractive on paper, it will be a prison for most. Some prisons serve good food, provide warm clothes, recreation halls, moderate work hours, and pleasant lawns—but they are prisons nonetheless.

Individuals must have the freedom to join or not to join. Acting collectively we can create a framework of legal order and be mighty in defense. Acting as private citizens, singly or in voluntary groups, we can do all the things we get personal satisfaction from. We will do them in our own way, making our own private compromises when necessary, with our own gains in view. We are not selfish, but we march to the beat of our own drums.

25. Equity and Equality

What leads well-meaning people to advocate a common rule? Behind the drive for uniformity lies a confusion, common in socialist thinking, between *equity* and *equality*.

Equity is fairness, to which every citizen is entitled. In the body politic we are all members equally: democracy assures each of us one vote on community issues; every person deserves the equal protection of the law. It is a serious mistake, however, to suppose that equity in treatment requires equality in the outcome. Equal citizenship does not entitle us to equal incomes or equal honors. Because humans differ greatly, equal rights to private freedom will surely result in *un*equal outcomes. No government can forbid this and remain democratic.

As private citizens, we begin with different talents, and use what we earn with different tastes and different values. Some learn more than others; some use their resources for travel, others for homes or boats; some gamble and go broke; some work hard and accumulate. All are entitled to a fair chance to maximize their own good—but all are not entitled to the same job, or house, or bank account. The role of legislation is abused when it enforces equality of result.

Over the long run, for most of us, fair treatment without forced equality yields results that are very good indeed. Competition, regulated reasonably, proves healthy. The maximizing of one individual's own good need not minimize another's. Life is not like poker, a zero-sum game in which each player's winnings must come from the losses of others. Quite otherwise. Private gains increase public benefits. Prosperous citizens pursuing their own ends contribute to attractive and decent community life. Openness in the community encourages variety of personal style and more widespread contentment. Private enterprise—in the arts and recreation and learning, as well as in economics—enlarges the total store of community production. In dividing a pie, it is not the equality of all portions, but the increasing size of each portion—and its taste!—that counts most. By redistributing wealth to ensure equal outcomes, the socialist imposes a structure inimical to the growth of the whole pie. And he deadens the flavor for all.

26. Trade

Markets, we have argued, are essential to prosperity and to freedom. The marketplace—of ideas as well as of goods—is central to democracy. What explains that centrality?

Human beings can reconcile their conflicting interests harmoniously only when they can *trade* what they have for what they want. Trading, in the most general sense, is one of the hallmarks of human association. The lesser animals are incapable of it; they must obtain directly from nature, be supplied by superiors, or do without. To exchange with one another, beings must be able to understand one another, to order their own goals, and to reason. Rational exchange is mutually profitable. In the central square of a rural village, or in the intricacies of a great industrial stock exchange, buyers and sellers can bring their several needs and wants into fair equilibrium without external compulsion.

Market exchange is the inevitable consequence of some having excess Ps and wanting more Qs, while others have excess Qs and want more Ps. The imbalance that creates the need for a market arises from the specialization of human labor. If every person could, by individual efforts, satisfy his or her needs for food, clothing, shelter, entertainment, and everything else, no one would ever need to trade—though many might like to, even then. Obviously humans are not self-sufficient in this way. The division of labor, and with it the market that permits the needed trading, are absolutely inevitable.

Marxists are offended by specialization. They condemn the division of labor as inhumane. Why? Because it leads inevitably to buying and selling, which they think evil. Differences in human employment will bring trade, as surely as night must follow day. Trade leads to some universally accepted instrument of exchange, which we call money. Karl Marx himself had a vision of a new world coming, in which the evils of trade would be forever erased, because the division of labor itself would be erased. Money, in all its forms, would be gone, eliminated. Well-rounded socialist men and women would take turns in doing all the many jobs in the world! This he proposed seriously as an ideal, but it has never even been approached in practice, of course. As though farming, and bridge building, and all serious employments could be treated like hobbies! Some small communes experiment with such principles. They do not last long; and while they do last they survive as parasites on a more productive economy—or they trade.

27. Subsidiation

If the division of human labor is universal, and the exchange of goods an absolute necessity, we must decide whether that exchange of goods is better conducted freely by the producers, or directed from above. There are no other alternatives. The exchanges within a society will be made through open markets, or they will be made on command. We choose markets because experience and reflection convince us that human affairs are managed best by those who are directly concerned. Within every social structure, and especially within governmental structure, we hold that decisions should be reached by the smallest group needing to decide jointly. *The exercise of power should be kept as close as possible to those over whom it is exercised.*

This principle of *subsidiation* is a corollary of democracy itself. It calls for decision-making power to be retained by the individual when the matter in question chiefly concerns the individual. It permits collective action, but calls for the placement of

authority as low in the hierarchy as is consistent with the achievement of common objectives.

We urge the retention of local authority over local matters.
It is foolish to suppose, for example, that local schools will be
more wisely administered by a distant state government than by
a board elected by the local citizens whose children attend those
schools. Local control will lead to much variation, in style and
quality, among school districts. Is that bad? There is no reason to believe a uniform standard imposed by others will be
higher or better than the standard we devise for and apply to
ourselves.

In a federal system, we are stout defenders of the rights of
states, as against the national government. States are quite large
enough. We know no reason to think people get smarter or better
when they arrive at the national capitol. We have very good
reason to think that bureaucrats in Washington, D.C., know less
about our problems in Florida or Colorado than we do ourselves.

On the world scene, we place great emphasis upon national
self-determination. As Americans or Britons, we know better the
sort of society we want to build for ourselves than can any spokesman for the United Nations who may never have lived among us
and cannot know what is good for us in our internal affairs. The
same is true for all other nations.

Some issues require action by large communities, of course.
States must enforce the criminal law; nations must regulate their
currency; all the nations must cooperate in the uses of the seas
and of outer space. The principle of subsidiation simply calls for
the limitation of each democratic legislature to matters of common urgency.

Beyond those, let all attend to their own business. In the last
analysis, democracy is justifiable—as other systems are not—
because it permits us to govern ourselves. We take *self*-govern-
ment seriously. We apply it first of all to the private selves with
which democracy begins.

Readings

(Other defenses of individualist democracy, arranged chronologically)

Classical

Date of Origin

(1776)   **Adam Smith,** *An Inquiry into the Nature and Causes of the Wealth of Nations.* Edited by Edwin Cannon. Chicago: University of Chicago Press, 1977.

(1825)   **James Mill,** *An Essay on Government.* Edited by Currin V. Shields. Indianapolis, In.: Bobbs-Merrill, 1955.

(1859)   **John Stuart Mill,** *On Liberty.* Edited by Currin V. Shields. Indianapolis, In.: Bobbs-Merrill, 1956.

Through World War II

(1922)   **Herbert Hoover,** *American Individualism.* New York: Doubleday, Doran, 1934.

(1937)   **William E. Hocking,** *The Lasting Elements of Individualism.* New York: AMS Press, 1976.

(1944)   **Friedrich A. Hayek,** *The Road to Serfdom.* Chicago: University of Chicago Press, 1944.

(1945)   **Karl R. Popper,** *The Open Society and Its Enemies,* Volume 2. 5th ed., Princeton, N.J.: Princeton University Press, 1966.

After World War II

(1949)   **Clare E. Griffin,** *Enterprise in a Free Society.* Chicago: R. D. Irwin, 1949.

(1950)   **Thurmond W. Arnold *et al.,*** *The Future of Democratic Capitalism.* Essay Index Reprint Series; New York: Arno Press, 1950.

(1951)   **Ludwig Von Mises,** *Socialism.* Translated by J. Kahane. New Haven: Yale University Press, 1951.

(1956)　　　　　**Francis X. Sutton, et al.,** *The American Business Creed.* Cambridge, Mass.: Harvard University Press, 1956.

(1957)　　　　　**John R. Commons,** *Legal Foundations of Capitalism.* Madison, Wisc.: University of Wisconsin Press, 1957.

(1957)　　　　　**Russell A. Kirk,** *The American Cause.* Westport, Conn.: Greenwood Press, 1957.

(1959)　　　　　**William F. Buckley, Jr.,** *Up From Liberalism.* New York: Hillman Books, 1961.

(1967)　　　　　**Ayn Rand,** *Capitalism: The Unknown Ideal.* New York: New American Library, 1967.

(1974)　　　　　**Robert Nozick,** *Anarchy, State and Utopia.* New York: Basic Books, 1974.

(1978)　　　　　**Yale Brozen, Elmer W. Johnson, and Charles W. Powers,** *Can the Market Sustain an Ethic?* Chicago: University of Chicago, 1978.

(1978)　　　　　**Michael Novak,** *The American Vision: An Essay on the Future of American Capitalism.* Washington, D. C. American Enterprise Institute, 1978.

(1979)　　　　　**Edward R. Norman** *et al.,* *The Denigration of Capitalism.* Washington, D.C. American Enterprise Institute 1979.

(1980)　　　　　**Milton and Rose Friedman,** *Free to Choose.* New York: Harcourt, Brace, Jovanovich, 1980.

(1980)　　　　　**Daniel P. Moynihan,** *Counting our Blessings: Reflections on the Future of America.* New York: Little, Brown, 1980.

A CONCLUDING NOTE ON DEMOCRACY IN GENERAL

Democrats—whether socialists or capitalists, or whatever blend of these—share principles more important than those that divide them. Beneath economic differences lies profound agreement—that the authority of government comes only from the people governed, and that the aim of government must be the realization of their will. Each side contends that it will accomplish that aim more surely and more justly. Voters must choose, at many junctures, between the socialist and the individualist approach. It is well to keep in mind, in choosing, what is *not* at issue in their dispute.

Both are representative systems, depending upon the honest election of the people's delegates for the conduct of common business. The machinery of representation may vary; the specific functions of the legislative assemblies will vary. For both systems, however, legitimate community authority flows only from the fair representation of the citizens.

Both systems can change. Each may be replaced by the other if the people wish it so. The socialist and individualist will both argue that the attractions of the other are illusory; but both are prepared to accept the decision of the people in making and implementing economic policy. This commitment to abide by the judgment of the citizens (even when convinced that judgment is mistaken) marks both systems as genuinely democratic.

Both, socialism and individualism, will break down if control falls permanently into the hands of a fixed majority—whether of one race or one religion or one national origin. Both depend upon the genuine opportunity of each citizen to be on the winning side in the controversies that arise. Both require great restraint in the use of political power once acquired. Both will be sensitive to the intensely felt needs of minorities; both will respect compromise; both, for the sake of peace in the community, will be willing to live with less than complete satisfaction.

Democrats, whether socialists or individualists, will appreciate the inevitable tension between society and the individual. Individuals claim from society the right to fair treatment under the laws. Society claims from the individual a fair contribution to the common weal. Both systems will recognize claims of both kinds. They will resolve conflicts between society and the individual differently, of course, but neither will insist that justice lies always on one side only. Both will search for ways to resolve such conflicts harmoniously.

Neither will be absolutist in spirit. The socialist will join in preserving great ranges of private life for individual determination; the individualist will join in finding great ranges of community life properly in the province of a representative legislature. Yet the mix of protected private powers with the powers of government will be always at issue.

Socialist democracy and individualist democracy are two relatively extreme points on a continuum, extending from the greatest reasonable emphasis upon what is common to the greatest reasonable emphasis upon what is private. That continuum itself will be better understood when the arguments for each of its end points have been appreciated. Between the extremes there are an unlimited number of intermediate positions that may be plausibly defended. Some of these are not clearly in the one camp or clearly in the other. Most real-life compromises between the two, however, though bearing traces of both, will also bear the fairly clear stamp of either an individualist or a socialist persuasion.

Each will claim that it is truly hospitable to democracy while the other runs against the grain of democracy in some ways. Each will contest the other's claims in this regard. In practice and in theory, however, both systems are feasible: democracy can be fully socialized or thoroughly individualized. Both are feasible not only as economic theories, but as systems of human government in which the people rule themselves.

They are forms of democracy. That is what marks them off from fascist authoritarianism on the right and from communist authoritarianism on the left—each of which claims authority *over* the people, for their own good, whether they like it or not. The democrat, socialist or individualist, recognizes no rights arising from the natural superiority of leaders or races. He does not grant the authority or inevitability of any dialectic. His government wields no authority whatever save that deliberately delegated by the citizens. All the risks and problems, the uncertainties and errors that stem from this base in the people are the unavoidable heritage of all democrats. But strength and justice also flow from that foundation. For good or ill, democratic socialist and democratic individualist are both committed to a decision-making procedure that takes precedence over their beliefs about ideal outcomes. In that shared procedure the members of the community, equal each to the other, decide for themselves what they will do, directing their own government. The surest practical test of democracy is the responsiveness of the government, in letter and spirit, to the voice of the people.

ADVOCATE SYNOPSIS
Fascism

Fascism is rooted in the inequality of human beings. Persons, although intrinsically precious, are endowed by nature with very different capacities and talents. These contrasting qualities of mind and character suit people for different levels of authority, different roles in life. Only fascism faces up to this reality squarely, choosing the most capable and most devoted leaders for the exercise of great power.

Human inequality results inevitably in hierarchy. *Successful government must recognize and employ natural hierarchies, assigning appropriate duties to each level in the social pyramid, and capitalizing on the variety of strengths and skills among the citizens. Fascism does not denigrate the masses—but it is aristocratic in spirit, trusting government not to the many, but to the best.*

Because democracy, whether socialist or individualist, is built on the myth of human equality, it results in perennial disorder and discontent. It denies the natural order of things, expecting people to perform in roles for which they are not fitted and in which they cannot be happy. Democracy thus invariably produces mediocrity in all spheres of life—in education, in the arts, and especially in national leadership. Democracy, counting votes, puts confidence in quantity: fascism, in quality. Democracy expects about the same from all; fascism draws the best from each.

Fascism rejects the democratic belief that government is based upon contract. Citizens are not separate atoms who simply decide to create a state. Society is not an artifact, but natural: the state, its highest form, is properly understood as an organic unity. *Its organs, social institutions, and its cells, human beings, are related not mechanically but internally. Each element is vital for the life of all the rest; each strives for the success of the larger whole. In that whole, the nation, all citizens can truly realize themselves.*

Every healthy organism must maintain internal discipline. The higher rule the lower parts, while protecting and cherishing all. With the authority to command, leaders take on heavy responsibility. With the benefits of state support and protection, citizens accept the duty to obey established authorities. Only fascism gives a rational account of authority at each level in the state, and of our proper respect for it.

This rational ordering of the elements of society is morally right. It is also most conducive to human contentment. The power to command is safeguarded by intelligence and strong character. Citizens are unified in purpose, enjoying security, prosperity, and civic harmony. When this natural discipline is abandoned, states degenerate or are conquered; everyone then suffers in the name of a false freedom.

True freedom, however, is the freedom to act responsibly within the bounds of rightful authority. We are most free when we realize our natures most completely. The organic state, in channeling and cultivating human activity, makes real freedom possible. To the nation, therefore, which is the ground of our being and the fruit of our striving, good citizens owe their deepest loyalty and affection. Only this organic world view can explain why citizens live with pride—and sometimes even die, heroically—for ideals far transcending their individual selves.

In sum: Fascism recognizes a great natural hierarchy, an organic whole, in which human institutions function and human beings thrive. In this transcendent system healthy relations between loyal citizens and their larger body politic can mature, and the lives of individuals can achieve fullest significance.

SYSTEM THREE
FASCISM

1. The Best

When the Roman legions marched to battle, a single soldier marched at their head, bearing aloft a bundle of twigs. Each twig singly could be snapped with ease; bound together, they were virtually unbreakable and symbolized the invincibility of a unified force. Each twig, like each soldier, was made secure by mutual reinforcement. These symbolic bundles were called *fasces,* from which the name of our theory of government—fascism—is taken. Often blamed for the brutalities of its crudest exponents, fascism has acquired an unfortunate reputation. But in recognizing the great strength of a unified body, the potential of which infinitely surpasses the powers of its individually weak components, fascism in fact is profoundly correct.

It is also deeply moral. The achievements of humanity flow not from the deeds or ambitions of persons singly, but from their joint dedication to common causes. Those larger wholes in which all citizens may make their powers effective are therefore supremely important. We fascists recognize this importance and seek to formulate the principles upon which the largest of these wholes—the state—is properly governed. Governing a state is the most serious of all human affairs; because our system is one in which states are most deeply understood, it is the only system in which state government can be truly wise and truly just.

Fascism has long suffered unfair abuse. We ask that our case in its defense be given a calm and thoughtful hearing. Reason and common experience are on our side; we shall be content with the outcome of an impartial judgment of our system and our arguments in its support.

A healthy, unified state is a great hierarchy, topped by devoted leaders with the deepest understanding and the highest capacities. The body politic they direct is made up of many, varied institutions, each properly subordinated to the interests of the whole, each doing its proper business. These, in turn, are constituted throughout by a citizenry that is dutiful, content, and loyal. The fascist ideal puts needed authority in appropriate hands, depends on the wisest heads to make the laws, and renders it possible for every person to do freely and fully what he or she can do best. These are high but realistic ideals; they have been defended (under differing names) by the greatest political philosophers, from Plato to the present day.

Fascism properly understood—not the malicious manipulation of peoples and powers, but the balanced disposition of authority in accord with the realities of the human condition—is both right and good. It is right in the sense that it is the political system human beings ought to live under. Real justice can be achieved for all only when the power to rule rests in the hands of the most capable, the best. We propose, in a word, a rational aristocracy; aristocracy is government by the *aristoi,* the best. Fascism is good in the sense that it is the one political system best calculated to advance human well-being; it promises satisfaction and peace of mind for individuals in every walk of life, prosperity and orderliness for society as a whole. We will begin by showing that fascism is entirely natural, that of all systems it is the one most in accord with our natures, and that it therefore (when not corrupted) works well.

2.   Hierarchy

We begin at the beginning, with the order of nature out of which man arises. Consider the vast array of natural species on earth. What feature of their organization is universally pervasive? Aggressiveness? Love? Territoriality? Familial loyalty? None of these, in fact. To understand evolutionary success we must examine it without preconceptions.

Struggle is a great part of life, but not by any means the whole of it. From the simplest creatures of a few cells to the noblest trees and mightiest mammals, the course of life from birth through maturation and decay is never safe or easy. The desperate search for sustenance in the first moments of life, the need to vanquish or ward off competitors, to hide or flee from predators, to feed and bring forth progeny—these unceasing struggles leave only successful species for our examination; the rest have died out.

Yet nature widely exhibits a loving side as well. Cooperation is often the key to the success of a species. The mutual support essential for survival is made concrete in the herd, the pack, and the hive. The helpless young of some species must be protected and fed with devotion by their parents. Each generation must be helpful as well as strong, bringing the next to maturity and reproduction in its turn. "Nature red in tooth and claw" is an incomplete image. Predatory struggle is common, yes, but so also is reciprocity and love. Only an enormous variety of capacities and instincts could yield the endless chain of generations in the natural order.

Nor is any one physical feature everywhere present or prized in the world of animals. Strength in slaughter, speed in flight, the hardness of a protective shell, or the cunning of a large brain—each may serve in some environments. Some animal species migrate; others remain in their territory. Some species are monogamous and loyal, others polygamous and uncaring. Some species are frail but prolific; others bear few young but rear them with substantial success. No shape, no organ, no capacity is universal in nature. *But one form of organization is: hierarchy.*

No matter the size of the creature or the ways in which it produces or feeds, hierarchical order is the single pervasive attribute of successful species of animals. In biological science as in common experience, hierarchy is so familiar and so omnipresent that its centrality is often overlooked. From the rigid hierarchies of insect life to the more flexible but equally vital hierarchies of bird flocks with established pecking orders, from warrens of rodents to packs of wolves and herds of wild horses with single powerful leaders, from the band of apes governed by the male who best combines strength and intelligence to the crudest beginnings of cooperative life for *homo sapiens,* animal communities (except for the most primitive) are everywhere hierarchical. These are but illustrations of a universal pattern.

The principle is absolutely fundamental: the success of every animal population requires that a natural *order* among its members be respected. The essence of this order is a sorting of the population according to capacities, the capacities of its individual members to do whatever that species must do to survive. The strongest (where life is simply brutal), the fastest (where it depends on chasing or fleeing), the cleverest (where survival depends upon cunning), and in virtually all cases the ablest and most responsible rise to serve as the natural leaders of the group. They defend and direct the group; they are obeyed by the others, and often served by them; they organize the whole.

3.   Inequality

Mankind is not exempt from the universal order of nature. We too, insofar as we are parts of this order, must sort ourselves into hierarchies appropriate to our condition. Human hierarchies will, of course, be far more complicated and subtle than those of lower creatures. Leaders among humans require, beyond strength and speed, a great range of talents—of which more shortly. But this principle underlies all: Among human beings, as among all other species, there are *kinds,* variations in natural abilities resulting inevitably in different roles for differing persons (and classes of persons) in the government of the whole.

That is the premise with which we begin: Human beings are not equal. The *in*equality of humans is not merely our theory; it is plain and indisputable fact. Human inequality is as natural—and even more evident—than the inequality manifest among other species.

"That all men are created equal" is the theoretical foundation of democracy. This foundation crumbles upon inspection; it is the figment of the imagination of an age. Much of the anxiety and frustration of our time may be traced to dogmatic insistence upon the truth of what everyone knows to be false in his daily life. Telling ourselves that humans must be equal, while seeing plainly that they are not, we establish as our ideal an equality that is not only unattainable but that also runs against the grain of all healthy and natural inclinations in social affairs.

This ideal of equality has been the bane of human life in recent centuries, erupting early in Europe and now afflicting all quarters of the globe. The pitiful quest for what cannot be has undermined peace and contentment. It cannot lead to order in the lives of men because it flies in the face of the natural order that distinguishes capacities, rendering degrees of influence and power inevitable.

Equality has been the *leitmotif* of every democratic movement. The democrat is contemptuous of rank. Typically, as in the French Revolution of 1789, all titles are discarded, all citizens counted as having equal authority. The result is havoc, of course. Legitimate authorities and traditional distinctions of rank do not create inequalities but recognize them. A political system that blinds itself to reality, and stakes everything on that blindness, is doomed.

No genuine democracy has ever lasted very long. Its members must persuade themselves that they are what really they are not—equal. They must pursue and live a gigantic lie: the lie that native differences of intelligence and talent do not rightly matter in distributing power, and that the most critical human decisions can best be made by counting noses. That principle is not only mistaken but perverse. Democracy therefore inevitably fails— and corrupts as it does so. It is, literally, degenerate.

4. Voting

Belief in human equality leads inexorably to government based on the count of votes. "One man, one vote," they say; the majority must rule. But the rule of numbers has nothing whatever to do with what is right or good. Majority rule is the rule of the largest part; in effect its advocates are saying that might does make right. That is a deeply immoral theory of government.

What we ought to do, and what is truly good for us as a community, is an objective matter. It should be decided by rational investigation, not by counting raised hands. In everyday affairs we understand this fully. When building a bridge we want to know how much weight it must carry, and the authority to build and test it lies rightly in the hands of those who know how to design for the expected stresses. Such judgments we do not dream of making by majority rule. Nor would we rely upon majority rule in prescribing treatment for the sick, or in preparing for a dangerous journey, or in making financial decisions—or in any sphere in which success depends upon reliable knowledge and good judgment. For the formation of any opinion of importance we need the facts, presented fully and accurately, and we want well-tested principles for their use. Naturally we turn to those who have the requisite knowledge and trained judgment. To build bridges we rely upon engineers; to treat the sick we rely upon physicians, and so on. Counting votes might be appropriate for a children's group deciding which game to play next. When matters are serious—safety or prosperity being affected by the outcome—we usually seek the help of well-informed persons; we aim to learn the truth.

That desire does not make decisions easy, of course. Engineers and physicians often disagree, and among competing authorities we may be unsure in whom to place trust. To reconcile such conflicts, however, we never simply count. we try to determine who among the conflicting experts is most expert, who really knows best. When we have found this out, or think we have, we rely upon that authority for guidance.

In matters of government should it be different? Is the use of political power a game and not serious? Do the decisions of governments not affect our safety or prosperity? Obviously they do. In matters decided by government—concerning taxes, schools, sanitation, transportation, and war—reliable knowledge and sound judgment are needed more urgently than in any other sphere. When rational, we want such matters decided by persons who know best. What madness it is, therefore, to establish as our governors the mass of uninformed citizens whose confused and half-baked opinions, mostly unfounded, we *count* to reach decisions! Democracy is a form of government chosen by a people that has lost its head.

We must keep our heads. And our very best heads must be heads of state. The political community, as Aristotle said, is the highest of all communities, embracing all the rest and aiming at good to a greater degree than any other community, and at the highest good. To direct this community aim, our well-being requires the very best of men and women. The system which places those best people in positions of highest authority is fascism.

Who are the best? This is not easy to say. The inheritance of power has often led to the rule of dolts. Wealth is certainly no guarantee of leadership ability. Very able people are often rich, and that not by accident, but wealth in itself, especially inherited wealth, proves nothing. The evaluation of good leaders requires a much finer screen than parentage or money. This much, however, is sure: some heads are better than others. All men are not equally suited to share in governing or in choosing the governors.

5. The Natural Division of Labor

The plain fact that human beings differ very greatly from one another is, in our system, fundamental. The critical differences among humans are those of character and intellect. Physical variations—of size and strength and color—are of little consequence in a species whose survival depends upon intelligence, fortitude, and adaptability. Varieties of *mind* and *character* are of critical importance, and they are enormous.

Our differences suit us for different roles in life. By direct experience we know that people differ profoundly in their inclinations, aptitudes, and talents. Training alone could not explain these variations; they result from differences in our natures. We all know persons having natural talent in the use of their hands as craftsmen or artists, persons who exhibit an ability to make things fit, or work, or who draw or carve beautifully from earliest childhood; others we know have a natural talent for speech and the use of words. Others again work wonderfully with animals; still others display a natural facility with logical and mathematical manipulation. Some are at home only with the concrete and the tangible, some only with the abstract and the theoretical. Some are fearful by nature, or cautious; others are courageous by nature, or foolhardy; some are meticulous and exact, others careless and sloppy; some are in every enterprise imaginative and forward-looking; others have narrower horizons and are content only with well-established routine. The varieties of humankind are great—but they are real and valuable. So valuable are they, in fact, that they account, in part, for the incomparable success and dominance of our species on the planet.

6. Self-Realization and Justice

We are different by nature. But by nature, too, we are alike in seeking to develop the talents that are in us, to perfect our abilities to do what our natural gifts permit and promise. Such self-realization is the normal focus of a happy human life. No prescription for unhappiness is surer than the pursuit of a career for which one is by nature unsuited. Training can do much, but it will leave the untalented musician mediocre and miserable if committed to a life of performance or composition. No training can make a timorous man a good naval captain, or transform a fine but inarticulate carpenter into a political leader. Instruction can bring to fruit what is natively in us; it cannot create capacities that were never there.

The appropriate deployment of inherent capacities and aptitudes is the key to a well-ordered society. Precisely that is the central theme of Plato's *Republic,* accounting for its penetration and its impact over the centuries. A just state, Plato explains, is one in which each element—each person, each institution—is doing its proper business, what it is fitted by nature to do best. Plato's ideal society is an aristocracy, of course; no other system meets the test of reason.

Plato's fundamental thesis—that the differing native capacities of citizens should determine their duties and powers—has always been sound. He applied this thesis to a small and simple community, calling it *The Republic,* though its government certainly was not republican in the current sense. Applied to a modern state, large and complex, the same thesis yields fascism. For

Karl Popper: The open society and its enemies.

Plato, as for fascists, the different chief functions in a society ought to be the responsibilities of different kinds of people. Plato viewed mankind as having three basic faculties; in whichever of these a person's chief strength lies (he believed) determines the class to which that individual belongs.

For the masses of mankind, the chief capacity is plain strength, and the chief motivation for action is the satisfaction of appetites, such as hunger or sex. Such plain folks are the productive foundation of a prosperous community; temperance is their characteristic virtue. Plato is not sneering when he calls them men of iron; iron may be common stuff, but it is strong, solid, and essential.

On a higher level are those whose emotions are stronger than their appetites. Their contribution lies in their capacity to respond to dangerous challenges, courage is their characteristic virtue, and upon them falls the duty of defending the state. Plato honors their spirit by calling them men of silver.

The stallions of appetite and emotion, as in Plato's famous metaphor, must be guided. Only reason is fit to give them direction, to be their charioteer. Only reason can know when to call for boldness, when to impose restraint. Persons in whom reason is dominant are entitled—and obliged—to hold the reins of the political chariot. They are the rarest and the best, and the government is rightly upon their shoulders. Plato calls them men of gold.

Too pat, we say. Neither human beings nor social functions fall so neatly into three divisions. True. But although Plato's categories are crude, the idea behind his categorization is sound. Now, as then, the reins of a good government must rest in the hands of those who are fit by nature to hold them. Human nature has not changed greatly since Plato's time. Gifts of mind and character still fit some for rule: the abilities and inclinations of others suit them for more subordinate tasks—making or trading, record-keeping or farming. A decent society, ancient or modern, Western or Eastern, must be rationally organized. Who says *organization* says *hierarchy*—as great political sociologists have repeatedly demonstrated. In the rationally-organized state each person will do his own work, for which he is best suited and in which he is happiest, and all will work for the health of the larger social organism.

Jeffrey J. Coggins

7.   The Organic State

The fascist view of society is consciously and thoroughly organic.
We view the body politic as an organism, not metaphorically, but
literally. It is not simply that states are like organic units—they
are organic units. Consider the ramifications of this profound
truth.

First, an organic conception of the state makes sense, as
nothing else can, out of the immense variety of human roles and
classes. The great range of human functions—making, serving,
trading, managing, and so on—would be a senseless chaos without some ordering principle. But it is not chaos. Each of the
countless human enterprises is a needed and natural aspect of the
life of the whole. Just as in any smaller organism, an animal or
a plant, the many functions vital to life are performed by organs
greatly differing in nature, so the functions vital to the life of the
social whole are performed by persons of greatly differing natures. The inequalities of men are by no means accidental; they
cannot be eliminated and they should not be regretted.

In a single human organism there are distinct jobs to be
done by the heart and the kidney, the hands and the teeth. We
are not surprised or offended by the differences in these organs,
or by differences in the types of cells that constitute them. Indeed, we know that our lives depend upon these differences, and
that we are healthy only when the sharply differentiated organs
are performing their functions, distinct yet harmoniously coordinated.

So it is with the social organism. Its organs are the institutions that perform the vital functions of its life: the factories,
courts, schools, labor unions, warehouses, transport systems,
and so on. Each major organ has sub-organic parts, and all the
parts are constituted—as in all organisms—by a vast host of very
small units, each of which is alive, and active, and integrally
related to its neighbors and to the overall hierarchy of units. In
the social organism the elemental units are individual persons.
There are tens of thousands, perhaps millions, of units in each
organ of the whole, and therefore, from the perspective of the
larger organism, no one of these is indispensable for life. Yet—
again as in every organism—these units, conjoined, constitute
the life of the whole.

States (the common name given to such social organisms) are related to their citizens as whole to part in a living thing. A state cherishes its members, protects them and cares for them, in the way a single organism protects and cares for its teeth, muscles, or genitals. Our organs are not simply mechanical parts we happen to be responsible for; they are we, and the failure to care for them properly will erode our natural power. The court that will punish us for inattention to our bodies is the court of nature herself; we will function less well, die sooner, and hurt. Organic responsibilities of care are likewise owed by a state to its citizens, and natural punishments will similarly befall it when those responsibilities are not met.

No one resents the fact that, within an organism, the many integrated organs are unequal in importance. Some organs of the state, energy production and central government, are the heart and brain of the whole; they are crucial to its life from moment to moment. Other organs are absolutely essential for long-term health—schools, for example, and heavy industry—but may malfunction for short periods with lesser impact. Still others—museums, for example, or theaters—are important for well-being, but not essential for life itself. An individual can live in reasonable comfort minus one finger but much less well without a leg: brain damage is ruinous; and heart failure kills. Work stoppage in an industry or inflation in the currency may be likened to injury or blood disease for an individual; they may be serious but not fatal. Defeat in war or economic collapse, like strangulation or cancer, is likely to kill.

Each individual citizen is engaged in some organic function of the whole, contributing to the whole by service in that role. Individuals are the basis of the entire system—and yet each individual must be replaceable within the system if the organism is to enjoy long life. Society is therefore constantly replenishing its institutional organs with healthy sub-units as individual elements age and die. New workers replace old; new managers, statesmen, teachers are constantly being prepared to replace those retiring. The state, like every organism, must plan for its future, even at some cost to its immediate comfort.

Healthy organisms continually groom themselves, paring away decayed or unhealthy tissue. That is not cruel; it is good hygiene, even when it hurts. Sometimes individuals, with pained regret, must sacrifice one of their own parts—as when we pull a bad tooth or amputate a gangrenous limb in the interest of the whole. States also sometimes face that unpleasant necessity, tolerating rot within themselves at their own peril.

Every organism runs risks; the world is full of perils. When we are forced to defend ourselves in battle we will be careful to protect what is most vital for life—head and breast—exposing as we must the arms with which we fight. So also with states, which may find themselves without alternative to war, and whose armed forces serve as shield for the vital parts and as instrument for attack.

8.   Subordination

The units of a healthy organism are mainly related as subordinates and superiors. The organs do not function of their own volition but at the direction of higher authorities within the whole. In the human organism, teeth chew and feet march not for themselves, but for the person in whom they exist as teeth and feet. Each part is naturally suited for its special service; each organ can function correctly only when properly subordinated.

So it is also with the body politic. There are those who fish and farm, and those who serve as ministers of state. Between the farmer and the secretary of agriculture lie differences of capacity and function for which both should be thankful. Naturally the farmer will be subordinate to the cabinet minister; naturally they are not equals, except in the sense that both are elements of the whole, though of unequal importance. No sensible farmer will be offended by that subordination or deny the inequality that makes it essential. All citizens—farmers, teachers, engineers, whatever —may take pleasure in their special abilities and will take satisfaction in the good performance of their various functions. In the strength and good order of the resultant whole all may take pride.

A corollary of subordination is purpose. Each subordinate member of the whole is assigned a mission. Each institution serves all. Each worker in an institution labors not for private goals alone but as part of a larger body—a hierarchy of larger bodies—that gives significance to the work. Purposelessness is the great sickness of modern life. Depression and boredom are the psychic marks of persons whose lives are without meaning, whose work has no rational aim. They are unavoidable when individuals do not understand their natural relations to the whole of society. One who seeks to be equal to everyone else finishes by being cut off from everyone else. Pursuing meaning for one's self, singly, results in finding no meaning at all. Only in a self-consciously organic setting can work be truly satisfying and life genuinely significant.

9. Respect

What attitude, then, is appropriate for a citizen toward his superiors in work and government? Dutifulness? Yes. And respectfulness? Yes, that too. The duty and respect each citizen owes flow not from any external imposition of authority upon him, but from the natural hierarchy of the organism in which all live. Each human being thrives only as a constituent part of some such larger body. All members of that body are naturally obliged to obey its rules. Citizens are not slaves to the state, any more than the cells of eyes or ears are slaves to the person. But we are conscious cells, and our consciousness is given content and form by the organic society in which alone we can mature as humans. We do not hang in space, freely. We have roots and ties on every side, bonds that both restrict us and give us nutriment.

If there is anything in the world to which respect is most fittingly given, therefore, it is that larger being that makes human consciousness possible. The state does not owe its life to me (though all citizens, viewed jointly, are its body), yet I do owe my life to it, in every sense. My parents' union, my upbringing, my sustenance, everything upon which my life depended and depends, I draw from the social organism. My debt to it (if we must talk of giving and getting) is literally beyond calculation. Not only am I indebted for food, shelter, and education, but for my language, my tastes and customs, for the very frame with which I view the world. I owe everything to the social organism. Indeed, I am what I am only *in it:* outside of it I could not have come to be, could not have survived, and would now quickly wither and die.

10. Awe

These debts I pay by the performance of my duties to the state. The state is the realization of that larger organic unity in a particular place and time. States grow and decline, like persons, engaging in a host of relations with one another, some amiable, some hostile. Of the larger scheme in which these great social organisms contend I cannot know very much. The great chain of social being extends backward in time beyond my speculations. Within my grasp is only the present condition of the world as I experience it, the recent past, and the short-term future. Although I cannot know the end points of the great chain, I can know something of that link—my state—in which I have being. Awe—going even beyond respect—is my proper attitude toward it. If the great scheme of things is Divine, as it may be, then its concrete manifestation in the world is godly, and I am right to worship it, not with empty rituals but with devoted service. That is part of what Hegel meant when he wrote: "The march of God in the World—that is what the state is."

11. Contract

Opposed to the fascist view of state and citizens is the democratic view of them, explicitly mechanical rather than organic. The democratic account of the state relies ultimately upon the notion of *contract,* of an agreement among independent parties to create the state as an instrument in their mutual service. Some democrats have believed that such contracts were actually entered into by the people; others use the notion of contract as a theoretical device to explain the relations of citizens to state, even if such contracts never were made in fact. The insurmountable difficulty of all such theories is not merely absence of evidence for actual contracts; it is the impossibility of an adequate account of an

essentially organic whole when it is viewed as an arbitrary conglomeration of parts agreeing to join together.

Whether contract is proposed as historical reality or as theoretical construct, we may ask: Who could the contractors have
been? What language could they have spoken—and how could
they have learned to speak it? Are they supposed to have had
customs and dress, principles of conduct, and ideals? Where did
all this social equipment come from? If, as in some primitive
cosmology, we imagine a band of heroic progenitors, springing
complete with language and ideals from the brow of the gods, to
utter the magic words of inception (or if we can convince ourselves that any equivalent fable is true), we must believe that at
one moment there was no body politic, and at the next, with the
document signed or the oath sworn, there was. Such accounts,
however refined, convict themselves of absurdity by supposing
what cannot be: citizens before states, organs before organisms.
The original human units supposed (in all contractual theories)
to have come together as creators of the state *could* not be real
—could not have reasoned, or bargained, or formed principles of
justice. They could not even have survived to the time of the
contract without the precious nurture provided by the social
organism of which they are products.

Established societies have sometimes formed colonies in
new places. These branches may alter the political constitution
of the motherland to suit new circumstances. But even in such
cases—the Mayflower Compact and the colonies that later
became the United States of America are the most famous—the
principles of the new community and its laws can be no more than
a version of the main trunk from which alone a stem may grow.

12.   Atomism

How could it be otherwise? Human culture cannot spring from
nothing; it grows slowly, organically. Human beings do not first
appear on the scene, articulate and fully dressed, to design and
form their social body. There are no fully human beings outside
social bodies. We act, speak, and believe as we do as a result of

the nurture given us by the social organism of which we are the fruit. Each generation sows new seeds; organisms arise in an unending organic chain. Any theory which supposes that the chain begins by deliberate choice, and which posits a ripe first fruit without organic source, wins the adherents it deserves.

Democratic theory, in sum, begins with a fundamental misconception of what human beings are. The democrat views the social world as consisting of a great host of atomic units, each separate and independent, coming together as the result of many individual decisions to form a body. Relations among humans (in this view) are necessarily external, tenuous, and dependent upon the sustained commitments of the individuals related. Contract thus becomes the glue of government. But human beings are not atoms, separate and independent, and the relations that bind them are not simply external and agreed upon, but internal and natural. The bonds among humans change, of course; they grow and wither. But they arise out of *natural* human relations—in the family, in play, and in work.

Organic ties do more than nurture us. They are the source of our deepest satisfactions. We are most human, our best and fullest selves, when as parents we teach and rear our children, or as workers we join with others in common projects, or as managers we deploy the work force under our command. We realize ourselves not independently, but as citizens of our country, actively and consciously fulfilling our organic social roles.

13. Authority and Authoritarianism

Each individual's role in life, or station, is therefore the key to that person's place in the government of the whole. The parts of an organism are never equal in government, but carefully subordinated on a hierarchical plan. Within that plan, as we know in our own persons, each element has a natural authority, certain few elements being in charge. Likewise in the body politic. The authority to direct cannot justifiably be distributed evenly amongst its members, most of whom have neither the inclination nor the talent for it. No, the role of director must be exercised by persons for whom it is a natural function. As the single animal must be directed by its brain, and the vessel making dangerous passage is rightly under the command of its captain, the government of the state must be in the charge of its natural leaders, skilled aristocrats.

It is therefore mindless to suppose—as many democrats do —that obedience to authority is humiliating, or that the exercise of authority by some persons over others is somehow wrong. In fact, respect for rightful authority is the mark of good sense, and deference to that authority does honor to both superior and subordinate, recognizing their proper relations concretely. We fascists do not flinch at that reality; we take pride in service as well as in command. For this we are called authoritarians. In its literal sense the name is fitting, and we would bear it proudly but for the sneer built into it. "Authoritarianism" carries now the suggestion that the authority exercised is somehow illegitimate. Some illegitimacy may arise in any system, of course; but when authority is legitimate, submission to it is just; we are not ashamed of that.

The term "despotism" fosters similar confusion. A despot, literally, is one who is strong, with great potency. There have been very many genuinely benevolent despots; in that sense we would not complain of this name either. But in present usage, "despotic" rule brings to mind only capricious and self-serving tyranny.

Likewise "dictatorship" suggests an arbitrary, even fiendish, abuse of absolute power. Evil despots and dictators there have been, of course; but their honorable counterparts—leaders with supreme power who have devoted themselves selflessly to their communities—have far outnumbered them. Authority wielded because of the merit of the possessor leads naturally to its humane and beneficial exercise. Wise leadership was essential to bring mankind from the primitive to the civilized state. The exceptions—Ghengis Khan, Nero, Attila the Hun—stand out precisely because of their remarkable infamy: just rulers, their strength dedicated to their peoples, are too numerous to identify or recall.

The placement of supreme authority in the hands of a very few persons, or of one person, we do not condemn. The mere fact that power is concentrated, however, does not ensure that its use will be intelligent or just. In recent as in ancient history there have been circumstances in which crude power has fallen into the hands of utterly incompetent and unbalanced persons. The resulting excesses—of the Nazi Party in Germany under Hitler, and of the Mussolini regime in Italy, as well as of Stalin in the Soviet Union, Generalissimo Franco in Spain, and others—must not be blamed on the system of political organization these evil men captured and corrupted. Aristotle long ago observed that though human beings are the noblest of animals when civilized, they can be the most vicious when in a state of barbarism. So it is with governments also. A system that has the greatest potential for decency and achievement has also the potential for indescribable indecency when distorted and misused. To identify our fascist principles with the barbarities of German and Italian dictators is not merely incorrect and unfair, it is painfully ironic. They practiced the most cruel and hateful brutality; true leaders of a unified people have no need for brutality, blending as they do firmness with compassion. The so-called fascism of the Axis powers in World War II cultivated unreason; the patriotic feeling we honor is restrained within the bounds of reason. Those regimes thrived on war; we make no bones about the need to prepare for war only to ensure for our citizens the blessings of peace. The vicious racism and bloodthirsty anti-Semitism of German and Italian dictators gone amok was beneath contempt. Genuine fascists recoil with horror from such barbarity.

In fairness we will agree that many of our principles were professed—although grossly distorted in practice—by Italian fascists. They gave our system its modern name, choosing the *fasces* as the symbol of an Italy that was to be united, organized, and humanized. They did achieve substantial progress until corruption set in. They did expose the shallowness of democratic egalitarianism; they did oppose the crass materialism underlying Marxist and other socialist enthusiasms. The realization of an organic, hierarchical state in Italy—until Mussolini's opportunism ruined everything—brought the people a degree of prosperity and a sense of purposefulness they had not known for centuries. As it is said, they made the trains run on time. Well, it is no bad thing that the trains—and all public institutions—run efficiently and rationally. That fascism could accomplish so much in so short a time in Italy, where chaos had so long been the normal state of affairs, remains a tribute to its enormous potential. But the life of true Italian fascism was cut off before it could become mature.

In Germany, Hitler's diabolic abuse of absolute power, and his intoxication by militarism, made the serious application of fascist principles virtually impossible from the start. Even so— fully recognizing the barbarity of Nazi practices—one should in fairness recognize the deep and universal satisfaction felt by the German people when, after a period of liberal-democratic disorder, they came again to experience the unity of their people, to know their lives had a purpose beyond themselves, and to enjoy the health and prosperity that a rationally organized state can bring. True fascism never received a fair test in Germany; it was utterly destroyed, first by German lunatics, and then by the understandably furious armed forces of the conquering powers in World War II. To think of the German Reich as the realization of fascism is a woeful but common error; Hitlerism is hardly an example of government by the best!

The contrast is the more painful just because, in a good society, power must rest at the top. At the pinnacle of a natural and healthy hierarchy, however, power is accompanied by high competence and deep understanding of the human condition. When—as was the case in Germany and Russia, and elsewhere at times—power is properly placed yet totally unaccompanied by the requisite human understanding, its misuse is inevitable and catastrophic.

14. Rationality and Irrationality

Power may be abused by a few or by the many. The form of a government alone cannot guarantee its right conduct. Our fascist form has this enormous merit, however. It places the authority of government in the hands of those who are most likely to have the intelligence and sensibility needed for its wise exercise. When power lies in the hands of an inchoate populace, abuses are far more probable and are likely to be more painful and more pervasive. Worst of all, the abuses of a democracy are more difficult to remedy or even to restrain. The reasons for this are many. Between a mass of people who do not have the capacity to rule and a few who are carefully trained for rule lie great contrasts, sensed if not understood by all. We now make these contrasts explicit.

Rationality first. The capacity to reason—to apply general ideas to particular cases and to understand causes and effects—is the chief mark of humankind. Some primitive rationality is required for every human role, however simple. To reason with depth and subtlety, however, is a capacity very unevenly distributed among humans. The ability to perceive critical differences among similar cases, and basic similarities in situations superficially unlike; to detect fundamental but hidden causes; to devise explanatory hypotheses and to confirm or disprove them; to envisage the outcomes of complicated chains of events and to weigh their merits; to apply abstract theory to apparent disorder in concrete situations—these are the talents (but not the only talents) of fine leadership. Such capacities are possessed in high degree by very few. For the exercise of great political authority, most ordinary people, although able to reason, cannot reason well enough. It is a fact, from which we should not hide, that the mass of citizens have mediocre minds.

Put the matter to test. Ask the man in the street about any affair of state of the most moderate complexity. His understanding of the issues is almost certain to be shallow and fragmentary. It may be nil. Where the matter is complicated—economic policy, say, or the relations of science and government—the judgments of ordinary folks are almost sure to be confused, incomplete, and unbalanced. Even their formulations of the problem are likely to be garbled. Democrats who honestly believe that citizens reason carefully and vote rationally on substantive political issues are deluding themselves utterly. (Some who make that claim are not fooled at all, of course, but have reason to hope that the rest of us will be.) Studies of voter behavior in a democracy have repeatedly shown the same painful ignorance—shocking to the ideological democrat, altogether predictable by anyone with sense: Most people have only the dimmest understanding of leading current controversies, and virtually no understanding at all of the complex but vital issues of trade, taxation, currency, production. Most voters are confused about geographical matters, woefully shallow in their historical understanding. They know next to nothing about the structure of their government, its principles and laws, its major departments and their functions.

The great majority of "qualified" voters do not know the names of their elected representatives; they cannot even recall *for whom they voted*, if they voted at all! About concerns of government, in sum, most plain citizens—artisans, doctors, truck drivers, and housewives—know practically nothing at all.

This state of affairs is not a temporary deficiency, to be remedied by informing and arousing the citizens. It has always been just this way, and it always will be. Imploring involvement succeeds with a few voters only, and even with them regarding only a single or a very few issues. The enthusiastic environmentalist (whose judgment even on environmental questions is often of questionable worth) is likely to know very little about tax reform; the committed civil libertarian is likely to be an ignoramus on the forms of energy production and their hazards.

This ignorance maligns the mass of citizens only in the eyes of those having unrealistic expectations of them. Democrats are pained and staggered when they face the facts about the electorate. But sensible thinkers do not defend democracy in serious affairs. We all know what the run of people are like. We know how narrow in vision, how limited in power of mind most people are. Fascists do not condemn the people for being what they are; we do not sneer at them, or exhort them to change, or expect them to be otherwise. We accept the world as it really is and people as they really are and always have been. We do not build our system upon some theoretical fantasy.

Most people are generally decent and honorable; that we also know. They are law-abiding, save for a few criminals who must be dealt with severely, and productive when their employment is suited to their talents. They are loyal when they understand their places and are content in them. What the mass of people do not have is the intellectual capacity for rule, or the inclination for it.

Most ordinary folks understand all this and look eagerly for appropriate governors to lead and direct them. When we oblige them to exercise a power for which they are not suited, we force the rule of unreason. By choosing governors through general election, we invite every form of chicanery from those who seek personal profit at public expense. We may expect absurd promises and even lies, empty oratory and inane slogans. Cheap plays for cheap votes are inevitable. We may expect people to vote chiefly for the candidates with whom they have shaken hands or passed a word of conversation, or for names they recognize or faces they like. We may expect popular political parties to support candidates on every irrational ground. And we get what we expect.

Election campaigns in a democracy would be amusing were the offices at stake only those of a school class or social club. But the matters at stake are deadly serious, and the inanity of holding popular elections to deal with them is nothing short of disgusting. Authority is put at auction; leadership is won by those who best exhibit the selling skills of prostitutes.

The people are thus preyed upon, their ignorance and caprice manipulated and used. Gathered into rallies and conventions, their passions are exploited by experts. They are led to support political parties as they do athletic teams, developing an enthusiasm that is no less real for its lack of reasoned basis. With buttons and stickers and half-baked arguments they back their candidate, just as they do their football team, and for the same reason: because an emotional identification has been teased into being.

The stimulants of irrational enthusiasm reenforce one another in mobs. Music and noise enhance the excitement, sheer numbers and proximity compound it. The reciprocal effects of shared emotion form the base from which those who can capitalize upon sentiment capture the highest offices in the land.

Politics in a democracy is not dirty by accident; corruption is essential to it, as those who have held elective office can testify. Hidden deals and "understandings" are common; mutual back-scratching by legislators and favor-seekers is standard practice. The informal motto of the U.S. Senate, taught to new senators upon their election, is: "Those who go along, get along." Beneath the surface everywhere, on levels high and low, lurks the power of money, the prize for shrewdness and the indispensable instrument for winning votes. All this is combined with public pretense of candor and scrupulous honesty, sometimes naive, usually duplicitous. "Principles" are warmly defended—but always formulated so as to permit the defenders to act later as their expedient interests require. Candidates (and all officeholders are candidates for reelection above all) are careful to present their views with minimal commitment, in words and phrases calculated to attract and never to offend—reducing much of what they say to empty slogans and sweet mush. "Character" is advertised, but the democratic election process does not really tolerate strong character that will tell the truth even when it is painful or that will pursue the right but unpopular course. Least of all will it tolerate the character that will admit error and the need to redesign policy. No, the "character" that election rewards is the hail-fellow well-met, the warm voice and manner, the dynamic speaker, the actor who can most sound as though he stands for something when in fact he stands for nothing—except office.

Proof of all this is abundant; the winner of almost every democratic election is mediocrity incarnate. Every careful student of the process has noted, and every ordinary citizen has often observed, that the popular favorite is the mushy-minded, the unctuous, the essentially unprincipled. Because such characters have the best chance for success, it is usually only they who run for elected office in the first place. Government by the many has no place for leaders of outstanding intelligence ("eggheads") or of true devotion to principle ("extremists"). It is not that ordinary people cannot recognize superior leaders, or do not want them; they can and do. But a system that bases office and authority upon the winning of great numbers of votes invariably attracts inferior, self-interested candidates who drive away the worthy. We see it every day.

15.   Wealth and Poverty

The irrationality of the masses, contrasted with the rationality of their superiors, is the root cause of the crude misuse of power by a democracy. Another factor not so fundamental perhaps, is yet very important and equally general. It has to do with money.

Equality of economic status is an utter impossibility. As an ideal it is as unjust as it is unattainable. The reasons for this can be reduced to two: first, people do not get money in the same way, and therefore cannot be expected to get equal amounts; second, people do not use the money they get in the same way,

and therefore cannot be expected to retain equal amounts even
if a forced equality of income be imposed. The latter reason is the
more evident, being a matter of everyday experience for us all.
Some are frugal in money matters, some prodigal; some are
forward-looking and build for the future, while others seem
hardly to care for the morrow. Some spend their entire incomes,
even living on borrowed funds, while others save and invest,
building security and wealth. There is correlation, no doubt,
between intelligence and the wise handling of one's funds—but
the chief point here is that, however evenly wealth may be distributed or acquired, it cannot stay even. And, of course, it never
does stay even, the persistent efforts of democratic utopians not-
withstanding.

The first reason for inequality of wealth, however, is more
basic. People acquire wealth in different ways and amounts, and
the differing amounts they acquire are the results of their greatly
differing talents and skills. Some socialist theorists say that everyone's work for the common weal is of equal value, whatever it
may be, and that all should receive equal amounts, or amounts
equal with respect to their needs. But the premise of this argument—the equal value of all work—is absurd. Menial jobs, requiring untrained labor and no brains, can be performed by
almost anyone and therefore do not deserve high wages. Skilled
work demands more from the worker, in training and in effort on
the job, and naturally wins more in return. Highly skilled professions, and managerial posts requiring subtle judgment and imposing weighty responsibility, demand yet more and return yet
more. The details of this long story do not need to be recounted.
In short, some acquire wealth and others do not; success in
amassing property generally results from superior talents in the
first instance and superior judgment in the management of
money in the second instance. A few, with much shrewdness and
very high energy, create great fortunes. Most people manage to
get along reasonably well, acquiring only a modest surplus of
income over outgo. A good many remain forever at the margin,
barely scraping by, or relying upon charity. That is the way it is
with money, always has been, and is likely to be.

By social action we may establish an economic floor beneath
which no one is allowed to fall; this concern for welfare will be
shared by every humane government. But if we seek to alter

fundamentally the natural balance in the distribution of wealth by forcing redistribution and imposing equality, we will fail in the end—and every temporary success will do injustice. Even in the democratic socialist states, in which equality is professed, the inequalities of income are vast. The chief result of socialist "reforms" has been that the highest incomes go to those with political influence, rather than to those with productive skills or talents.

Because economic inequality is inevitable, government by the many invariably leads to government by the poor. Power in the hands of the poor must bring unrest and strife. The natural order is upset; populist leaders are called upon, by their well-meaning but intellectually-limited constituencies, to make everyone well-to-do. *They* were wealthy when they ruled (the implicit argument runs), now *we* rule and we will have their wealth. But, of course, that cannot be. Affairs of state are turned on their head.

The first step may appear reasonable. Let us take from the rich and give to the poor, the democrats propose, through steeply progressive taxation effecting a lawful redistribution of income. This soon fails to achieve its purpose. All the wealth of the upper classes, when distributed among the masses, brings no noticeable improvement in their condition. The reverse occurs, in fact. Apart from its injustice, a policy of consistently "soaking the rich" proves a disincentive for hard work and the creative use of money; it prevents the aggregation of capital which alone can provide jobs and the foundation for economic growth. Crude economic egalitarianism soon disrupts the economy, leading to unemployment and bad times. Populist ignorance achieves the very opposite of what was sought.

The demagogues whose policies bring on such economic misery will, of course, deny this charge. Some of them will not even understand what has taken place; those who do will not tell the truth publicly for the sake of their own popularity. Who will oppose or criticize the will of "the people"? So a second, more drastic step is taken to placate the masses. This time expropriation replaces taxation. The levelling of incomes is not enough; property ownership itself must be levelled. Estates are confiscated and redistributed in small parcels to the peasantry. But agricultural productivity depends upon mechanization, automation, and all the economies of large-scale operations. So-called "land reform" programs, appealing to the masses, prove economically suicidal.

With the hope of regaining productivity and reestablishing economic equilibrium, yet more drastic steps are taken. In the name of the masses, the elected authorities, now on a path from which they cannot turn, *nationalize* productive property, in industry as well as agriculture. Nationalized industries cannot be distributed in small parcels, of course. They must be owned and operated by the "people's" government—which is to say by the leaders who promise well-being in the future, demand hard labor in the present, and themselves enjoy the perquisites of management and the comforts of wealth. Good demagogues make bad managers, however—bad industrial planners and bad supervisors of production and distribution. Every socialist democracy, in its own way, vividly illustrates this process of economic deterioration.

The leaders of these governments by the poor (to which all democracies degenerate) are cornered by their own shallow policies. Desperation leads to excesses of unreason. Scapegoats for the anger of the masses must be invented. The old order is thus more bitterly attacked than ever, its remnants reviled and persecuted as villains seeking to subvert "the people's democracy." The pains of egalitarian disorder and general mismanagement, however, cannot be avoided.

While the old order is publicly assailed, its economic brains will be quietly called upon. Hierarchical and competitive institutions will have to be reintroduced, but new "democratic" language will hide the move. The continued irrationality of democratic leaders seeking to play Robin Hood corrupts hierarchy itself. The powers of wealth and political authority go to a few —but now to an incompetent few who acquire and hold their offices by pretending to wield their power in the name of the people. Hypocrisy becomes so blatant that "the people's democratic leaders" are drawn to every extremity to keep the show going. If the masses cannot be successfully brainwashed, it may be necessary to build high walls of bricks and barbed wire to keep them from fleeing to some land where the economic order has not been so thoroughly scrambled.

That is the summary history of democracy extended—as it always is, sooner or later—to the economy. The government of the many gives to the poor enormous power, which is readily manipulated by the greedy and ambitious. Politicians whose authority rests only on their ability to win votes are inevitably tempted to promise, and then to attempt, to make the poor rich. They succeed chiefly in making the rich poor, and the poor still poorer. *Inflation* (when money cannot be legitimately saved for public projects, it is printed recklessly and the currency debased) and *depression* (the mismanagement of industry leads to uncontrollable glut in some spheres and painful shortages in others) are but the most obvious signs of the instability that results from government by popular election. The first great factor leading democracy inexorably to ill-health is intellectual incompetence; the second, yielding catastrophe sooner or later, is economic egalitarianism.

16. Knowledge and Ignorance

Ignorance is a third factor. In spite of widespread opportunities for schooling and the general encouragement of education, the masses are without much learning and always will be so. What can schools be expected to accomplish? Basic literacy, elementary history and geography, the manipulation of simple numbers can be mastered by almost everyone. Fine. Serious culture, however, is not within the competence of most persons. Science and mathematics, penetrating study of literature and philosophy and social relations—all vital for wise political leadership—are essentially alien to the masses and beyond them. The rule of the many, therefore, yields judgments characteristically uninformed and shallow.

In a democracy almost everyone "gets an education," but most, including the leaders, are very poorly educated. Numbers do not make up for quality. If the mass of children are compelled to complete secondary schools, the level of instruction in those schools must be literally degraded. And it is; most American high-school graduates read and write at primary-school levels. School administrators in democratic school systems do not report this too loudly, of course. The people, although generally honest, do not care to have their incapacities advertised.

From fraudulent secondary schools that all must attend and from which almost all are graduated, millions go on to colleges for which they are more unsuited still. These must be degraded, in turn, to serve as instruments of mass education. Standards of university work are lowered so that more of the masses (inadmissible in earlier times and now intellectually unchanged) may enroll and eventually "get their degree." In some communities, every high-school graduate, regardless of past performance or tested abilities, must by law be admitted to a public university, which is thus further demeaned. There, professors teach at the high-school level and must also provide the remedial instruction in reading and arithmetic that may bring students up to that level. In the once great public university of the City of New York, only financial stringencies, not intellectual rigor, made it essential to require that all new students be able to read at an eighth-grade —13-year-old!—standard. High intellectual standards are a hindrance to the rule of the many; indeed, they prove ultimately incompatible with it.

What is true of the school is true of every cultural activity in a democracy: music, art, and literature must be pop; the ultimate standard of achievement is mass appeal. The pictures seriously discussed by major critics are of soup-can labels, or gigantic canvases on which naked girls, dipped in paint, have rolled. The music for which great throngs gather is a combination of simple rhythms and great volume, usually accompanied by mindless lyrics and inane glitter. Best-selling books (read only by the democratic literati) are novels of sex and adventure, without depth or subtlety. Network television caters to vulgar tastes and shallow minds.

Language itself, the chief and finest instrument of human intelligence, is corrupted. Precision, eloquence, and clarity in speech and writing grow rare, and are replaced by teen-age slang, the repetitive lingo of sports reporters, and mindless obscenities. Politicians and clergymen hide behind meaningless platitudes calculated to offend as few as possible. Sustained philosophical argument, avoided by nearly everyone, is relegated to academies having no influence on public business. Its place is taken by ephemeral products of half-baked reflection: letters-to-the-editors columns in newspapers, and that trademark of democratic culture, the "philosophical" comic strip. Where everything is for the people, everything must be debased to a form in which the dullest can digest it.

The passion for equality, once aroused, must be catered to in every sphere. In work, in schools, in the arts, there is a movement to suppress distinction, to reduce all to that low level the masses can attain. Advancement on the job comes to be based not upon merit but upon seniority. Everyone can "put in his time"; to reward what some can do and others can't begins to seem unfair. Fairness itself is thus corrupted. When seniority won't suffice, preference in jobs commonly goes to those who "get along with others," who smile much and are disliked by few. The arch virtue of life in a democracy is unoffensiveness.

The discipline of training, in the trades as in the arts, comes to be despised. Fine workmanship gradually disappears. High achievement—in musical composition or carpentry or any craft—requires a long apprenticeship, instruction from experienced masters, and a gradual rise in accomplishment and recognition. Only a few have the requisite devotion and discipline. Even fewer have the talents that make such discipline fruitful. To avoid distinctions of talent or accomplishment, a democratic society will revise even the standards of merit. Simple subject matters, handled primitively, are widely acclaimed. Speedy gratification is commonly sought; gaudy carelessness replaces painstaking subtlety. Paint smeared on a canvas without discipline is lauded as fine art. Geometrical designs that please unsophisticated eyes and "human interest" photography—the boy with his dog—share easy honors. Let the clay be fired when imperfectly shaped or glazed; the roughness will attest to the plainness of its makers and increase the vessel's arty appeal. Vessels actually used will in any event be plastic with cute designs. Let the parts of a musical composition be played in random order, or by the several instruments at random; discipline in the composition of the whole will be thus undetectable, and therefore unnecessary.

"Mastery" becomes a bad word, for if there are masters there must be journeymen and apprentices. To equalize all, the surest method is to lower standards of workmanship. Whoever sets his hand to the material must be an instant artist, whatever the result. The archetype is no longer the "masterwork," of which there are few, but the "happening," of which there are limitless numbers. This is the natural career of the arts in a democracy.

The passion to equalize the unequal reaches its apogee in the schools, "the training ground of democracy." Distinctions in intellectual accomplishment must there be eliminated, or explained away, or as a last resort disguised. Sorting better or poorer students by ability is despised; it is thought too cruel to tell anyone, but especially a child, that he isn't capable of learning mathematics or Spanish at the same level or speed at which others can. All must learn mathematics—or reading, or geography, or whatever—at the same mediocre rate in the same mediocre classes. Quick students and slow ones are mixed deliberately, on the pretext that it will be socially and intellectually beneficial for both. In fact, the refusal to sort by ability leads to the frustration of all, the embarrassment and self-deprecation of the poorer students, the boredom of the bright and the waste of their talents. It is "good for them" only if our aim is to homogenize society, keeping all to a universally mediocre standard.

Honors programs are cancelled as undemocratic. All cannot be honored equally, and an intellectual elite must not be permitted to emerge. If honors cannot be done away with, the egalitarian aims to render them meaningless by spreading them so generally as to cancel any distinction in their award. Grades themselves, distinguishing students who achieve more or less, become anathema; let the grading system be simply pass/fail—but let no one fail. If grades cannot be eliminated, nearly the same result may be achieved by awarding the highest grade to virtually everyone, inflating the academic currency and (as in every inflation) driving out good currency with bad. When such devices fail to suppress intellectual distinctions, the egalitarian seeks to redirect evaluation altogether. Not achievement in learning but "effort" will be graded. Everyone can try; why should we evaluate two students differently who try equally hard? If this results in distinctions flowing from character, the school can take the next step and evaluate neither achievement nor effort, but "citizenship." Good school citizens need only be in class and be quiet, which everyone can do. Education should draw out the best in each; education in a democracy expects the same from all. The schools degenerate into custodial institutions.

Among educational institutions, differences in quality are similarly suppressed. It becomes indelicate to send one's child to a better—i.e., a more demanding—school; the ordinary public school for everyone is the democratic way. Some universities remain elite (Harvard and Oxford, California and Michigan) because faculty and students are more accomplished there, but that will be admitted only informally. In legislative chambers the word "elite" will be used only in the pejorative sense; universities will not be recognized as second-rate, although most of them are. Honesty might offend.

Democratic pretense hides what democratic artifice cannot change—that a few people are very smart, a few are quite stupid, and most are of middling ability. Some can learn much and quickly, others little and slowly. To recognize these human differences honestly, and deal with them efficiently and justly, institutions of differing qualities, using differing methods, must be devised.

Democracy denies this reality, refusing to recognize critical human differences, disguising them if need be for the sake of self-deception. Fascism takes account of these differences. We recognize that humans unequal in talent can be happy and virtuous in different ways. For high government posts, fascism demands the very finest qualities; it demands persons whose mind and character naturally fit them for leadership. Democracy relies upon the man in the street. Some ancient Greeks carried this spirit to an extreme: Leaders were not popularly elected, but chosen at random by lottery. That culmination of the egalitarian's conviction is admired by many modern democrats. Like children at play, we must take turns at rule.

Government by the many is inevitably disastrous. The irrationality, the poverty, and the ignorance of the masses illuminate our fundamental premise: Recognizing great native differences among humans is crucial for a healthy government.

In exhibiting the dangers of ignoring or suppressing natural inequalities, we do not merely attack democratic principles but support our own. The alternatives are sharply limited. If political power is not to rest in the hands of all, it must rest in the hands of some. To understand the failure of democracy, therefore, is to grasp the case for fascism. A few among us, by virtue of natural talents, are far more suited for leadership than the mass of humankind. These few should govern. Human beings are not equal and cannot be made equal.

17.   Equality Reexamined

Some democrats respond: "Variations in the native capacities of human beings do not justify differential voting power among citizens, because each citizen remains an equal in the community of persons. Each has but one life to lead; each possesses that spark of humanity for which all else is instrument. To seek to bring all persons to the same level of learning or judgment is foolish, we agree—but we deny that unequal capacities render democracy foolish. Democracy supposes only a deeper equality that *is* universal. This fundamental equality of humankind is what makes democracy just and authoritarianism unjust."

Behind this screen of words we find not reality, but the democrat's ungrounded faith. What is that "deeper," "fundamental" equality? All humans are humans; no one denies that. To insist that all humans are *equal* just because they are *human* begs the very question at issue. Of course we all share humanity, but while sharing it we have differing natures and talents, and therefore appropriately differing roles and powers in the social organism. Once the critical inequalities have been admitted, the insistence that somehow, beneath them, a mystical equality remains is an irrational conviction contradicted by good social science and by everyday experience.

The democrat's talk about "deeper levels" and "sparks of humanity" is rubbish. If such notions justify equal roles in government, they must also justify equal roles in all important affairs —in science, medicine, and sports. No one seriously believes that. When there is important business at hand, the democrat conveniently forgets deeper levels and sparks and attends, as a rational person, to critical differences of talent and skill. In the operating room, the patient is quick to agree that all men are not equal. Employers or foremen or coaches put aside all talk about fundamental equality and spend much of their time discriminating the best from the many. Democrats who deny the ubiquity of inequality are led to hypocrisy and absurdity.

Democrats who admit great native differences among humans, recognize their importance in science or industry, and still insist that those differences may not count in government, must harbor a naïve view of the talents government requires. Knowledge and astute judgment they acknowledge to be essential in managing the laboratory or the locker room—but managing the city or the state is (they suppose) a job all can do with equal skill. Directing finance or forestry, they know, demands training and intellect—but directing the body politic they think demands just run-of-the-mill common sense. They cannot otherwise justify government by universal voting. But if there are great differences in the native powers of human beings, a system of government that ignores these differences is dangerous.

Consistent democratic theory, moreover, will ascribe the right to vote to *all* humans, without regard for age or mental health. Children are no less human than their parents; if humanity itself is the criterion for equal voice in government, individuals five years old have as much claim upon that voice as individuals twenty-five years old. Ridiculous? Of course. The inference need trouble only those who tell stories about some fundamental equality shared by all human beings. If they specify any set of humans who are not entitled to vote—idiots, felons, the insane, infants—they must explain how democratic theory can justify that deprivation. There are very good reasons to discriminate in the distribution of political power, but the consistent democrat must be systematically blind to them. Any attempt to ground the essential distinctions everyone makes in practice on differentiable capacities to reason or judge destroys the whole democratic case.

"Your problem," the democrat may rejoin, "is that you insist upon thinking of the equality of humans as an empirical fact, a feature somehow visible, tangible or measurable. It isn't; the fundamental equality of humankind is nonempirical. It is a fact, but one that cannot be confirmed by science or established by evidence of any objective kind. Our confidence in this universal but non-empirical truth about humanity is the ultimate foundation of the democratic system. Ridicule that foundation if you please; you cannot refute it."

It ridicules itself. We only point to its meaninglessness. Unlike all the qualities and relations of people we know anything about, this supposed equality crucial for democracy is claimed as a reality that cannot be verified. We are told that it is just *so,* and that we are to believe it on the democrat's assurance, without evidence, and without any possibility of evidence! Religious beliefs about heaven and hell, and other supernatural matters, are often defended in such ways. Politics differs from religion, however, in that its arena is this empirical world; the powers of government must be tied to claims for which there is at least some rational evidence.

The desperation of the democratic theorist leads, at last, to basing the system on a mystery, on a claim for which, conveniently, no evidence can ever be given. Even ghosts in haunted houses are more credible than that. To defend democracy by insisting upon the key role of entities for which evidence is impossible in principle, and whose reality therefore cannot be refuted, is to abandon the canons of reason itself.

"If we cannot prove that all human beings *are* equal," the democrat is driven to reply, "is it not reasonable, at least, to treat them *as if* they were equal? Let the equality upon which democracy is grounded be understood as our postulate, an hypothesis which, if warranted, requires the equal distribution of the ultimate powers of government." The *wishful* character of democratic theory is here exposed. Reality is not its foundation; there is no evidence for human equality and there is overwhelming evidence against it. Yet we are to base government on hope, to make believe that humans are as some would like them to be, in order to justify a form of government that, realistically, is neither appropriate nor wise.

The pretense called for is totally unwarranted. The practical results of that "hypothesis" of human equality are pernicious, as we have seen. Ordinary human experience gives no reason to suppose that such equality is an appropriate postulate. The reverse is true. Most people have a direct acquaintance with human *in*equality, and an intuitive appreciation of it. Most of us know very well that there are a host of roles and responsibilities for which we have neither the ability nor the inclination. Most of us were not born to be leaders and know that. In performing important but subsidiary functions, most humans need to be given direction; they want to be led.

18.   Leadership

Leadership in the social organism is a very specialized function. The tasks of overall management require capacities that few possess. The exercise of great authority entails great responsibilities.

Leaders are never for a moment free of care. Only a childish view of leadership glorifies the power of rulers while ignoring their heavy burdens, the incessant anxieties of those who must make the critical decisions affecting all.

Good leaders are commonly not happy. They may take satisfaction in the fulfillment of immense responsibilities, knowing that few could have done better. But that satisfaction is normally accompanied by intense strain. Leaders are aged by their duties, pushed to the limits of their physical endurance, drained of their spiritual energies. When their turn at the helm is at last done, they hand over their trusteeship with some regret but much relief. In his ideal republic, Plato even suggested that true leaders may have to be forced, against their inclinations, to reenter the cave of worldly struggle. Not the comfort of particular persons, he taught, but the health and good order of the whole is the paramount consideration. To that end leaders also must do the work for which they are by nature fitted.

When it is understood that the assumption of leadership is natural for some, and that the subordination of others is equally natural, the common fear of fascism dissipates. Government by the best must be government by a few, yet it is not for the benefit of a few but for all. It offers every citizen the fullest opportunity to realize himself, to do what he was born to do and can do with greatest satisfaction. The great hierarchy of stations and duties is the natural condition of humankind.

Most people take comfort in the recognition of this natural order. Where common goals are clear while distinguishable functions must be performed, at work or in play, equality is hardly ever thought of. The body—a town, a university, an athletic team, or whatever—must first of all choose a leader. One person, or a few persons, must be given the power to organize the rest. Jobs must be assigned, plans developed, priorities established. If anything is to be accomplished, there must be a president and executive committee, a premier and cabinet; other members must understand their individual roles in the common enterprise. Most of us, most of the time, are set to tasks by superiors who supervise our contributions to the larger whole. We receive and complete assignments, report to our supervisors, are rewarded or reprimanded, and go on to other duties for which our abilities and training suit us.

In this organic process we feel the pressure of orders from above with differing degrees of compulsion. But orders they remain for all except the highest authorities. There is no humiliation whatever in accepting and obeying them. That is what life is all about.

19.   Discipline

Discipline is absolutely essential in a rational civil society. The democrat's belief that being subordinate is shameful stems from egalitarian delusions. Everyone naturally recognizes superiors and inferiors in the various functions of life. Respect shown to superiors—in manner and in form of address—is not mindless servility but mindful service. It is recognition of proper place, yours and mine and theirs. Obedience to the commands of superiors provides the thrust that energizes the social body. The shared spirit of obedience is a pervasive moral bond. A body whose members will not perform their assigned duties will soon disintegrate. No organism can thrive whose parts and cells take upon themselves the "right" to decide what they are going to do and when. That is an organism diseased.

Most people have an intuitive grasp of this healthy subordination, if not a reasoned understanding of it. Most people want to obey. Of course they do not want to obey just anybody, or the command to do just anything; but they are prepared to receive reasonable assignments from legitimate authorities. Most of us know, when not misled, that contentment and well-being lie in fulfilling our assignments as well and as enthusiastically as we can. Internal as well as external rewards do not come from cheating or defying the boss. On that path lies misery. The workman whose joys lie in honest craftsmanship, the student who is diligent in learning, the teacher whose highest pay is the growth of his students—these are the happy, healthy people of the world.

If the duties assigned are reasonable, the rewards for satisfactory performance fair, the punishment for negligence or failure appropriate, decent people will rarely disobey their rightful superiors. Defiance of proper authority is generally understood to be out of order. Rebellious spirits may be tolerated, even admired, in youngsters exploring the world and themselves. But obedience is the norm, for children and adults. Disobedience, when deliberate and continued, must be punished. The needed discipline is developed in the early training of children. The youngster who is never firmly forbidden gratification, never spanked when disobedient or disrespectful, is, as the saying goes, "spoiled rotten." In maturity, discipline rarely needs physical sanction; it comes to be our second nature, self-imposed. The physical punishment of adults is justifiable only on rare occasion, as a response to criminal conduct. In those communities where respect for authority is well-developed, and standards of self-discipline are high, we are very likely to find peace, productivity, and self-understanding. Complete autonomy—each legislating for himself without ordered authority—is unnatural. It is a literally crazy ideal.

Good superiors are therefore vital. They promote general well-being and make satisfaction possible for their subordinates. Obedience to superiors—in work or play, in war or religious service—gives comfort and pride. Relations with a superior are properly both formal and very human. We address him or her with respect: our judge, "your honor"; our conductor, "maestro"; our superior in any mundane context, "sir" or "ma'am." Respect and readiness to obey may even be expressed with a salute or other physical gesture of submission.

Such concrete marks of hierarchy will never disappear. Democrats may scorn them, but sensible folks are not ashamed of their honest place in the real world. A domestic servant, whose duty is to clean and run errands, rises when her employer enters the room. She honors him and herself in so doing, giving an open sign of the relation between them. That relation is but one tiny thread of a great fabric. Within that fabric many different jobs, some menial, must be done. When that employer reports to *his* superior, he is not likely to sit unless bidden to do so, or to neglect respectful forms of address. Of such relations is the larger social fabric woven.

20. Sexiness

Giving and taking orders have been vital for the survival of the human species through countless generations. Now the drives to command and to obey are literally in our genes. The natural disposition of some to assume command, and the natural readiness of others to obey, are part of what attracts the sexes to one another for mating. The almost universal dominance of the male and submission of the female is not merely "cultural," as any clearheaded reflection upon the size, strength, and general character of the two sexes immediately reveals. The healthy of both sexes want it so. Virility in males is most often associated with strength. Men are most attractive when powerful, assuming protective but firm command over others. Women—whose native capacities are neither less nor greater than men's, but different —are most alluring when subtly yielding. In a word, submission to a fitting authority is downright sexy, for superior and subordinate alike.

This sexiness is not limited to relations between the sexes, although its roots are there. Within the hierarchies of single-sex institutions—a girls' school, a military unit, and so on—the libidinous pleasures of command for some, and of obedience for others, can be missed only by those who have their eyes shut. Carried to extremes these tendencies may engender sadism or masochism. In most humans, however, these natural inclinations are not carried to extremes; they provide the inner motivation to assume the sometimes arduous roles for which nature has fitted us. Of all systems of government, only fascism recognizes this deep sexual connection. Only fascism can bring the genetic inevitability of obedience and command to concrete realization. The pride and excitement that come with the exercise of authority (and with submission to it) are deeply human satisfactions. The democrat strives in vain to eliminate them.

21.   The Historical Record

In vain, we say, because the inner drive toward hierarchy is difficult to suppress and impossible to eradicate. Successful human societies must have order, and social order entails organization by quality. All human history gives testimony to this necessity. Tribes and clans, states and nations—political communities of every kind—have required, in their earliest stages, the development of a class of leaders or chiefs. Inevitably, every body politic has formed a natural aristocracy, or it has died. Whether warlike or peaceable, whether hunters or farmers or merchants, whether primitive or civilized—men must be led. Some rise to lead; the rest are naturally fitted to follow. This has always been the way of the world, and it always will be.

"Not always," answers the democrat. "The rule of the masses has been uncommon in human affairs, true, but it has emerged at times, and in some periods it has thrived." Is this so? Democratic experiments have been the exception to the rule in human government, we agree. But has democracy ever truly thrived? We say not. Consider.

In the long view of human history, the lifespan of democratic governments has been very brief. A few years is usually the most that can be strung together before the system reverts—by default, miscalculation, or force—to a more natural one. Those city-states the Greeks called democracies were hardly that; most of the men and all of the women there were not full citizens but underlings by whom the menial work was done. Equality for the Greeks extended only among the upper crust of male citizens— and even that degree of democracy led to perpetual bickering, weakness, and early downfall. Democratic Athens was crushed by fascist Sparta and never recovered. All the Greeks infected by the notion that the many ought to govern themselves, fell soon and stayed long under the imperial Roman thumb. The Roman republic in turn, hardly a true democracy, pressed a crown upon the Caesars when its need for leadership was desperate. Every people craves a monarch to whom loyalty and submission may be given.

From Roman times to the recent past—and in all the generations of men so far as we know them—democracy has been an object of ridicule. It has played no truly constructive role in most human history.

In recent times those countries in which democracy has re-emerged are either unstable or fraudulent, or both. Most modern democracies, born in a flush of enthusiasm for human equality, have quickly tumbled when political reality had to be faced. The republic of equal citizens envisioned by the utopians of the French Revolution fell quickly to the Directorate and then to Napolean Bonaparte. The democracies of Latin America are notoriously short-lived, overthrown by military juntas whenever crisis demands stability and firm leadership.* All democracies eventually topple because with the masses on top they are top-heavy. Like a cork with one end weighted, there is only one posture in which a state can stay afloat.

Countries in which democracy has had a longer span of apparent success are either less stable or more hierarchical than commonly thought. American, French, and Canadian governments have proven vulnerable to catastrophe and resort quickly to martial law. In the long history of nations, their lives are short. England, during most of its history and all of its most successful years, was not a democracy at all but an imperial aristocracy, topped by a powerful monarch. Much that appears democratic in some lands is pretense, obscuring the fact that real power rests in the hands of a few families or corporate groups. In the United States the concentration of effective authority in the military-industrial complex, the "power elite," as American sociologists call it, has been repeatedly demonstrated and is widely admitted. Democracy cannot withstand the inevitable resurgence of hierarchy; if it is not cultivated openly and intelligently it will grow corrupt in secret. A mass of people cannot rule itself; a people that parades the trappings of self-government must shelter another reality beneath.

22.   The Iron Law of Oligarchy

All human societies, not only political bodies, thrive on strong leadership and wither without it. Great productive corporations are never democracies; they are directed by a hierarchy of managers who are responsible for decisions involving great sums of money and the deployment of much human energy. Power always lies at the peak of these hierarchies. Assembly-line workers and

---

*Bolivia—appropriately named after the great republican, Simón Bolívar—has had nearly two hundred different governments, and sixteen constitutions, since its founding as an independent "democracy" in 1825. Elections there are invariably fraudulent; power rarely passes peacefully to the winners. The only respite from turmoil comes with hastily-organized and ill-executed military take-overs.

office clerks are essential, of course, but it is to the managers that they must be subordinate. Successful churches have been those hierarchically led. The Roman Catholic Church is not a democracy; its long life and great prosperity is attributable partly to its astute mode of government. Successful political parties, however much they contend otherwise, are not democracies. Even "social democratic" parties that have professed the equal distribution of power, ironically have stayed long under the firm command of a few powerful and indispensable leaders.

The historical evidence is overwhelming. Scholarship and everyday experience combine to assure us that strong leadership, duly ordained and loyally obeyed, is the natural shape of order and the natural craving of mankind. What Robert Michels called "the iron law of oligarchy" is everywhere the underlying rule of human society. Organization entails oligarchy. The democrat denies this, either knowing the true state of human affairs, in which case he is a hypocrite and a fraud, or honestly, not recognizing the true state of affairs, in which case he is a fool and a danger.

23.   Fascism and Freedom

"But democracy means freedom," says our critic, "and its loss means the loss of freedom. Fascism must be rejected because, under it, we cannot be free."

This is empty rhetoric. In the first place, democracy does not mean freedom; it may or may not promote freedom. Often it does not. In the second place, the argument suggests, falsely, that we are more free if the laws we are obliged to obey are made by the many. This is a confusion. Every government must have laws; democratic regimes, like all others, are forced to limit the conduct of individuals to protect all. No citizen of any government is an iota more free because those limits have one author rather than another. It is not who makes the laws that determines our freedom, but their content. In the third place, if the argument suggests that the laws made by an ill-educated many will somehow be better than those made by a well-trained few, it is wholly spurious. The reverse is true. Laws made by the many, as we have seen at length, are likely to prove greatly inferior.

What underlies this confused appeal to "freedom"? Perhaps it is the assumption that in a democracy "free"individuals join together, as independent units, to form a government as their instrument. Freedom (in this view) is the natural condition of atomic citizens, to be restricted as little as possible by the laws. This atomistic conception of society has earlier been shown utterly wrong-headed. A healthy social system is no more the product of a contract among free and independent citizens than my body is the product of a contract agreed to by my independent organs, or the free cells of my body. There are no such free and independent beings; there never were and never will be. Such "freedom" is myth and foolishness.

Conceived in that way, freedom becomes a pernicious deception. In many democracies it is in practice equated with license, the right to act entirely according to our own private rules. But human beings cannot be wholly autonomous. Self-legislation for everyone is a corrupt ideal that cannot be realized. The attempt to do so would bring chaos. Were the single units of a social body to act independently and without unified control, all would be conflict and disorder.

True freedom is the opportunity to act within the range of alternatives appropriate to us. That range cannot be set by each individual for himself; it depends on the kind of person he is and his role in the larger scheme of things. Parents are not properly free to care for their infant children or to leave them to die, as they choose. Children are not properly free to obey their parents or not, as they choose. The "freedoms" of pilots to take unnecessary risks, or of statesmen to make impetuous threats, and so on and on, are very nicely done without. Real freedom is freedom with responsibility—action for which one is answerable. Democratic prattle about freedom is dangerous because where there is no hierarchical order there can be no true individual responsibility.

In our view, on the other hand, answerability for action makes good sense. Every citizen is responsible to some higher authority. The larger system within which freedom can be realized is the social organism itself; concretely this is the state and its instruments. Latitude there may be in the *ways* of doing one's job, or fulfilling one's duties—but not in *whether* one does so. There are many ways to care for infant children, but limits upon neglect of them; many judgments must be made by the keen pilot, but they must be made in keeping with the rules of safety. The freedom to make all one's own rules—taken even as ideal only— is plain lunacy. The range of appropriate alternatives is some- times small; there may be but one path open. The truly free person understands the rightness of restriction; the performance of duty to others becomes his chief source of satisfaction.

24.   Fascism and Free Speech

"But some activities," the democrat may answer, "should be absolutely free. For pilots and parents, restrictions are readily justified. But in matters pertaining to an individual's own body and style of life, and especially in speech and in publication, no external restraints can be justified. This democratic ideal of free- dom you ought not to mock."

We do not mock it; we reject it as deeply mistaken, though often honestly professed. To maintain that people should be free to say and publish whatever they like, and live however they choose, sounds appealing. In fact such freedoms are neither pos- sible, nor tolerable if they were, and no reasonable government will guarantee them. The classic example of the crowded theater in which surely no one may be permitted to shout "Fire" falsely is unanswerable. This is only one of countless circumstances in which the ideal of *absolute* freedom is monstrous. We may not freely defame another's character in speech or writing; slander and libel are rightly crimes which, if that ideal were taken seri- ously, would be crimes no longer. We do not permit the public utterance of frauds, the writing of false documents, the use of speech or publication to aid an enemy in wartime, and so on without end.

Speaking and writing is sometimes restricted, democrats may rejoin, because of the immediately harmful consequences of certain acts performed through speech. It is not the speech that is then forbidden, say they, but the harm it inflicts. Just so; that is precisely why the restriction of speech and publication is always a matter for a wise government to determine. Treasonous words may be more harmful than bullets. Teaching that corrupts the morals of the young is deeply injurious to all. Shall we protect it because it is "only" speech? Is the unrestrained portrayal of violence rewarded and vice honored no more than words and pictures? What shall we say of arbitrary discrimination against racial groups ("Whites Only") or among religious groups ("Jews Need Not Apply") with words? The answer is obvious, showing how shallow is the advocate of the total absence of restrictions upon speech.

In matters of personal conduct, completely unrestrained freedom is equally absurd. The sexual excesses of some may harm or seriously offend others; private dirt may endanger the public health; personal habits may create noises or nuisances that society cannot permit. Is the claim only that all should be free *barring* considerations such as these? But "these" are all considerations of collective well-being; they have no limit of kind or number. That is why there is no aspect of any person's life that can be allowed to be absolutely unrestrained. Everything one does or says may have important consequences for the social body, the state. Absolute freedom never makes sense. It is a pernicious ideal.

All citizens are threads in the fabric of society. Because we emphasize the *weave* in that fabric, we are called totalitarians by our critics. The term is meant as one of abuse—but in its descriptive sense we do not reject it. That thistle, too, will lose its sting if we grasp it firmly. We are totalitarians; we try to see things in their totality; we understand that each human being is but a tiny element in a whole far larger and greater in importance than he. We see that there is no aspect of an individual's life—not his speech or habits, his property or family, his work or ideals—that does not lie within this totality and have some bearing upon its health. When immoral conduct, degenerate art, or a mistaken scientific theory proves injurious to the whole, we think it essential for responsible authorities to act. Their job is to protect the whole; like everyone else they must answer for what they do and for what they fail to do. Withholding guidance, protecting what is unhealthy, refusing to confiscate what is plainly noxious, are derelictions of duty by the established authorities. Some conduct is evil; some arguments are fallacious; some reports are lies. It is cowardice not to say so; it is malfeasance if responsible leaders do not use the legitimate authority of the state to protect its interests. This is part of what government is for. Judgments, and actions based upon judgments, are inescapable. These are the duties of wise leaders. If this be totalitarianism, make the most of it.

If freedom be conceived as the opportunity to act intelligently within reasonable bounds, fascism will maximize it. If freedom be conceived as the absence of restraint, it is neither a proper ideal nor a feasible objective. Many who sing the praises of freedom do not understand what it entails. True freedom goes far beyond selfishness. It is responsible conduct, designed to serve others as well as ourselves. In acting for and within our ordered community, we are most truly free. *Loyal* freedom is our proper ideal.

25. Loyalty

Loyalty is not a mindless attachment to a place or a person. It is the thoughtful, rational dedication of one's self to a larger cause. Emotion is part of it, surely, but its foundation is reason, the understanding of one's place in the scheme of things. Recognizing our debts to parents, teachers, the society at large, knowing our selves to be parts of many wholes, each within the one largest whole we call the state, we come to see that we have no individual interests distinct from those of the institutions in which we flourish. In our schools and families, our teams and offices, and above all in our nation, we become all that we can be.

Our loyalty, therefore, is owed to the whole system of causes that give purpose to our lives. The player is loyal to the team and will sacrifice personal acclaim for its success and honor. In like manner we must be loyal to the great team called nation. The good team player needs to develop individual skills, strength, and endurance. He trains hard, but not for himself alone. He may be replaced on the playing field by one who runs faster or is less tired, but the team's victory remains the chief goal, and whatever his personal disappointment, he is joyful when the team is unified and triumphant. An athlete is judged outstanding partly because of technical excellence, but importantly also because of excellence as a team player, blending individual skills with others, to bring out the best in them and in the whole. The ultimate plaudits come only when, at the moments of greatest stress, he "gives everything he's got." He is devoted. He is loyal.

One's team is usually not of world-shaking importance—a school, a club, a company. Yet the virtue of selfless service in smaller settings is essentially identical with the virtue demanded by the great teams in one's life. It is no accident that team sports are the common games of youngsters; by developing team spirit and the capacity for self-effacement, they provide the moral training needed for good citizenship. One carries out his assignment, gives his all, and finds elation and fulfillment in loyal service and collective achievement.

26.   National Loyalty

Now magnify that team loyalty a hundredfold. Blend with it the family loyalty that arises from common blood and shared daily life. Enrich it with the mutual affection that comes from decades of cooperative service. Thus may one begin to appreciate the intensity of the loyalty a good citizen feels for his country. He is suffused with a feeling of devotion to it; he knows himself in union with it.

We fascists say proudly, "Everything for the state; nothing outside the state; nothing against the state." When we say it, our shallow critics think us to be irrational slaves to an external power. Nothing could be more false. We know ourselves as effective and dutiful members of a social system that is our own larger body. If we are not loyal to our country above all, we betray ourselves and are nothing.

The concrete forms of national loyalty are sometimes burdensome; we must accept without quarrel the decisions of legitimate authorities, even when we do not like them. We must accept the duty of obedience to duly-appointed officers who may be stern and demanding, and whose larger missions we sometimes do not fathom. Our superiors may be unpleasant persons, sometimes perhaps unkind or unfair, and yet we owe them obedience in the pursuit of our common purposes.

Loyalty is not normally heroic. Most often it is neither specially painful nor specially exhilarating. For most of us, most of the time, being loyal simply means doing our duty, obeying with good spirit the orders given us, and seeing to it that the persons subordinate to us conduct themselves in accordance with the interests of the whole.

Nations differ and conflict. Human history always has and probably always will exhibit bitter contests among nations for space, for wealth, for supremacy. Most citizens of most nations honestly believe that their own country really is the best of all. In defending fascism we do not pass judgment upon competing national traditions; history will do that. The Englishman who knows himself to be a part of an old and settled order, and a speaker of the language that serves all the world in trade and diplomacy; the Italian who feels deeply the richness of his artistic heritage and the beauty of his land; the Russian and the American who sense intuitively the great space of their lands and the power and variety of their peoples; Egyptians and Frenchmen, Australians and Peruvians—indeed citizens of every nation—are loyal to their institutions, their codes of law and morals, their land and their culture. The real constitution of the nation, its unwritten makeup, is re-created in the acts and attitudes of each of its citizens. Loyalty to the constitution is in all our bones.

The links between our selves and our nation are often indirect. Many duties flow not from laws but from the missions and rules of the institutional units within which we are organized. Loyalty to the nation, therefore, takes concrete form in loyalty to the school in which we study, loyalty to the athletic teams that represent us, loyalty to some profession that practices under national auspices or to some business or factory or hospital that is part of the national corpus. The school or team will be part of a league of schools or teams; the business or hospital part of an industry or welfare system. Each loyalty fits into a higher loyalty, and all fit together in the end. We live our lives within sets of institutions, successively more encompassing, organized in uncounted layers and forming a great pyramid. This living pyramid gives meaning to all elements within, and what is (or seeks to be) external to it is either alien or useless. This is why we insist that all activities—in the arts as well as in the professions, in scholarship as well as industry—must serve the national whole.

Some contend that a scholar or a scientist owes his highest loyalty not to his country, but to "truth," or that an artist must be "true to his art" even if untrue to his people. Such views make the fundamental error of social atomism; they assume, falsely, that the scholar or the artist stands outside the social pyramid and can therefore determine independently what is true or worthy. Not so. Truth itself, its formulation and its verification, is tied to the institutional structure that makes a scholar's work possible. His scholarship, its presuppositions and material conditions, can develop only within the social body and are meaningless without that body. His first and last duty, therefore, are to it, and his quest for truth is genuine when given purpose by service to the whole.

So also with the arts. In the Tenth Book of *The Republic,* Plato puts it bluntly. Every artist, like every other citizen, must be asked what contribution he makes to the whole state, to all of us living together. Disruptive and unhealthy art, like corruption everywhere, we must root out. We do not say that innovation in the arts is always dangerous. Indeed, changing conditions require continuing exploration by artists and scholars both. But innovation has no value for its own sake. Artistic merit, in the last analysis, cannot be independent of social needs. Literature and theater that subvert morals by portraying sexual perversion or violence in a deceptively agreeable way must be thoughtfully censored. Distorted ideology and manipulated history do not deserve to be protected. The title "artist" does not give license to lie or do damage to the nation.

The sometimes dubious reputation of art and artists results from widespread antisocial aestheticism. The products of a deviant artistry that ignores common moral standards are generally unwholesome. "Arty" and "bohemian" people are rightly suspect. The moral weakness of the *aesthete* is conveyed even by the tone of that word; if one is cut off from the lifeblood of his nation, his work will be rootless and pallid.

True artistry is imbued with the spirit of a people; its creativity flows, consciously or unconsciously, from a national tradition. Not just folk ballads and country dancing can be art, of course—although we do respect and love these as genuine products of a people's culture. But artistic genius, when realized concretely, will embody some ideal that springs from the life of the nation. Great Italian and German opera grasps in theme and form the genius of those peoples; to understand Verdi or Wagner is to understand the Italian and German soul. Great Russian and Spanish literature molds national ideas into language and story. The themes of Dostoievsky are profoundly Russian; the cadence of Cervantes is profoundly Spanish. The greatest artists invariably exhibit this national character. It underlies their imaginative recreation of the spirit of their people and their time. Great works take shape within their organic settings, contributing to the organisms that made them conceivable. Arts and scholarship— Japanese *Noh* drama and Dr. Johnson's *Dictionary*—are eternally linked to peoples and places. Pursued in proper spirit, they are among the highest manifestations of national loyalty.

27. Patriotism

The noblest form of loyalty, however, is the sacrifice of life itself. Self-sacrificial heroism makes sense in an organic view of the world; in an atomistic democracy it is inexplicable. If the state were no more than an instrument devised to protect life and property belonging to its citizens independently, why should anyone give up his life or property, or risk them seriously, to defend the state? Sacrifice, when society is seen in that light, is insane. A rational person would not suffer death or injury to protect the tool that he devised to guard himself from death or injury! Yossarian, in *Catch 22,* is at least consistent in his individualism; out there in battle they are shooting at him, and he thinks it crazy to go voluntarily into such mortal danger.

Crazy it would be, if his own life and property were the individual's ultimate concerns; but they are not. More important by far is the well-being of the whole that is each citizen's larger self, and to which he owes everything. For its sake I can rationally risk my life, even give my life, knowing that no action could be more worthy. Great sacrifices for the state make sense because in it are realized my highest ideals, far beyond my life and my property. The state is a system of order in which I participate, a great living body of which I am but a tiny part. It is my life's blood, and more; it is fatherland and motherland, and more. It is *Patria,* and when I carry its flag through the most terrible adversity, singing its anthem, I am most myself, strongest and most serious and most joyful.

Whoever sneers at patriotism must live a thin and contemptible life. He cannot know the exaltation—the feeling of fitness and the mix of humility and pride—that comes with the celebration of one's country.

> *Breathes there the man, with soul so dead,*
> *Who never to himself hath said,*
> *This is my own, my native land!*
> *Whose heart hath ne'er within him burn'd*
> *As home his footsteps he hath turn'd,*
> *From wandering on a foreign strand?*
> *(Sir Walter Scott: "The Lay of the Last*
> *Minstrel," Canto VI.)*

The individualist must indeed be wretched. "Concentrated all in self," he approaches everything as a potential tool for his own, self-regarding pleasures. In the symbols of his country, its flag and its songs, he grasps nothing but colors and tunes. He is embarrassed when others salute with respect and emotion.

Inwardly, however, even the most cynical individualist cannot deny his intimate connections with his national community and its ideals. No man is an island; every man *is* a part of the main. The false ideals of equality and popular rule having been widely inculcated, feelings of national spirit may be for a while suppressed, but they cannot be eradicated. At special moments in one's life, as when returning to one's homeland from a long stay abroad, that spirit resurges spontaneously. Some would have us deny with our heads what our hearts know beyond doubt. In fascism, head and heart are consonant. The intellectual justification of an organic political system is consummated by the patriotism that gives focus to the emotions.

Heroism *is* truly admirable. Many who would like to sacrifice themselves for noble causes have not the strength to do so. Few have the courage to risk injury or death for the sake of what is beyond them. Some fine human beings, through their heroism, teach us what we might also be; in their acts our idealism is given concrete example. The proof of the universality of this instinct is the honor accorded to heroic sacrifice even by professedly atomistic societies. The ridicule of heroism is offensive to us all.

28. War

Heroism will not be ridiculed when the life of the nation is threatened. Then patriotism is no joke, and the principles that should infuse all social life come to the surface. When a nation struggles to preserve itself, no citizen will doubt its organic unity, or its need for leadership that is decisive, authoritative. Fascism may be a word now out of favor, but its substance is what every citizen craves when his country is at war. Then our leaders must be strong and wise, our government in the hands of the best. Everyone detests killing and waste and yearns for international harmony and human warmth. Sensible people do not relish bloodshed; the claim that an authoritarian system thrives on war is vicious myth. Just the reverse is true; war (whose causes are many and various) leads nations and peoples back to an authoritarian order by exposing the critical inadequacy of populism. The horrors of war bring at least a realization of who we are and what we are, as a people, and what we must do to survive. The symbols of patriotism are no objects of derision then. War is serious, and it makes us so. Serious people understand how their government must be organized.

War is also a fact of international life. So long as there have been human communities there have been wars among them. In the course of human history there has been hardly a day without conflict between societies struggling for hegemony or for survival. We fascists try to recognize honestly the inherent flaws in human character. No one can know what the future holds, but we do not see humans becoming any better than they have been, nor do we think it likely that wars will soon disappear. Talk about "the war to end all war" or "the war to make the world safe for democracy" is plain silly, testifying to the shallowness of the philosophies that encourage it.

Realistic citizens are wise to retrieve from the miseries of war what is of value. The trappings of democracy are then largely put aside, the combatants obliged to assume their strongest and most natural stance. From war we retrieve the consciousness of national unity, the reality of national spirit, and the understanding that leadership and power must rest at the top, while responsibility and obedience must infuse the whole.

Grieved by the losses inevitably sustained in war, we deploy our forces so that the men and equipment lost will be most dispensable. The most valuable national organs—central planning of strategy and supply—we most carefully protect. In childhood romances the king leads his army into battle; the nation that acts out such childishness soon learns the cost of fallen leadership in times of crisis. War reinforces a lesson of deep importance: Some are more fit to plan and direct, others more fit to obey and follow. When success is really a matter of life and death, we are all authoritarians.

National conflict is the rule, not the exception. When states are not engaged in mobilizing hostile armies or preparing for espionage, they nevertheless remain in deadly competition with one another. National interests invariably overrule any policy of altruism or pacifism that threatens survival. In commerce, in science, in exploration, in diplomacy and, most obviously, in armed conflict, every nation is always fighting for its life.

Our natural human condition and its limitations cannot be ignored. We live and die in bodies politic that rise and fall in the course of history. Every individual imagines at times that he cannot die, and every nation acts at times as though it too will go on forever. Death comes to all; but sooner by far to those, humans and nations, who do not prepare wisely to meet the perils of life by keeping themselves strong.

Struggle against a recalcitrant environment, and often against hostile neighbors, is the permanent and inescapable condition of human societies. Victory—health and prosperity for the whole and its parts—comes most surely to those most rationally governed.

The success of every human society depends upon the strength and health of its internal relations. False ideals of equality and autonomy will ruin us, causing us to suppose that we live as atoms and cooperate only out of selfish calculation. Ideals of duty and obedience tie us together, giving each—a frail twig taken separately—a share of the strength of that great bundle of branches bound firmly into unity. Our ties are the principles of just government, under which at every level the best command.

That is fascism, the natural and healthy condition of human beings in society, good for each and all together, and supremely
right.

Readings

(Other defenses of fascism, chronologically arranged)

Ancient and Classical

Date of Origin

(4th century B.C.)   **Plato,** *Crito,* and *The Republic,* in *The Work of Plato.*
Edited by Irwin Edman, Jowett Translation. New
York: Modern Library, 1965.

(1st century A.D.)   **Plutarch,** *The Life of Lycurgus of Sparta,* in *Plutarch's
Lives.* Berkeley, Calif: University of California
Press, 1974.

(1513)   **Niccolo Machiavelli,** *The Prince.* Translated by
Luigi Ricci. New York: Modern Library, 1950.

Nineteenth Century

(1808)   **Johann G. Fichte,** *Addresses to the German Nation.*
Translated by R. F. Jones and G. H. Turnbull,
Chicago: Open Court, 1922.

(1821)   **Georg W. F. Hegel,** *The Philosophy of Right.* Translated by T. M. Knox, New York: Oxford Uni-
versity Press, 1967.

(1841)   **Thomas Carlyle,** *On Heroes, Hero-Worship, and the
Heroic in History.* New York: Oxford University
Press, 1975.

(1870)   **Heinrich von Treitschke,** *Politics.* New York: AMS
Press, 1916.

(1886)   **Friedrich Nietzsche,** *Beyond Good and Evil.* Translated by Walter Kaufman. New York: Random
House, 1966.

Twentieth Century

(1905)   **Inazo Nitobe,** *Bushido: The Soul of Japan.* Rutland,
              Vt.: Charles E. Tuttle, 1969.

(1906)   **Georges Sorel,** *Reflections on Violence.* New York:
              AMS Press, 1975.

(1925)   **Alfredo Rocco,** *The Political Doctrine of Fascism.* New
              York: Carnegie Endowment for International
              Peace, 1926.

(1928)   **Giovanni Gentile,** *The Philosophic Basis of Fascism,* in
              Readings on Fascism and National Socialism. Ed-
              ited by the Department of Philosophy, Univer-
              sity of Colorado. Denver, Colo.: Alan Swallow,
              1960.

(1930)   **Alfred Rosenberg,** *The Myth of the Twentieth Century.*
              New York: AMS Press, 1979.

(1932)   **Benito Mussolini,** *The Doctrine of Fascism,* 3rd ed.
              Translated by E. Cope. Firenze, Italy: Vallec-
              chi, 1938.

(1933)   **Adolph Hitler,** *My Struggle.* Translated by Ralph
              Manheim. Boston: Houghton-Mifflin, 1933.

(1936)   **Mario Palmieri,** *The Philosophy of Fascism.* Chicago:
              The Dante Alighieri Society, 1936.

(1939)   **Ernst R. Hüber,** *Constitutional Law of the Greater Ger-
              man Reich,* in *National Socialism,* Division of Eu-
              ropean Affairs, U.S. Department of State,
              Washington, D.C.: Government Printing
              Office, 1943.

ADVOCATE SYNOPSIS
Communism

Communism is rooted in the laws of historical development. It provides the only scientifically correct account of how human societies have become what they are, and how they will progress. Unlike Western democracy and fascism, communism emphasizes not the way governments make decisions, but the substance of what is decided. It seeks and promises a society which is no longer divided into economic classes. It aims at a world order based on material prosperity and economic justice. It will eliminate the exploitation of man by man.

Scientific communism—called Marxism after its greatest theoretician—is built on the principles of dialectical materialism. Dialectics, employed by all great philosophers from Plato to Hegel, is the study of the universal patterns in change and development. Marxism applies this dialectical analysis to the material foundation of human life, to basic human needs for food, clothing, and shelter, and to the changing modes of industrial production.

Human history exhibits a pattern of relentless opposition between those who control the productive forces of society and those who do not, unending conflict between oppressors and oppressed. In every age the resolution of these dialectical conflicts has led to renewed opposition at a higher level, with oppression taking new forms. Marxism explains the successive phases of this continuing struggle, each dominant class replacing its predecessor as it wins control of the material substructure of society. Each resulting revolution in the course of history brings new productive powers and new economic cruelties. The long chain is culminated by the cataclysmic conflict, now in progress and already international in scope, between the capitalists and the working class, between the bourgeoisie and the proletariat.

Capitalism, like every preceding stage in history, contains the seeds of its own destruction. It is based on the private *appropriation of goods that are* socially *produced. This internal contradiction will be dialectically overcome only when production and appropriation, making and taking, are brought into full harmony—when both are fully socialized. This cannot be accomplished (as Western "socialists" and vulgar communists believe) by nationalization or state ownership. The concept of ownership itself must be eradicated, superseded by new relations between people and things.*

Marxism elucidates the stages of this complicated but inexorable process. It shows why capitalism necessarily results, even today, in the alienation and exploitation of working men and women. It explains the inevitable accumulation of wealth under capitalism, and its centralization into fewer and fewer hands. It shows how these tendencies produce increasing tension between the classes, and then increasing misery among the workers. It traces the development of these trends from their beginnings in Europe, through their growth in North America, and to their consummation throughout the globe over which capitalism extends its tentacles. Marxism explains the struggle of the capitalists to retain their wealth and power, resorting first to collusion, then to monopolies and cartels, then to colonialism and other forms of imperialism, and eventually to war.

The revolution of the proletariat against bourgeois exploitation is shown to be dialectically inevitable. Workers and peasants, led by a devoted and intellectual avant-garde, will ultimately create a world in which private property has been abolished, and material abundance is available for all. When the division of society into classes thus comes to an end, national states, which are the instruments of class oppression, will also wither away. In the highest phases of communism alienation will be overcome, universal equality and full self-realization achieved, in accordance with scientific principles. All will work— creatively and with satisfaction—and all will benefit justly.

In sum: Communism applies the dialectic to the material foundations of human history, and thus provides a scientific and coherent account of the inexorable course of social development. It explains the proletarian revolution now in progress, and it points to the classless society being born, in which human society will at last live up to the supreme principle of justice: From each according to his abilities; to each according to his needs.

SYSTEM FOUR
COMMUNISM

There is only one correct account of how governments obtain power and how they ought to use it: communism. Communist theory—its critique of Western democracy, its predictions and prescriptions, and the proof of its truth—we aim now to explain and defend.

This explanation cannot be short. Although the basic ideas are simple, their applications are complicated. The great changes in perspective our theory provides need to be assimilated gradually. We cannot and would not coerce agreement. But whoever gives our argument thoughtful attention will in the end be convinced that we are right. Our account of human history and government will be plainly stated and systematically proved. The intellectual persuasiveness of that proof accounts for the fact that most of the people of the world have judged it sound. New millions steadily join our ranks as rationally enthused advocates of the communist cause.

1. Substance and Process

Communism differs fundamentally from all systems of political democracy, and from all authoritarian systems, in this: They focus primarily on how decisions are made, contesting over who shall have authority; we focus primarily on the results to be achieved—leaving the bickering to them. Correct decisions may be reached in differing ways; whether a method is well-chosen depends upon whether, under existing conditions, it leads to the right results. Democrats are correct—sometimes—in believing that the people can jointly choose the correct path. Fascists are also correct—sometimes—in believing that intelligent leadership is crucial and that leaders must often be vested with great authority. Neither is correct in supposing that procedure is the main thing. Democrats and fascists alike are hypnotized by forms while painfully inattentive to content, to truth.

In contrast to them, we are more interested in *what* the decisions of government are than in *how* they are made. The instruments are important, but substance is what really matters in the end. The objective conditions of life are what sensible people really care about. So what counts most is not how the laws are enacted, but what they say; not how economic policy is set, but whether, as a result of that policy, the people are rich or poor. Governments, whatever their procedures, often make bad decisions. The chief thing about a good government is that it makes correct decisions, that it goes wrong as seldom and as little as is reasonably possible. We are not so silly as to claim that communist governments never go wrong; of course they do. But we do claim that communism is fundamentally on the right track. The substance of what we aim at is right—historically inevitable and morally just.

2.   Science and Philosophy

This concern for truth obliges us to deal with things as they are, not as we would like them to be. We offer not a fabric of hopes and wishes but a *scientific* account of economic and political development. Science and sound philosophy are not separate realms. The philosophy we defend—dialectical materialism is its technical name—can be shown to explain scientifically, with remarkable completeness, the course of human history. It can make sense out of the apparently chaotic present, and although it cannot magically foretell the future, it can provide a rational vision of what the world is moving toward.

Moving toward. Moving. All persons and all things are constantly in motion, in development. With that simple but profound truth we begin. Our view of the world seeks to understand movement and trace its direction. History, for us, is not simply the description of what was, collected in books; it is the dynamic course of events out of which everything that is has come. No satisfactory explanation of human government can be given by a theory—democracy, for example—that prescribes how things should be shaped without fully grasping how things came to have their present shape. Theories that do not respect the laws of historical development are futile, even dangerous. We begin, therefore, with an account of those general laws of development that provide the key to real understanding.

3. Dialectics

Motion itself does not need to be explained—but the patterns of motion do. Heraclitus, the Greek philosopher who taught that everything is in flux, also grasped this fundamental point: Movement, physical or mental, takes one direction or another in response to the pressures of opposing forces. The archer, mastering the tension between the bent bow and the taut bowstring, controls the flight of his arrow. That simple illustration reveals a deep truth about motion in every setting: Its direction and speed are the products of tension between conflicting forces. Such opposition cannot remain static; there must eventually be a resolution, at least temporary, that synthesizes the pressures previously in conflict. All change, all development transpires in accord with laws of tension and reconciliation, exhibiting intelligible pattern and rhythm.

Dialectics is the name of the study of those patterns underlying all change. Its roots—the same as for the word "dialogue"—are the Greek words for "between" and "speaking"—in one word, interaction, Dialectics is not itself science, but it is the instrument of all truly scientific understanding. To be known fully, a thing must be known in its movement and the stage of its development appreciated. In some matters stability is an aid to understanding, of course; objects of knowledge are often treated as though static. But no penetrating science can ignore the fact that things and events are never frozen in time. Interaction and historical development are unceasing. Genuinely scientific knowledge of any subject matter must be dialectical. In every sphere we must discover and apply the laws of growth and decay.

Great minds apply these laws with new insight in new spheres. Heraclitus was deep, but crude. Plato was far deeper, his philosophical reflections self-consciously dialectical in form. In his dialogues, the quest for understanding is pressed onward by the tension among disputants, by the conflict of claim and criticism, objection and reply. As resolution in argument seems to come within grasp, it, too, is opposed. Dialogue never ends. The profundity achieved by Greek philosophy lies precisely in its exposure—only partial but very deliberate—of the dialectical character of all true knowledge.

Every real advance in theoretical understanding, from Classical Greece to the present, has relied, directly or indirectly, upon the dialectic. The culmination of Medieval thought, the *Summa Theologica* of St. Thomas Aquinas, was a magnificent achievement in dialectic. Centuries later the critique of human reason reached extraordinary depths in Kant's "Transcendental Dialectic"—in which are exhibited the inescapable contradictions encountered in the quest for ultimate knowledge. In the physical sciences with Galileo and Einstein; in biology with Darwin and Pasteur; in history with Gibbon and Toynbee—in every sphere deep thought takes dialectical form. Even the greatest moralists—Jesus and Socrates—taught through dialogue with their disciples.

4. Hegel

To advance the spiral of human understanding, it was essential to explain the logic of dialectic itself. The one man who did most to accomplish this was Georg Wilhelm Friedrich Hegel who, in spite of some serious failings, was the greatest dialectician of all time. Writing at the turn of the nineteenth century, he uncovered at last the central pattern of the universal dialectic.

Before Hegel, disorder was rampant in the world of intellect. The physical and moral sciences were at war; mathematics and biology, logic and chemistry, appeared to run like rabbits, sense-lessly in all directions. Hegel revealed the integrity of the intelli-gible world. In striving to complete the circle of learning, he exhibited the interrelatedness of developments in every sphere. Before Hegel, history could be viewed as a story whose chapters might have one ending or another, depending on the strength or luck of the characters. After Hegel, history must be understood as a rational whole, the intelligible explanation of the necessary relations among past, present, and future. Sometimes wrong-headed and dogmatic, Hegel nevertheless glimpsed and formu-lated—not perfectly, but for the first time as an integrated whole —the dialectical system of the world.

Dialectical logic was not invented by Hegel; it was explained by him. It is simple in outline, profound in application. Its impor-tance cannot be overemphasized; it plays a key role in every true scientific inquiry and is absolutely fundamental for scientific com-munism.

The central concept in dialectical logic is *contradiction*. This notion is not easy to grasp fully. Development in every sphere is the product of conflict between opposing forces; that much was well understood by early dialecticians. Hegel identified and characterized the interrelations of these forces; he saw the rational connections between each conflict, resolution, and the rise of the next conflict, and thus he was able, for the first time, to expose the inner nature of the process and the larger continuing progression of contradictions which underlie all history.

Previous philosophy had been committed to a quest for sta-bility, for fixity. No system was thought adequate that did not at least pretend to reach the unmoving base upon which all else could be built. To achieve this end, philosophers sought vainly to rid their systems of all contradiction. Aristotelian logic—for more than two thousand years the discipline of Western intellect —was both cause and result of this quest. Aristotle taught that, given any two propositions that contradict one another, one of the two must be false. This principle of non-contradiction, the pillar of Aristotelian logic, has profoundly hindered most science and the development of logic itself. The principle is not entirely wrong, but it is gravely incomplete. The acceptance of this partial truth as though it were the whole truth has reinforced the perennial but doomed search for a perfectly stable world cleansed of contradiction.

There is no such world. Contradiction, real opposition and tension, is not just chaff to be sifted away; it is the heart of progress, to be cherished as the inner motor of dialectics. Opposing forces naturally seek resolution. Where *thesis* and *antithesis* meet in conflict, there is, inevitably, some *synthesis.* These are the three phases (or moments) of every dialectical situation. An original contradiction cries out for resolution; in time it is resolved through the development of a different whole that is both new and not new. That synthesis is an outcome of the conflict; it retains some elements of both the thesis and the antithesis in opposition, yet it is in some degree novel, shedding those aspects of the earlier forces that cannot fit the new frame. Each synthesis, as Hegel explains, retains the truth of its thesis and its antithesis —is formed of them and yet is not them. Within the great system of the world one may say both that there is nothing new under the sun and that nothing remains the same for an instant.

Every contradiction seems at first paradoxical and troubling; we are tempted to seek to explain it away. In fact, contradiction is neither paradoxical nor bad. Nor is it eliminable; if it were it would long ago have been eliminated. Then where does it come from? It doesn't come *from* anywhere; it's not alien to the world but natural to it and present in all things. The dialectical opposition to every thesis (whether an idea, or a physical state, or a biological entity) is to be found *in* that thing, not outside it. So everything is precisely what it is, Aristotle being correct that far, *and* everything is what it is not! This audacious and at first astounding revelation was Hegel's remarkable contribution: Everything carries its own contradiction *within itself.* Contradiction thus cannot be the enemy of science; rather, it is in fact its core, the ground of all development and growth. The syntheses to which contradictions inexorably lead, once achieved, emerge as new theses, to which new antitheses also arise from within. This process of contradiction and resolution is constantly recapitulated, with ever-changing content, at higher and higher levels. The progression has no end.

There can be no completed account of the dialectical history of the world, obviously. Hegel overreached himself in seeking to provide that account. Yet there are determinable features and directions in world history; their detection and description has been the ongoing task of dialectical thinkers after Hegel. Most successful among these successors was Karl Marx, whose dialectical science gives the most profound insight into the present state of society as well as a penetrating glimpse of human destiny.

5. Dialectics in Everyday Life

The abstract account of dialectics may sound esoteric, but it operates concretely in our everyday lives and is immediately experienced by everyone. For example: Each of our emotions and states of mind contains its opposite within itself. Great joy is invariably tinged with sadness, as the tears it brings indirectly show. Our loving and hating are inextricably bound together. When we indulge in profanity, we reach for what is holy to us. In mathematics and science, the most powerful ideas lead inevitably to their own contradictions: action entails reaction; the concept of limit drives us to think of the unlimited or infinite. So it is also with aggression and cooperation, with order and disorder, and on and on, each thesis evoking its antithesis with logical necessity.

Immediate physical experience teaches us that bodily equilibrium is the product of opposing forces kept in balance. Good health is not static but dynamic. The growth of plants and animals, the waxing and waning of energy and interest, the sharpening of appetites followed by their satisfaction and then their redevelopment in new forms—all such rhythms give direct and incontrovertible evidence of the dialectic in our own lives.

Evolution is the most vivid illustration of the dialectic at work on a grand scale. The development of species was a shocking idea when the natural world was believed to consist of a fixed order of unchanging kinds of plants and animals. We are no longer shocked; species of the natural world are now known to evolve, each possessing at every stage the possibilities for alteration from within. Mutation and the responses of populations to the challenge of their environments has carried life from a primordial slime to the heights of human culture. The same fundamental process that underlies the development of species can also underlie the development of nations and classes; it accounts for the birth and death of civilizations. *Dialectics* is everywhere the key to world history—first in the sphere of material nature, ultimately in the sphere of human spirit.

Each human life is a microcosm of the whole. In birth, reproduction, and death, we each live the dialectical cycle. Our earthiest drive—sex—produces the strongest passions both of self-assertion and of devotion to others. In the act of sex itself we are at once alone and intimately in union with another. From this union of two comes new life. Here is the most incontestable, bittersweet illustration of the dialectic in us and in everything.

Communism begins with this dialectical approach to the world and all that is in it. We strive to understand the dialectic in human life and in human history. The perennial puzzles of human government can at last be solved, with dialectic as the first key.

6.   Materialism

A second key is needed. Dialectic can be wrongly applied; even Hegel derived monstrous results by misapplying it. Philosophers must never forget the concrete world of material reality from which human consciousness arises. Absorbed by the interplay of ideas, the dialectician may fail to keep his feet on the ground. The products of our brains, our analyses, must be applied to the *matter* out of which we are made. Materialism is the second key to the understanding of human history and government.

Like dialectics, materialism has a long tradition, extending back to speculations of Democritus and Epicurus in ancient Greece. But a fully coherent formulation of materialism could be seriously undertaken for the first time only in the nineteenth and twentieth centuries, as the intricate chemical and physical details of matter came to be revealed. The powerful forces interacting even within the smallest elements of matter have only recently been discovered—and even now are not fully understood.

Scientific advances finally set the stage for the unification of the two great principles—materialism and dialectics—upon which a scientific history of humankind depends. Matter could be analyzed for the first time dialectically, and the dialectic could for the first time receive a mature, materialistic statement. *Dialectical materialism,* an objective account of the history of matter, was possible at last. The dialectic materialized, or materialism dialecticized, has led to a comprehensive and definitive account of man and his condition.

7. Marxism

What has all this to do with politics? Our critics are impatient with dialectical principles and materialistic premises. They want to know how dialectical materialism bears on the organization of government. Will rule under communism be democratic or authoritarian? By the many or the few?

We will explain fully. Our system incorporates rule both by the many and the few. Government will be democratic and authoritarian—and neither. Contradictions like these are unavoidable; they should be cherished, not despised. Forms of government change, like everything else; political devices must reflect the dialectical history in which they are rooted. To select the appropriate device for any given circumstance, one must trace that history and comprehend the present as one phase in it.

Communists have been working on this historical analysis for almost a century and a half, with ever-increasing refinement. New chapters of the dialectical advance are being exposed with the passing of each decade, the whole account becoming ever more detailed and more convincing. Of course, no one ever can encompass all of human history; we are social scientists, not fortunetellers. But a general formulation of our views has been given by a few truly great thinkers, of whom the greatest was Karl Marx, 1818–1883. So powerful was his analysis of history, so rich and synoptic his understanding of the human condition, and so humane his vision of our future, that as scientific communists we are proud to call ourselves Marxists.

Karl Marx did not invent dialectical materialism; truth cannot be invented. Important scientific principles are discovered, first presented as hypotheses and gradually confirmed or disproved. Einstein did not invent the theory of relativity, or Darwin the theory of evolution. The theory of relativity expresses true features of the real world, quite dimly understood by most. It has been confirmed beyond reasonable doubt. The theory of evolution explains the actual development of natural species, including the human species. It too has been confirmed beyond reasonable doubt; and if some dogmatists stubbornly refuse to accept it, that doesn't affect its truth in any way. Most of us accept relativity and evolution as confirmed theories; in doing so we are Einsteinians and Darwinians. That doesn't reduce us to mindless idolaters. We simply recognize the genius of some thinkers who, gathering data and insights from all sides, fit the previously disorganized pieces into one comprehensive theoretical whole.

Marx is another such thinker. Einstein's physics was built on Newton's discoveries before him; Marx's dialectic was built on Hegel's discoveries before him. All great thinkers see as far as they do because they stand on the shoulders of other giants. In calling ourselves Marxists, and our system Marxism, we pay tribute to an intellectual giant who for the first time made sense out of a mass of historical and philosophical material never before understood.

Marx's work did not just happen accidentally. He lived at precisely that juncture in history when the inexorable dialectic of human events could be deciphered. Friedrich Engels, Marx's learned collaborator and loyal friend, observed that only an unscientific utopianism would suppose a great man with a splendid scheme could spare the world centuries of suffering just by being born earlier. Utopians have no grasp of the dialectic of history. Marxism, like every great advance, has a natural and necessary place in the course of historical development.

Other philosophers, most notably V. I. Lenin in the Soviet Union and Mao Tse-tung in China, have contributed greatly to the development of dialectical materialism. A host of minor thinkers have added to its depth and accuracy. By some the facts have been corrected; by others the predictions have been adjusted, or the application of theory to practice refined. Marxists are honest scientists. Marx himself was contemptuous of blind followers. He was a forceful critic of what others had said, and he gladly gave credit where it was due, even to his bitterest opponents. He always rendered an honest report of the facts insofar as he was able to ascertain them.

In that spirit, contemporary Marxists are far from being in complete agreement on the details of our theory. We reject the stupid idolatry and dogmatism of some who call themselves Marxists or Maoists. Every honorable name has been used by some narrow-minded or unscrupulous people for their own ends. Democrats will recall that atrocities have been committed in the name of democracy; Christians know the same of Christianity, and so on. Like them, Marxism should be judged not upon the basis of the acts or character of particular leaders (though Marx and Engels were good and honorable men), but on the basis of the argument and evidence for and against it.

Marx's genius brought materialism and the dialectic together in a profound and detailed analysis of human history. His historical materialism remains the core of the communist system. The best evidence for its truth is that it renders the growth and decay of human societies intelligible as they had never been before, and that it answers objectively and coherently questions about government that had never been answered satisfactorily before.

8. Historical Materialism

Historical materialism begins with real human individuals and the concrete conditions in which they live. We examine them and their social structures empirically. We do not begin with what men ought to be or become. We start with premises asserting the material basis of human life: that humans must have food, clothing, and shelter first of all; that survival requires social organization providing these; that the material environment must be mastered—tools made, necessities produced and distributed, children protected. We begin at the bottom, where mankind began, with economic needs in a perilous and recalcitrant world.

In this we reverse the procedure of traditional philosophy, which began (like Socrates) by trying to define "justice" or (like Descartes) by trying to prove the reality of the ego. In fact, abstractions like these are the product of material circumstances and therefore cannot explain those circumstances. We do not denigrate abstract reasoning, but we insist that it is useful only when rooted in the material conditions of human life.

With this beginning we avoid entanglement with the empty logic-chopping of most academic philosophy. Definitions of justice and proofs of the reality of the ego are irrelevant to most human lives. Philosophers have been led astray by their emphasis on thoughts instead of things. Dabblers with words and systems come to believe that ideas control facts; some even hold that the ultimate constituents of the world are concepts or relations! Idealism—not in the everyday sense of having ideals, but in the technical sense of basing first principles upon ideas rather than matter—has been the great pitfall of philosophy.

German philosophy of the eighteenth and nineteenth centuries exhibits this vice plainly. Hegel and his followers, having grasped the essentials of the dialectic, mistakenly applied it chiefly to ideas, spinning out great webs of theory from their own brains. Although elegant in appearance, such theories prove to be no more than concoctions, unable to explain the real substance of human life.

Marx saw that this German philosophy was at once profound and wrong-headed. Its dialectical spirit he honored and retained; its philosophical idealism he condemned and rejected. This idealism he replaced with his own scientific materialism—doing justice to the paths of the dialectic in history by applying it to matter. Human history is the course of material demands and material satisfactions, an advancing series of material contradictions and new material syntheses. Equilibrium and disequilibrium in human history could at last be accounted for scientifically. "In direct contrast to German philosophy," Marx wrote, "which descends from heaven to earth, we ascend from earth to heaven." We—Marx and all of us who remain his followers and heirs—do not set out from what men imagine, conceive, or say, but from their real condition, their daily needs and work. From that material base we may discover why they imagine and conceive what they do.

Marx said that he found Hegel standing on his head and set him right side up. Head work had been treated by Hegel (as by all idealists) as the foundation of philosophy, when in truth it is its fruit. What is top and what is bottom had been confused. The Hegelian dialectic needed to be turned upside down to permit the development of dialectical materialism.

9.   Class Struggle

The main line of that development, the essential outline of human history, was sketched by Marx and Engels in the *Communist Manifesto* in 1848. In that great essay, the dialectical character of the long chain of class conflicts was first revealed. They exposed the principle connecting the links of that chain: tension between those who control the material bases of human life and those who do not.

Class conflict is the key to human history—indeed it is the substance of all recorded history. The dialectic is realized concretely in contradictions arising in the struggle to possess land, factories, houses, food, and money. Each society has its special economic base or substructure; the history of that society is the account of struggle between those who control that base and those who are controlled by it. Each such struggle leads to the next in dialectical pattern.

"Freeman and slave, patrician and plebeian, lord and serf, guild-master and journeyman, in a word, oppressor and oppressed, stood in constant opposition to one another, carried on an uninterrupted, now hidden, now open fight, a fight that each time ended, either in a revolutionary reconstitution of society at large, or in the common ruin of the contending classes." So argues the *Manifesto,* and so we argue still. Whatever adjustments of detail are needed, it remains clear to all who will open their eyes that every age, including our own, has been shaped by its material roots: how things are made, grown, and distributed.

Karl Marx is the symbol of that understanding, now a great and permanent acquisition of human knowledge, largely absorbed by the social sciences. The names and personal histories of his followers, who have continued to piece together the intricate dialectical patterns of history, are not very important. Sometimes we err, overlooking, misplacing, misinterpreting some pieces of that great puzzle. What matters is that, bit by bit, around the globe, communist scholars have contributed to the overall understanding of dialectical history. Individuals are honored for notable breakthroughs, as in every science, but the truth is what we are after. From this point on, therefore, as we explain communism and defend it, we ignore the names of the contributors and focus on the substance of the system: socialism made truly scientific.

10.   Substructure and Superstructure

The fundamental facts of any age or any place are those pertaining to its material base, its economic substructure. Upon this economic foundation there develops, during each stage of human history, a great complex of derivative institutions, including schools and churches, literature and art, legislatures and courts. Surrounding these, in turn, are the customs and beliefs of that society—the patterns of thought and dress, the codes of morality. All of this is superstructure, in one way or another the product of the economic substructure. Economics lays down the conditions of life; all other features are molded, consciously or unconsciously, to fit those conditions. Ideology—proverbs and principles, commandments and constitutions—is all superstructure. Superstructure is important, of course, but secondary. It can be explained as the reflection, in thought, language, and art, of what is more fundamental: the system of production and distribution.

The relations between substructure and superstructure are the keys to historical understanding. To illustrate: When ownership of land is the base of the economy, it is also the chief source of power, and the real rulers will be the gentry who own land. The legal system will then exhibit great sensitivity to the needs of landowners in matters pertaining to the use, sale, or rental of lands. The landless—serfs or sharecroppers—will be politically powerless, and servile in order to protect their lives.

When heavy industry becomes the base of the economy, art and morals, as well as politics, will reflect the values of new masters. Vanderbilts and Carnegies become the new aristocracy; they are the real powers behind the government and the patrons of the arts. Laws are changed to permit investment with limited liability; the tax structure is adjusted to protect capital and reward speculation. Not humble poverty but affluence is the mark of good repute; honesty is justified as good business, and thrift emerges as a notable virtue. In everything, money becomes the index of worth.

Where the economic system is feudal, religion is feudal also; the organization of cardinals, archbishops, bishops, and priests reflects the deeper hierarchy of the substructure. When production encourages private enterprise, religion does too; every man becomes his own priest. Nothing in the superstructure is without economic roots.

11.   Oppression

Control of the substructure by one class results in oppression of the many by the few. Not bad people, but a bad system has this result. Landlords and bankers are often morally good—yet an economy that permits their domination must have cruel results. "Classes" are no more than economic groups. Hence the history of all hitherto existing societies can have been only the history of class struggles.

Like the class conflicts which produce it, oppression takes different forms in different times and places. In an agricultural society the key to production is arduous manual labor, often of slaves. The substructure will then be controlled by slaveholders, who oppress their human chattels. When the key to production lay in the skills of artisans, guilds became the instruments of oppression, guild-masters ruling journeymen and apprentices. When the key to production became machines and factories, their owners dominated the lives of workers by controlling wages, hiring, and firing. Oppression is simply the exploitation of the class without economic power by the class that has it. They have it because they control the substructure—the means of production and distribution.

Oppression is one manifestation of dialectical conflict. Aristocrats against commoners, employers against employees—each struggle in turn is between thesis and antithesis, elements at once incompatible yet mutually dependent. There are no nobles without commoners, no slaveholders without slaves. Exploitation by the dominant group is successful only when those dominated prosper enough to yield spoils. There can be no employers without employees—and while management must squeeze out the most work for the least pay, excessive squeezing can undermine the manpower pool essential for production. At the other pole, workers must seek the highest wage for the shortest hours—but pressing their interests to the extreme may threaten the viability of the enterprise that gives them employment. Classes with opposing economic interests depend upon each other for their very existence as a class. In each phase the thesis, forced by economic necessity to nurture its antithesis, prepares the way for its own overthrow.

The course of class struggles is not random; it advances inexorably in accord with the dialectic. Thesis gives rise to antithesis. Their synthesis contains new contradictions, which grow and are inevitably manifested in the conflicts of new classes. Tension, reconciliation bringing new forms, then new tension—so the world moves.

12.   The Capitalist Revolution

The explanation of world history given by dialectical materialism is invariably confirmed by the detailed record of all human societies. Traditional versions of history, focusing upon the rise and fall of kings and empires, mislead; they obscure the truth. Accounts of battles, treaties, glories, blunders, and the like are the surface of history, not its substance. Whatever may be thought or said about national interests and religious beliefs, the interests people really defend—in battle or in diplomacy—are those of their class. The struggle that underlies all other struggles is for control of the economic substructure.

With this realization the major events of history come into sharp focus. Consider the centuries of feudal domination of Europe as an illustration. How and why did that apparently stable system collapse? The power of the feudal lords was rooted in their control of land, then the core of the substructure. So long as the superstructure—the laws, moral codes, and political practices that had come to reflect that agricultural foundation—remained in harmony with its substructure, equilibrium under feudalism was maintained.

But the seeds of its own destruction lay within the feudal system itself. Even as its lords relished their power, a new class gradually arose within the system, destined to revolutionize it.

The prosperity of feudalism had brought influential tradesmen into being—makers and merchants whose wealth was not drawn from land. This "middle class," whose base was the city and whose power lay in manufacture and commerce, gradually emerged as an historical antithesis. These burghers and the landed aristocrats despised one another, but at the very time their interests were clashing, they depended upon one another.

Cleverly and ruthlessly the old regime kept a leash on its antagonists for generations, even for centuries. But the old regime was doomed. Not for tactical reasons (e.g., defeat in battle) or for moral reasons (e.g., inferior ethical standards) but for dialectical reasons not then understood, feudalism had to be replaced. Agriculture was being replaced by industry as the chief source of productive wealth. The substructure of the society itself was being transformed—and with that fundamental alteration, revolutionary change was impossible to contain.

Growing manufacture required new and more raw materials, faster and more reliable transport, new systems of credit and exchange. Invention and organization sped the manufacturing process. The scale and the profit of manufacture leapfrogged upon one another. Laborers, needed to transform the raw goods —wool, iron, timber—into marketable products, were drawn to the cities, which mushroomed as factories became their core. By mid-nineteenth century Europe was transformed from a rural into an essentially urban world. Its substructure itself had been revolutionized.

Yet the superstructure lagged behind. Legislatures remained under the domination of landed gentry gripping their political privileges. Stumbling agriculture was given artificial support by laws devised to protect inefficient producers from the competition of cheap imported grain. Borrowing and lending were still taught to be morally wrong. The entire system of markets, manners, and even theology that had served as suitable superstructure for the old order became a burden and a block to the new order. That old superstructure was now a ball and chain from which the rising bourgoisie had to cut themselves loose. Eventually the feudal superstructure was demolished, and the bourgeosie was freed for growth.

The dialectical class struggle between feudal lords and bourgeoisie took a thousand forms, hidden and open, civil and brutal.

In the end the doomed superstructure was replaced by a new one devised to suit the new masters of production and distribution. Bourgeois economics had to have laws and morals to accommodate its operations. It got them. It had to have a political structure that would accommodate its burgeoning demands. It got that too. Only in this dialectical frame can the economic and political history of modern Europe be truly understood. Urbanization, colonization, the shift of power to the manufacturing north, and the enfranchisement of the workers—all these are but aspects of what is rightly called the industrial revolution.

The battles of that class war were not all bloody, but the results were genuinely revolutionary. Leaders and boundaries changed, but more important were the changes in the style and spirit of all European life—even global life. The feudal thesis was overcome by its capitalist antithesis. The contradiction implicit in the earlier system had led to its own destruction.

This has been the repeated pattern of human history. The class dominating the substructure creates, deliberately or inadvertently, a superstructure reflecting its own economic needs. When the economic base changes, the superstructure becomes outmoded and must be cast off. A new superstructure is molded to fit the newly dominant class—and the process begins afresh.

The bourgeosie was therefore truly a revolutionary class in its time, and no one paid fuller tribute to its genius and impact than did Marx himself. Under bourgeois dominion, the face of the world was changed almost beyond recognition. With astounding productive powers, with transport and communication of previously unimagined efficiency, capitalism permanently transformed the economic foundations of human life. The modes of dress, travel, work, talk, play, the making of war and even of love were revolutionized by the bourgeoisie. The texture of human life and the substance of human interests were radically altered by the revamping of the economic substructure. A new superstructure arose inevitably. New laws, new morals, new wants and hopes and ideals, even new religious forms, reflected the interests of the new lords of life. One word epitomizes that great set of superstructural changes: *capitalism.*

Slowly at first, and then from the time of the French and American revolutions in a swift and inexorable flood, capitalism became the order of the world. Pockets of the old order remained here and there, but the industrial revolution could not be halted. The dialectical process is invincible.

13. The New Revolution

There is a critical turning point in every dialectical process—a synthesizing leap at which the previously contending elements reform into a new whole. The technical term for these critical points is "node." In human history these nodes may extend over some time and are called *revolutions.*

The capitalist revolution is long over. It began in embryo centuries ago, reaching maturity generations ago. Over centuries, capitalism gradually solidified its grip on the world until reaching its apogee in the middle years of our century. But by that time its replacement was already leaving its embryonic stages to enter a vigorous youth. What remains of capitalism now is a great shell, imposing but crumbling. Its deteriorating superstructure exhibits the marks of senility and disorder. As a world system, capitalism has already been shattered; it struggles to shore up foundations permanently eroded by a dialectical process it does not fathom.

The new revolution is well underway; its infancy is long behind us. Its growth will bring the final collapse of capitalism. It rides now the rising crest of the wave of history. It is the most far-reaching, the most radical revolution ever. By some it is ignored, by some reviled, by most in the capitalist world it is misunderstood. It is recognized as a competitor for power and therefore condemned by capitalists as demonic, when in fact it is genuinely humane. This new revolution—some call it the proletarian revolution, though the name is a bit outdated—is our cause and the hope of mankind. Those who understand it will cease to struggle against it.

Our revolution is like all earlier ones in its general pattern: The economic substructure changes fundamentally; the old superstructure collapses and is replaced. That collapse is unavoidable because of the incapacity of the old system of human relations to control the economic forces of the new order. The forces of production outgrow the system of ownership and exchange that previously managed them, requiring a new set of economic relations. But now it is the capitalist system which is the old and inadequate order, unable to manage the economic forces that had first been unleashed within capitalism itself. The magnificent achievement of capitalism was its exhibition of the potentialities of human labor when intelligently organized. Until the bourgeosie took charge, economic enterprises everywhere were small, isolated, jumbled, operated by one or a very few individuals. Capitalism did a stupendous thing: it *rationalized production.* Factories and wonderful machines were its early products; the assembly line and mass production were trademarks of its heyday. The fruit of its maturity was vertically-integrated production: from Ford's cargo ships come Ford's ores for Ford's foundries, out of which pours the steel for Ford's trucks and cars; Ford ships them, Ford sells them, and Ford even lends the money to buy them. At its prime, capitalist production displays a computerized intelligence that boggles the mind, global trade with electronic credit that renders cash unnecessary, and incredible automation at the worksite—all bring order and productive power to a degree formerly undreamed of. We travel to the moon, split the nuclei of atoms and fuse them, control the weather, even duplicate the processes of life itself. Capitalism brought to life the power that lies in the lap of *social* labor.

However, the capitalist system of *appropriation,* of ownership and control, which had developed to accommodate these productive forces, came eventually to hinder those same forces, and proves now to be absolutely incapable of controlling them. Here lies the central point: while capitalist *production* is *social,* capitalist *appropriation* is *private.* Goods and services are provided through the most ingenious integration of human effort and intelligence —then bought, sold, owned, and exploited not by the workers who created them cooperatively, but by individual capitalists. The mark of capitalism is the inescapable strain between collective making and private taking.

"But this," it will be replied, "is the nature of capitalism. It is a competitive system of private enterprisers who produce for profit and their own benefit. It has faults—but that competitive struggle has led to the wealth you just praised so highly. How then can you deride the essence of that system—the private ownership of productive property?"

We do not so much deride capitalism as we seek to understand it; we see it as one essential stage in human history. We give credit to its accomplishments, but we also point to the fundamental contradiction within capitalism which is its essential characteristic. That contradiction must lead to its ultimate downfall.

Economic systems do not collapse fortuitously; they die when at last they cannot cope. Each is destined to fail when it confronts forces more powerful than it was designed to handle. The emergence of those forces within the system itself reveals in each, in turn, a fundamental internal contradiction. Each economic system carries in itself, in its essential nature, the seeds of its own destruction. The root contradiction of capitalism, leading dialectically to its supersession, is the contradiction between social production and private ownership. The system of private ownership ultimately proves incapable of managing its own productive powers. Those powers rise up against their masters, overcome them, and demand a wholly new system for the management of human affairs. The revolution of the proletariat —the workers and peasants inevitably exploited under capitalism —is a critical step in that inexorable process.

14. Surplus Value

We must now explain how this proletarian uprising is forced by the capitalistic process itself. Again we shall be looking, although now in much greater detail, at the operation of the dialectic. We have seen that politics and government are rooted in material needs and their satisfactions. The heart of dialectical materialism, therefore, is *economics,* which absorbs all history and politics. But the frame of economic analysis must be correctly dialectical.

The essence of capitalism is this: The capitalist, having first accumulated some money and machines, buys raw material and hires workmen to process it. To make things he can sell, he employs people to whom he pays wages. The capitalist owns what they produce, sells it for profit, buys more machinery and raw material, hires more labor, and so on. We are all well-acquainted with the process. What makes the system work? Profit, of course.

Businessmen must make a profit; that is their essential aim. But *what is profit?*

The explanation is simple yet powerful. Profit is the value (measured in money) that was in the products sold but not used up in paying for raw materials, machinery, or labor. Profit is surplus value.

Capitalist production creates value in the shop or factory that was not there before. Who creates it? Obviously human beings do—those who make the goods and run the machines. Doesn't the profit come from the machines? No, the machines must be paid for at full cost and maintained and replaced at full cost. From machines alone there is no profit possible. From the raw goods then? No, the iron ore, timber, raw cotton, or whatever, is also paid for in full by the capitalist, as are the machines. There may sometimes be a good buy here and there, but the profitability of an industry cannot have its source in bargains. The answer becomes clear as we reflect upon the matter. The capitalist's profit comes essentially from the work of his employees—from their productivity. Their labor produces value, much value. The capitalist sells what they produce and pays them. They cannot know how much value they produce, (though of course he does) and they hope (and often believe) that they are receiving a fair wage. It may be fair in the sense that it is as high as the wages of employees of competing capitalists. But wage earners *never* receive a truly fair wage. There is no such thing. Profit depends absolutely upon the *un*fairness of the wage, since profit is reaped only when, after the machines and raw goods are paid for, there is more value produced by the workers than they receive in wages. That *surplus value* is the goal of every businessman; the greater it is, the more profitable is the business. Capitalism lives and thrives only upon the surplus of value its laborers create.

Thus, the men and women who produce value never get back all that they produce. Much of it is harvested by employers in ways that cannot easily be seen through. Assembly-line workers are paid by the hour; clerks, salesmen, managers, and engineers are paid by the week or the year; but all wages are purchases of the *time* of the workers who produce. Owners (in most circumstances shareholders) produce nothing. Of course, the owner of a business may also work in his own plant and pay himself a salary, but *as owner* he is totally unproductive. Capitalists, though sometimes corrupt, commonly harbor good intentions. Yet they *steal* from the working classes that portion of the value produced called profit. The system of production based on private ownership of the productive process is one that absolutely must exploit workers. Wage labor is both the instrument and the mask of that exploitation. If the exploitation is not successful (i.e., if enough surplus value is not extracted), the business "fails"—it doesn't make a profit. The importance of this point cannot be overestimated: Capitalism does not exploit workers occasionally or accidentally, but *invariably and systematically.* That exploitation flows not from capitalist malice, but from the essential nature of capitalism: it must take from workers more than it gives back. Their creative power is its lifeblood, which it sucks. That creation of value, by the workers cooperatively, is intensely social; the capitalist appropriates it privately. The interests of employee and employer are deeply, fundamentally opposed.

"But I give them jobs!" replies the offended capitalist. "If it were not for me, where would they be? And I pay them well, so well that they have been and (if it were not for some agitators like you communists) would be quite content with their wages and standard of living. I work hard, run great risks, and deserve my profits. It's my money, and in a free country I can invest it as I like, within reasonable bounds. Business investment is good for everyone. I do no more than put my money to work (as you would, too, if you had managed to save some capital), and if I invest it wisely and profitably, let that be a model for others who, like me, may provide jobs for the unemployed, acquire wealth for themselves, and do both in an honest and productive way."

That story is shallow, confused, and misleading. The capitalist apologist is not usually lying—he just does not understand the essence of his own system. First, it is not *the capitalist* who provides jobs; the jobs are part of the productive process itself, a process that can go on very smoothly without private owners. Second, the contentment of the workers with their wage slavery is indeed often real—but that is because they also do not see how the system really works. The fact that the workers *think* they are paid fairly does not make it so; exploitation is often hidden and does not have to be recognized by the victim to be real. Third, the work of management is indeed often hard. Owners who contribute productive work are to that extent workers, and we do not seek to deprive them of anything their labor rightfully earns. Surplus value is our target—the profit reaped from products made by the proletariat but appropriated and sold by the bourgeoisie. That surplus value owners do not deserve. In a just system there will be no surplus value; all value will be returned to its producers, to the masses who work. In a just system, obviously, there can be no capitalism either.

15. Labor as a Commodity

The deepest misunderstanding is exposed when the capitalist says, "I only put my money to work" by "investing wisely." It is as though he thinks a system permitting such "investment" were ordained by God as eternally right rather than a mere stage of human history. Consider what this investment entails.

Profit in any business, we saw, comes originally from productive human labor, of hand or brain. Capitalist investment—whether in a small shop or through the shares of a great company—seeks profitability through the *buying of human labor*. Capitalism, because of its essential nature, must treat the work of human beings as a *commodity*. This is the real secret of capitalism, the dirty secret that Marx was the first to expose. Human creative power, human energy and time, human imagination and intelligence—all these the capitalist *buys* for cash. This is deeply immoral. No decent social system would put the most profoundly human values—human work and creation—on the market. It is by buying and selling what should be priceless that capital is "put to work."

The system encourages, often obliges, those of us who are not capitalists to sell ourselves to those who are. It is, without exaggeration, a system of generalized prostitution. The evil of ordinary prostitution lies not in sex but in sale. One who gives sexual favors promiscuously is not for that reason a prostitute. The word itself is from the Latin, *pro* (before) *statuere* (cause to stand); the original prostitutes were those who were made to stand exposed before the potential buyers, exhibiting their charms. It is immoral because it involves the sale of what never, under any circumstances, ought to be sold. The seller as well as the buyer of "love" in a brothel is debased by giving or taking money for the physical acts of intimate human affection. Our repugnance for prostitution flows from its placement of sex, precious to every healthy human being, on the market. It treats as a commodity what must never be so treated.

The market for labor is unwholesome in precisely the same way. The applicant for a job is a prostitute. He, or she, comes to stand before the prospective employer to be looked over. Skills and charms are displayed, in competition with other applicants, in the effort to persuade the buyer that this seller has qualities really worthy of purchase. "From me," says the petitioner silently or aloud, "you will get energetic, loyal service that will justify my price. I've done it for others—read what they say about how nicely I performed—and I can do it for you. Put me on probation and try me." Thus do we prostitute ourselves, not meaning to be wicked. We do not see ourselves as we truly are. The office boy who dresses neatly and comes running when called is in the same position as the young call girl who is anxious to please her employer. Both are drawn into a life of prostitution; they may have little alternative in a system they neither control nor understand.

Productive human labor is beautiful and satisfying. In a life lived decently, our labor will be given freely and passionately—as sexual energy is expended—in the service of others. A system that entails the selling and buying of labor cannot be honorable. We do not contend that humans should not labor, any more than we would contend that everyone should remain a virgin. But the circumstances under which we lose our virginity make a world of difference. So also do the circumstances of our productive work. Humans should no more willingly put their work on the market than they should put their genitals there.

In a brothel, what changes hands is viewed (by sellers and buyers) as of little consequence—a few dollars for a few minutes' use of a few organs. The great brothel of capitalism is far more obscene—it sells us whole. Our days from morning to night, our best energies from youth to age—our work—we are forced to sell. They buy. Their inspection of us and our talents is no different, in principle, from the inspection of needy, eager whores. Instead of examining breasts and buttocks (which some capitalists also do!), they examine skills and character, our most human qualities. They will not pay for our work unless they can make a profit from it. And we compete to serve them, not greatly different from slaves parading naked in the slave market. Working people under capitalism are wage slaves.

Wage slaves are kept in line by the power their employers have over their livelihood. The fundamental contradiction of capitalism—between social production and private appropriation—becomes first concretely manifest in the inevitable antagonism between the hired and the hirer, the worker and the boss.

16.   Alienation

Workers are forced to spend their time and labor on things that are not and will not be theirs. Assemble and polish, design and repair, distribute and sell—what? Products that belong to the bosses. We make them, they take them. The goods in our hands belong to others. To us who create the value—and the surplus value—the *products* are alien.

Workers are alienated from the *process* of their labor as well. When producers are alienated from their products, their work becomes tedious and boring. Because maximal surplus value must be extracted, the work is tiring, often dirty, and sometimes dangerous. Workers in a capitalist system generally despise their work, laboring only for the paycheck they must have. Bought they may be, but only for the hours of their labor. At quitting time they run from their place of work as fast as their legs will carry them. Who has not witnessed the office workers' rush to the elevator of escape at the moment the clock permits, or the happy exodus of laborers from the factory as the shift whistle blows? Upon release from the prison of their jobs, they sigh with relief.

This alienation between human beings and the work that should be their satisfaction is the bitter fruit of capitalism. The power to create is distinctively human. Yet creative work, under this system, becomes burdensome toil in hateful places. Alienated from the products, alienated from the process, the workers are alienated also from each other. Being cogs in a great machine, they cannot—during hours of work—relate to one another in human ways. They are no more than "hands"—replaceable as nuts and bolts and, like them, disposable when rusty or broken.

Machines are the glory of capitalism. Until the bourgeosie had exercised its intelligence in the productive process, the power of machines had hardly been imagined. But machines are used by capitalism for the ever-greater accumulation of capital, and that is pursued by exploiting the labor purchased to work on the machines. Where capitalism flourishes, therefore, what should be the means becomes the end; the machine becomes the master of men and women who operate it.

Machines, from the simplest levers to the most complicated computers, are *labor-saving* devices. Humanists have long dreamed of machines that would eliminate the need for most arduous toil. The dreamt-of machines are here. But the uses to which they are put in a capitalist system are "labor-saving" only in a demonic sense. They save labor time—thereby allowing the capitalist to increase productivity and profit with the purchase of relatively fewer laborers. *The capitalist* saves labor, the cost of labor, while the laborers are bound ever more tightly to the machine, their tasks becoming ever more mechanical and mindless. What could and should serve the purposes of humanity comes to serve the purposes of capitalist enrichment.

17. The Market

How things are made, under capitalism, contrasts with how they are distributed. The rationality of production, thoughtful planning and cooperative labor within the factory is the antithesis of the irrational frenzy that reigns in the marketplace. In the auto industry, for example, the intricate assembly and subassembly lines, the split-second timing, the sophisticated analysis of alternative procedures are all critical to productive efficiency. A thousand discrete but complementary activities, from the rolling of steel to the fitting of upholstery, are all coordinated vertically and horizontally with an overriding integration that makes one's head swim. It is genuinely wonderful, and it is possible only through cooperative efforts. One office could never do it; no single person could even comprehend the whole in all its detail. Yet it is all intelligently planned. In the telephone system, in the oil industry, everywhere under capitalism, the same rationality is displayed in production.

All this, however, leads to the market—to a system of distribution without intelligence or plan. The market is not merely *asocial,* it is *antisocial.* It operates not only without cooperation or integration but on the opposing premise that each of its elements will seek to mislead and stymie the others, to outsmart and take advantage of them. The result is churning disorder.

Sophisticated capitalist assembly plants produce millions of automobiles, carefully ornamented and lavishly advertised, for sale in a market in which there may or may not be purchasers. The products may fail to meet demand or pile up in yards and warehouses because unsaleable. Luxurious sedans are produced by the thousands, to enter a market in which small cars are in demand. Redesigning and retooling is no sooner completed than the market demands vehicles of a yet different kind. Expensive public transport systems are laboriously installed—and the market calls for more private vehicles. A storm of private vehicles is produced, the public-transit system is allowed to deteriorate badly, and the shortage of oil leaves us humiliated. In agriculture the disorder is even worse. The market sends the price of rubber (or coffee, or sugar, or beef) soaring, so extensive plantations of rubber trees (or sugar cane, etc.) are born. As all the new trees begin to produce, the market is glutted with rubber (or sugar, or beef, etc.), prices drop, farmers suffer, and the enterprise proves a social catastrophe. When harvests are good, grain piles up in elevators by the millions of tons, unwanted and rotting. When the grain is needed to feed the hungry, it is too late—to save storage costs the grain has been sold off at a loss as food for cows. The story is repeated endlessly, with pigs and peaches and petroleum: surplus and shortage, unpredictable fluctuation of supply and price, resulting bankruptcy for some and windfall profits for others. The market is blind; its ignorance, born of competition, makes planning for genuine human needs impossible.

Even the cultivation of humans themselves relies upon "market forces," thus disordering the availability of human skills. The academic market is a good example. When the going price for school teachers, engineers, or professors of history is high, a thousand competing institutions rush pell-mell to produce them. At first, other institutions fall over each other to buy them up. Suddenly the market is glutted with engineers, the newly trained teachers are without jobs, and after years of study there are more professors of history available than anyone knows what to do with. Neither demographic nor cultural change means anything to the market. The sophistication of the productive process repeatedly contrasts with the crudity of the distributive process. Social production and private appropriation wage an ever-sharpening dialectical war.

18.   Crisis

That war ends only when the system of appropriation is brought into harmony with the system of production. This great change cannot take place painlessly. In the final phases of the revolution, the root contradiction of capitalism grows blatant; the productive system rebels outright against its capitalist fetters. These phases have already begun.

When the development of productive forces is so great that the reigning superstructure cannot control them, economic revolution is forced. So it is now. For many decades we have been witnessing—first in Europe and North America, now in Asia and the rest of the world—the productive power of capitalism simply out of control. What begins as market aberrations and localized distress—here a "recession," there an "energy crisis"—becomes a series of economic catastrophes. Surplus becomes glut, shortage becomes need; glut becomes inundation, need becomes desperation. Lacking intelligent control, the system experiences a series of cathartic explosions: inflation, depression, unemployment, panic. Repeated cycles of boom and bust are only the most tumultuous manifestations of the dialectical contradictions of capitalism.

Every temporary recovery leads to the next wave of disorder, broader and deeper than the one before. How many times can the capitalist system rescue itself from near chaos? Its managers have proved more ingenious and more tenacious than Marx and his early followers ever imagined. Communists have often erred in promising the final capitalist collapse by a specific time. Speculation is understandable, but prediction is dangerous; miscalculation gives capitalists false hope that their system may go on indefinitely. It cannot. Even war, the cruelest measure to consume glut and stimulate demand, cannot put off forever the ultimate breakdown.

19. The Law of Capital Accumulation

The inner workings of the capitalist system make its world-wide collapse inevitable. Capital in itself is without fruit. It is paper or coin that has no intrinsic value but only represents the congealed value of human labor. Capital is "productive" only when *invested,* when used to buy labor power. Labor power is the only commodity on the capitalist market that has the capacity to produce more value than it costs. Capital and wage-labor are in dialectical tension; they produce one another, depend upon one another, yet necessarily oppose one another. Laborers depend upon capital investment for their wages; capitalists depend upon exploited labor power for their profits.

Labor thus creates the value that is capital; that capital buys more labor, which creates more capital. Thesis and antithesis reciprocally support each other's accelerated development. The greater the quantity of capital accumulated, the greater the quantity of labor that can be bought and the greater the profit made. With these profits capitalists seek new "investments," new labor pools to exploit, new markets and new worlds to conquer. This is *the law of capital accumulation.*

Some primitive accumulation is required for a base. Funds must be gathered in order to start a business, to "take off." For the vast majority who lack inherited wealth, the power to borrow, or an income that permits substantial savings, capital investment is not possible. Most people, therefore, are locked permanently among the wage earners, the exploited. It is not a joke but an established economic principle that under capitalism the rich get richer while the poor get children. Poor families need the puny wages children can contribute; for the exploiters child labor makes possible greater profits still.

"The continual retransformation of surplus value into capital," Marx wrote in *Das Kapital*, "now appears in the shape of the increasing magnitude of the capital that enters into the process of production. This in turn is the basis of an extended scale of production, of the methods for raising the productive power of labor that accompany it, and of accelerated production of surplus value." So the accumulation that is the condition of capitalist production is its product as well. Accumulation gives impetus to the capitalist system, and the system constantly increases the accumulation. Those who have, get; those who do not have must sell their labor for wages.

A two-line poem by Sarah Cleghorn encapsulates the drama:

The Golf Links

> *The golf links lie so near the mill that almost*
> *every day*
> *The laboring children can look out and see the*
> *men at play.*

20. The Law of Capital Centralization

Profit comes from the productivity of labor; real productivity is increased when the labor power purchased is set to work on more powerful machines. The more powerful the machines, the more they cost. More and more of the capitalist's investment, therefore, needs to be devoted to plant and raw materials, to what Marx called "constant capital." Mass production and automation, upon which mature capitalism depends, require fixed investments of staggering dimensions: the rolling stock and roadbeds of the railroads, the power plants of the utility companies, warehouses, ships, computers, and heavy equipment, all great in size, complexity, and cost. The need for these causes an inevitable shift in the *technical composition* of capital: An ever-greater percentage of accumulated wealth must be devoted to *constant* capital, fixed investments; an ever-smaller percentage of the whole remains for *variable* capital, purchased labor, which alone can be squeezed for surplus value.

This hidden change in the nature of capital is the technical side of everyday events with which we are all familiar. In business the big fish eat the little ones. Because profit making demands an ever-larger scale of production, capitalists who can accumulate fastest (by borrowing or squeezing) can expand fastest, then buy bigger and faster machines, employ more workers, and grow. Capitalists whose accumulation falters find themselves unable to enjoy the economies of scale, unable to afford the expensive technology that makes possible the profitable employment of workers, and finally unable to survive in the dog-eat-dog world of the market. Competition weeds out the small and the weak until, in a given sphere, only a few great producers are left. They may then collude to share the available market, or they may continue to compete until only one or two real capitalists are left in that sphere.

This is the *law of the centralization of capital*. Its operation is everywhere evident. In advanced capitalist countries, the small grocery store and the small butcher have virtually disappeared. They are literally swallowed by the giant food-market chains whose great masses of centralized capital permit them to purchase in such quantities, and advertise and ship with such coordination and on such a scale, that the smaller capitalists are driven from the arena. The publishing industry, once populated by a host of small, moderately-profitable enterprises, is now dominated by a few giants who buy up the smaller firms, absorbing those smaller capitals into their own. These publishing giants are absorbed, in turn, by the great conglomerates of capitalist industry—International Telephone and Telegraph (ITT), International Business Machines (IBM), and so on. The small publisher or grocer may fight doggedly to retain his independence and may survive for a while; but the economic necessity for amalgamation and conglomeration spell doom for him in the end. The clearest case is again that of the automotive industry, once the sphere of many inventive small makers. But automobile production soon forces a scale of production—huge investments in constant capital—that reduces the number of profitable firms to a dozen, then half a dozen, then three or two. Finally there remains only one really profitable enterprise left in each national automotive market, one *general* motor firm. Would-be competitors, who could in fact be swallowed at a gulp, are allowed to remain operative for the sake of the appearance of a "competitive" market.

Centralization is more ominous than the capitalist imagines. For the expanding corporations it brings huge profits, growth in size, sales, and dividends. But by exposing the sham of "free competition" it actually kills the market through which capitalism had prospered. We are all free to compete with U.S. Steel and the Bell Telephone system. Centralization also exhibits the uselessness of the owners themselves and the fact that the private investors of capital are parasites, sucking private wealth from the value produced by the social labor of others.

21.   The Law of Increasing Misery

Extreme centralization leads to the demise of capitalism by forcing the deterioration of the condition of the working classes. This critical truth is almost invariably misunderstood by our critics. Marx formulated, in *Das Kapital,* what is called the *law of increasing misery.* Writing in the nineteenth century, he had sufficient data to sketch correctly the outline of capitalism's rise and fall, but insufficient data to give a detailed account of the twists in its later historical path.

He reasoned as follows. The inexorable shift in the technical composition of capital (relatively more devoted to fixed investment and less to labor) must result in a squeeze of the working classes. Only variable capital buys the labor that can be made to yield profit. When centralization forces the capitalists to put relatively less of their investment into that truly profitable commodity—while profits must be maintained and even increased if they are to survive in a cutthroat market—they are obliged by economic necessity to wring the needed profits from a steadily decreasing investment in labor. To survive they must extract ever more surplus value from the work force. The exploitation of the working class therefore must increase, even at the cost of their misery, until at last they will rise up in a rebellion from which they have nothing to lose but their chains.

The historical realization of this process is more convoluted than early Marxists believed it would be. Since the scale of production increases fastest in the heavily industrialized countries, Marx supposed that the working classes there—in Germany, Britain, the United States—would be the first to feel the crunch of this dialectical pressure. The unification of the proletariat, and its rebellion, he therefore expected first in those countries. The communist revolution (it was thought) would begin in the West, spreading to parts of the world undergoing the same process but in earlier phases of development. To see why it did not happen that way—and yet why Marx's analysis is fundamentally sound— we must look closely at the behavior of investment capital and at the ways in which labor can be exploited.

Exploitation of wage earners takes two forms, *relative* and *absolute*. Some fraction of the value each worker produces each day is stolen by the capitalist. The theft is difficult to detect, because the worker knows little of profit margins and sees only that portion of the value produced which comes back in the pay envelope. The measure of the worker's exploitation is the surplus value he produces but does not receive. The more effort that goes into surplus value, the more the worker is exploited, even if absolute wages rise. Higher wages may be due partly to inflated currency. But there may also be a real increase in the absolute value of the wage received; the worker may truly get more—while being exploited more than when his wage was less. This happens because the steadily increasing investment in constant capital, machinery, makes each hour of labor much more productive. When the productivity of labor leaps up, while the wage of laborers creeps up, the *relative surplus value* increases. The gap between what the wage earners actually produce and what they receive grows larger.

Marx used hours of the working day to illustrate. Suppose the value of the worker's daily wage is actually produced in six hours of one person's work. Suppose he is paid that wage for a ten-hour day, a short working day in Marx's time. His exploitation is then at the 40 percent level. Suppose, with new machinery, which can never be squeezed but must be paid for in full, the worker then produces the value of the same daily wage in five hours. Exploitation rises to the 50 percent level.

This increase in relative surplus value accounts for the steady accumulation of capital earlier described. But the increasing costs of fixed capital investment, with the consequent decline of the profit margin, oblige the capitalist to squeeze the labor force ever more tightly. Increasing relative exploitation eventually does not suffice; then the pressure falls directly on wages, forcing an increase in the *absolute* exploitation of the workers. This pressure cannot be successfully resisted by laborers. The automation of industry has by then created a great mass of unemployed (Engels called it the "great industrial reserve army") who, desperate for jobs, will gladly accept the increasingly inadequate wages, if any employed workers are so brave or so foolhardy as to quit in anger. Heads of families can't quit, of course. They endure a steadily increasing exploitation, both relative and absolute, about which they can do nothing singly, until they are submerged in misery.

Even joined together in labor unions there is nothing they can do to ward off economic depression and epidemics of unemployment that grow more severe with each passing decade. By refusing to work they can sometimes bring individual capitalists to their knees. But strikes can do no more than keep capitalists reasonable, and to be kept reasonable they must be kept in business. If the power of the labor unions is used to compel unprofitable agreements, the employer's consequent retrenchment or bankruptcy throws yet more workers out of a job. Labor within the capitalist system, even when unionized, must play by that system's rules and endure its consequences.

Tolerable misery eventually becomes intolerable oppression. Intermittent layoffs become permanent and widespread unemployment. In breakdown the system shows itself incapable even of maintaining its slaves in their slavery. A desperate working class comes at last to unite everywhere, turning to revolution because there is no reasonable alternative.

22. Monopoly

Three sets of events delay this inevitable outcome, convoluting the path to revolution.

First, when the market results in widespread distress, its disorder is counteracted by the capitalists themselves. Great corporations—IBM, AT&T, Standard Oil—constitute monopolies or trusts that can maintain some order in the market. When so-called antitrust legislation is enacted to keep the market competitive, informal collusion among corporate giants yields the same result. Supply and demand are rationalized. Available raw materials are apportioned, rates of production silently agreed upon, prices informally fixed. Genuine competition largely disappears from major industry; its fraudulent banner—a mixture of theater and ancient history—is displayed to soothe the masses. Some marginal economic activities—pet shops and plumbing repair—may be left to the chaos of a free market. Private property is for a while protected from the wrath of the people by devices which, in keeping some order, slow the rate of exploitation while ensuring its continuation.

23. Labor Unions

Only through the unity of the international working class—the solidarity of the workers of the world—can the proletarian revolution finally succeed. That solidarity comes slowly. Labor unions must first fight just to establish their legitimacy, even among workers themselves. Once established, the unions will be dealt with by the capitalists in whatever ways will best protect profits. The upshot is hard bargaining in which the aim of management is simply to placate the workers cheaply enough to keep the system afloat. Mollified by shorter hours or better pay, the working classes of the industrial countries do not achieve unity quickly. Groups of workers are played off against one another. Union leaders, bought with fat salaries and secure positions, bicker among themselves and fight for scraps from the capitalist table at which they secretly covet a seat. The unionization of labor, although advancing the revolution in the long term, is in the short term a second cause of delay by playing into the hands of the capitalists.

24. Imperialism

When the capitalist system appears to lose control over its own productive forces, it fights for new ways to counteract the glut and depression, and new places to invest accumulated capital profitably. The capitalist quest moves imperially outward, and the process of exploitation takes on global dimensions.

New markets, new sources of supply, and new labor pools are sought in Africa, Latin America, and Asia. The underdeveloped, underindustrialized portions of the planet inexorably fall into the net of capitalist expansion. The history of that expansion is scandalous. It first takes the form of outright possession —as the Congo was long the personal possession of the King of Belgium. Later it appears in the form of ostensibly benevolent colonialism that is in reality ruthless exploitation—as exemplified by the British in India, the Dutch in the East Indies, the French in West Africa. When at last "political independence" is formally achieved by underdeveloped countries, capitalist imperialism simply changes its garment. The exploitation of raw materials and native labor falls now under the direction of mammoth international corporations based in Europe, North America, and Japan which, singly or in consortium, contrive to drain local wealth in the interests of distant capitalist shareholders. American oil companies openly collude in dividing the rich spoils of Middle Eastern oil, abetted by greedy sheiks who enjoy incredible luxury while Arab masses suffer penury. Great mining companies exploit Andean nations for their tin and copper; giant fruit companies quietly but firmly rule the "banana republics" of Central America and the Caribbean through local puppets.

Imperialism is proof of the need for global economic order. By providing some temporary economic stability, it delays the revolution yet longer. But by forcing capitalism to break through the national frame in which it is at home, it advances the planetary character of economic disorder. Imperialism is, as Lenin justly called it, the "highest stage" of capitalism. Even he did not see all of its twists and turns, all the devices the capitalist system would invent to save itself from ruin. Nor can they all be seen yet. But Lenin did see that with imperialism comes the *internationalization* of the substructure. The proletarian revolution, ever more self-consciously, becomes the revolution not of German or American or any national proletariat, but the revolution of the world-wide working class. This brings the next dialectical node perceptibly closer.

North Atlantic imperialism has had some productive consequences. Roads and ports were built to exploit new markets; elementary education has been encouraged to exploit new labor pools. But always the real objective is profit. Television and radio are used to create new wants, new attitudes, even new needs. Goods are manufactured with carefully built-in obsolescence. The conspicuous consumption of the fashionable becomes the trademark of Western culture. No society is too sophisticated or too primitive to be immune to the penetration of the capitalist market-makers—electric toothbrushes and portable color television for jaded appetites; Coca-Cola, Volkswagens, and Singer sewing machines for all; global interpretation provided by the BBC and *Time* magazine.

Markets and sources of supply are only half the story. The other half is the role of imperialism in providing scope for the investment of capital. Vast sums of accumulated capital must be put to work profitably. The banks, nerve centers of the capitalist system, pay interest upon the billions of dollars held. But how? Bills and coins do not have babies; money stored in safes is useless. Ways must be found to build, buy, and sell fruitfully. The opportunity for profitable investment in the home markets having been reduced by virtual saturation, it is the underdeveloped lands of Asia, Africa, and Latin America that draw these capital investments, promising a renewed enrichment of the profit stream.

Profits come more often in torrents than in streams. But, as earlier in the home country, they always and necessarily have one source only—the exploitation of labor. The labor pool exploited now, however, is not in Detroit or Glasgow, but in Chile and South Africa. Imperialism is undertaken for profit; profit comes from exploited labor in the imperialist domains. Class antagonism, and ultimately class warfare and class revolution, moves from the narrower stage of the industrial centers to the wider stage of world commerce. Profits for giant American rubber and textile corporations now come from the exploitation of sweating laborers in Malaysia and Taiwan. With the value they produce, the unions of Akron and Los Angeles are bought off. The profits of the massive insurance consortiums of London and Hartford are not produced where premiums are collected. They are produced wherever in the world it is found possible to buy and to milk the labor power of human beings at near subsistence wages.

Imperialism leads to war. Spheres of influence inevitably collide. Each capitalist enterprise must expand or die; aggressive capitalist powers must eventually fight for their lives by fighting for territory and markets. The systematic contradictions of capitalism—not the personal villainy of capitalists—make world wars inevitable.

The Japanese demand for a "Co-prosperity Sphere" in Asia and the Pacific; the perennial German push to the east into Poland and to the west into France; the Monroe Doctrine and Marshall Plan of the United States, and her military outposts virtually everywhere—all these are by-products of the inexorable quest by capital for profit-making outlets. The flags and mottos are national and ideological, the excuses are idealistic and altruistic. But the underlying explanation of modern global wars lies in the struggle of imperial powers to protect capitalist enterprise. Because that is a life and death struggle, it must, sooner or later, take the form of armed conflict.

The ultimate explosion of the system need not take place *in* the industrialized countries. The shift of capitalist exploitation to the workers and peasants of developing countries explains why the revolution first appears there, and not in Europe or North America. In the so-called "backward" lands, the exploitation of labor has been most oppressive—and the net of capitalism tears where its cords are weakest. Knowing the history of exploitation in Russia and China, we should not be surprised when the first concrete manifestations of the proletarian revolution appear there. But the revolution spreads irresistibly and must eventually be world-wide.

25. The Revolutionary Process

The pieces of this dialectical puzzle are gradually falling into place. In Africa, Southeast Asia, Central America, and the Caribbean, working-class consciousness is now rising; corrupt capitalist regimes are falling one by one. The wealth and power of the entrenched enemy, fighting for its life, will make this struggle long and hard. Control of military forces, ownership of press and television, educational advantages—all render the capitalists formidable. Revolutionary parties will be outlawed. Tenacious capitalist elements will subvert shaky communist governments when they can. Hostile bourgeois powers will refuse to recognize or trade with new revolutionary governments. Even armed counter-attack will be tried, as against Cuba at the Bay of Pigs.

There will be fraudulent communists, too—leaders claiming to act in the name of the working class while in reality seeking power for themselves. There will be stupid communists who insist upon armed revolt before the objective conditions for successful revolution have developed; they will cost us lives by the thousands. There will be those who once honestly sought the solidarity of labor but, bribed by bourgeois luxuries, turn traitors to their class. Some communist leaders will be so swept up in the enthusiasm of revolution that they may indulge in needless brutality against the vanquished capitalists. There will be bloodshed, a great deal of it, as there has been already. There will be anxiety and distress, even as we strive to avoid these by-products of revolution. We will be as gentle as circumstances permit, but the revolution will advance, in spite of all opposition.

The aim of our revolution is deeply humane. As its leaders grow more confident and more experienced, they will grow more patient, too, and more understanding. If the proletarian revolution is sometimes armed and bloody, it need not be so everywhere. Our objectives are the good of humankind; we aspire to a society in which people may finally rid themselves of all exploitation and realize their potential. This will come sooner or later, but it is important for human beings now living that it come as soon as possible. That is why we communists advance our cause so vigorously. The dialectical laws of history make the overthrow of the old order inevitable, but the makers of history are ordinary human beings who must bring this process to reality through their own activity. We therefore proselytize, agitate, and educate —we do all we can to bring the revolution quickly and decently to its fruition. The tide of history is ours; but this knowledge does not excuse indolence. In the service of humanity we strive to ease the pangs of birth as a new social order is born.

That birth will be painful. Powerful institutions must be destroyed; to perform their positive functions without their negative features, new institutions must be developed. Attitudes now almost universal must be profoundly altered; convictions intensely held must be shown delusive. All this requires time, patience, and persistence. Thorough revolution matures slowly, by stages, but will emerge victorious at last.

We do not threaten, but promise. A few parasites who now live on the labor of others will have to be eliminated or reeducated, of course. What they stand for must be eradicated. But even they are genuinely welcome to join us in the great struggle, and when they become our comrades we shall bear them no enmity. A classless society needs no scapegoats, harbors no grudges.

Some bourgeois intellectuals—like Marx and Engels themselves—grasp the pattern of dialectical history and its ramifications. They cut themselves free of old class ties, join the proletariat, even become leaders of the revolution. This recruitment is now more and more common. University scholars in all countries join us in increasing numbers. At first pained by the conflict between their indoctrinated national loyalties and scientific truth, they learn that the vigorous pursuit of communist goals quickly provokes persecution by bourgeois authorities who realize that our revolution spells the end of their privileges. The fight for freedom of inquiry thus becomes entwined with our own, and the revolution draws closer.

Violence may prove to be unnecessary in some parts of the globe. Marx himself sometimes thought that where the citizens have confidence in their own collective judgment, as in Britain or North America, the proletarian revolution may be a peaceful one. Foresight, pressed by objective needs, may bring radical changes through established forms of government. That will require widespread understanding of the economic dialectic, and the developed class-consciousness of the masses. The old order must be overthrown, but the objective conditions for that overthrow may emerge so completely as to render the revolution, although disruptive, speedy and relatively painless. Capitalism, as Lenin used to say, may drop like a ripe fruit. We will do our best to avoid violence, and to restrain it if it comes. The proletarian revolution is necessarily radical, but it is not necessarily bloody.

The chances of peaceful revolution are not good, however, in many countries. The grip of private owners must be broken; where that grip is very tight, the breaking may be a grim business. Yet the revolution will certainly come; its inevitability is not of our making. If there is a useless struggle against historical necessity, the fault is not ours.

26.   Dictatorship of the Proletariat

How will the revolution be led? For us, recall, it is substance, not forms, that matter. We therefore have no *a priori* commitments to specific forms—to oligarchy or to democracy, to armed forces or to elections. Defenses of one or another form of government have usually been disguised defenses of class interests. What counts for us, however, is not how the decisions are made but whether in fact they advance the revolution and bring the classless society closer.

Will the leadership of the proletariat be autocratic or democratic? Both, and perhaps neither. Effective leadership will surely take different forms in different times and circumstances. We take historical development seriously; we do not attach ourselves to particular sets of institutions that may be obsolete in one context, premature in another. There are many ways to make a revolution; we judge each by its results.

But do we not advocate "the dictatorship of the proletariat"? Yes, but this dictatorship, if such it may be called, is certainly not our ultimate objective. Marx and Lenin did use the phrase, correctly observing that forceful instruments may be needed to bring the revolution to fruition. But its end is justice, even when its tool proves painful. Sometimes the dentist must pull a rotten tooth.

Objections to the dictatorship of the proletariat have been shallow. Where authority is used justly, in the interests of the masses, its structure need not be feared. Recall that the proletarian revolution will encounter the entrenched forces of the existing superstructure. Everything—the army, the laws, the police—everything under bourgeois control will be pitted against us. Although destined by history to triumph, we become the target of vicious hostility. Like the tender shoot of a new plant, the emerging revolution needs to be protected. We nurture it, promote it, protect it with every means possible. Of course we infiltrate; of couse we are obliged to be cunning and sometimes deceptive. If forced to it, we will even resort to threats and to terror. We have used such instruments, and we will use them. We are in a war, a total war, that will lead to an unconditional surrender for one side, a permanent victory for the other. It is the war of classes, the dialectical, revolutionary war that will decide the fate of all mankind. In such struggle no means may be ruled out —even those offending bourgeois democracy or transcending bourgeois morality. Strict hierarchical organization on a military model, with the attendant unquestioning obedience to authority, and even sometimes ruthless tactics may be essential. If such means genuinely advance the proletarian revolution, they will prove, though brutal on the surface, humane in the long run.

We can hear the anguished objections of bourgeois moralists: "Does the end justify the means?" Our answer is simple: yes. What else can justify means, if not ends? Our end is a truly decent world, and it is of such profound importance that sacrifice—of ourselves and of others—is justified to attain it.

We will need to consolidate our gains as the revolution progresses, building a secure base for the international revolution. Early victories are naturally partial, only national in scale. These first centers of the revolution—the U.S.S.R, China, Cuba—we must protect from the hostility of multinational capitalism. In 1917 the new Soviet government was subjected to armed attack on Russian soil by capitalist forces aiming to obliterate that first great revolutionary achievement. Half a century later, after the agonizing costs of the war against Nazi tyranny, the U.S.S.R., still the bastion of twentieth-century Marxism, was surrounded by the armed forces of bourgeois democracies whose ostensible objective was "containment." They are still out to get us—and they will succeed, temporarily, if we let down our guard.

The dictatorship of the proletariat was—and is still in some countries—our protective instrument. We organize our forces, during transitional periods, to solidify the rule of the proletariat. Ours is not a dictatorship in the Hitlerian sense; it simply insures that the people's true interests will determine the course of the nation. The phrase may not have been happily chosen; it was intended to emphasize the dialectical negation of the dictatorship of the *bourgeoisie,* by the dictatorship of the *proletariat.*

Our critics complain that the means employed by the dictatorship of the proletariat are sometimes "unlawful." You play dirty, they say; you don't obey the rules. We answer: *Whose* rules? The complaint against our "bad sportsmanship" is revealing; it assumes the whole set of bourgeois values we reject. The capitalists control the media of persuasion—newspapers, television, periodicals, and radio—so completely that the audible voice of "the people" can only be their voice. Any forceful breaking of their grip is—from the bourgeois point of view, but not from ours—a violation of the rules.

There can be no real contest for power within capitalist rules. The tasks before us now transcend those rules. We say it again: Material justice is our aim—the justice of subtantive results, not mere procedures. Capitalism is grounded in the exploitation of labor; it impoverishes and oppresses the masses. In the struggle to destroy it we also break its rules. We don't give a fig for the hypocritical restrictions of bourgeois morality. The morality of the proletariat guides us; we build *its* superstructure, obey *its* rules. It is silly to criticize the dictatorship of the proletariat for its "immorality." If it achieves what must be achieved, it is profoundly moral.

The capitalists are the ones who cheat systematically. They will quickly enough break their own rules to advance their own interests. They do that all the time. They even change the rules, if that is expedient, to suit themselves. That's what we shall do, openly. All the rules will be changed, by us, to suit *proletarian* needs. Every class must have its day. When we have ours, we will free working people everywhere from the grip of an economic system that is outmoded and cruel. That is what our revolution means—and the dictatorship of the proletariat is only one phase of that revolution.

27. The Communist Party

The revolution requires both strategic and tactical wisdom. Timing is critical; the objective conditions for action must be cultivated, then recognized and exploited. Leaders—Lenin and Mao are splended examples—must combine philosophical understanding with toughness and administrative effectiveness. Reinterpreting abstract principles so as to make them applicable to wholly new circumstances is demanding work. We do not idolize the heroes of our revolution, but we honor them for their brilliant and self-sacrificing leadership. They took nothing for themselves; they gave themselves completely to the proletariat and to humanity. The revolution advances like a great phalanx, its point thrusting into the future. The diamonds at the very tip of that point are our leaders.

Just behind them come the cadres of Communist Party members who transform principles into action. The contradictions of capitalism, the nature of its exploitation, the stages of the revolution—all must be explained and illustrated for widespread understanding. Bourgeois values must be uprooted; a new, proletarian frame of reference must be established. The working classes must be helped to become class conscious.

In every land these are the tasks of the Communist Party, whose members are the more enlightened elements of local populations. Each national Party, however, is an integral element of an international movement. Our march is global. In that march the Communist Party carries our intellectual and spiritual banners. It is our avant-garde.

There is only one such movement, not several. In each country there is but one Party, one set of authorized leaders. We are engaged in a long and bitter war to overthrow what has been the ruling system of the world and to replace it by another. In the battles of that war we will experience reverses as well as successes. While fighting those battles, there is no time for wrangling among ourselves. The Party is and must be single and unified. It possesses the scientific, dialectical understanding needed to determine what is next to be done. Radical and permanent changes of social structure require extraordinary leadership. The Party provides that leadership; we, the people, follow proudly. Party discipline must be maintained.

Direction given by the Communist Party is not only firm, it is intellectual, theoretical. Wise leaders do not act on impulse, but thoughtfully, with broad perspective and depth of understanding. Lenin, for example, was a scholar and philosopher; in addition to his many tactical writings, his *Notes on Hegel's Logic* gives an interpretation of the dialectic most bourgeois leaders could not even comprehend. Compare his treatises with the drivel produced by (or ghost-written for) American presidents: *Why Not the Best?* or *Six Crises.* Mao wrote delicate poems as well as deep philosophical essays. It amuses us that bourgeois critics give the thoughts of these great intellects only their most simplistic interpretation, without even beginning to appreciate their dialectical richness. There are simple meanings in the thoughts of our leaders, of course, to stir the enthusiasm of plain working people—but there are also many levels of deeper meaning to be retrieved from them by the student of dialectical materialism. Even the most intelligent of the bourgeoisie have been largely blind to those meanings and insensitive, therefore, to the intellectual force of our movement.

In deciding upon the correct line of action, we encourage uninhibited debate within the Party. All considerations are weighed, alternative analyses reviewed. We listen to everyone. Self-deception we try hard to avoid. The truth is our objective; our philosophical framework is well-calculated to uncover it, though of course we are not infallible. But once a policy determination has been made, after thoughtful deliberation, by our leadership, we argue it no longer. Solidarity is essential for the success of the revolution. Party decisions therefore bind us all.

Policy in Communist Parties is formed at the top, our best minds responding to historical developments. If "democracy" requires that we rely upon well-spread ignorance when deep knowledge is at hand, then we are not "democrats." But if democracy requires that policies be chosen *in the interests* of the people, the good of the masses being the ultimate standard of judgment, then ours, and only ours, is a truly democratic system. Our leaders are dedicated to the well-being of all, even at the sacrifice of their own comfort. Marx, Lenin, Mao, and their true disciples led spartan lives, reaping no riches, seeking no personal glory for themselves. Rarely did they take so much as a holiday from their labors. In that spirit our Party leaders command us still, out of thorough knowledge, for our own good.

The work of Party members, especially in the early stages of the revolution, is arduous. Objectively, the conditions for revolution must be promoted. The interests of progressive countries, serving as the bastions of communism, must be advanced. Members must undermine capitalist regimes in every feasible way. They must work within the law, and, where necessary, outside of it. They must work openly, capitalizing upon bourgeois principles of "freedom of speech" and "freedom of travel," and the like. They must also work clandestinely, in cells so well-insulated that they cannot betray one another even if they would—all the while centrally coordinated by the international Party. They must work under our own name, that of the Communist Party, and under the name of every other organization, real or fabricated, that will join us on particular issues. "Socialist" parties, activist liberal organizations, and civil-rights groups must be won over, at first infiltrated clandestinely if that proves necessary. Labor unions must remain a prime target, as Lenin emphasized, since it is there, above all, that working men and women may be found and reached. When infiltration fails and openness is inadvisable, front organizations must be created, bearing names appropriately attractive to the target groups. In this struggle Party members must not and will not be deterred by considerations of propriety. Nice guys, as the American saying has it, finish last.

Subjectively, our Party must win understanding and sympathy. We must explain our cause and our aims in terms that all segments of the populace will find palatable. We must exhibit the inhumanities of the capitalist system, expose its exploitation of the international proletariat, its imperialism abroad, and its bribery of unions at home. We must do this honestly and without exaggeration, so that independent investigation will confirm our claims, reinforcing our credibility. We must explain—first in simple terms, but with ever-increasing depth—the workings of the dialectic and the inevitability of the collapse of the bourgeois superstructure. Above all we must—within the context of hostile bourgeois intellectual life—drive home to ordinary people the nature of the class struggle that is in progress, and in which they are inescapably involved. With unfailing perseverance and patience, in schools and universities, in clubs and political parties and labor unions, we must raise the class consciousness of the people. We must strip off the disguises of national interests, the romance of flags and armies, the deceptions of advertising and national propaganda. We must overcome the continual bombardment of the capitalist press, radio, and television, pulling the masses of the people to a clear understanding of their true class interests—as the producers and the rightful possessors of wealth. When, subjectively, class consciousness has been sufficiently raised, and when, objectively, conditions for overthrow have ripened, the revolution itself will shortly follow—as it has already in some places.

28.   The Classless Society

The aim of that revolution is the total replacement of the capitalist system—by what? By a world without classes, a *classless* society. Hitherto, classes have been the form in which dialectical conflict was manifested. Until the proletarian revolution is complete, therefore, classes, their needs and values, remain the essential levers of social action. The conflict of proletariat and bourgeoisie differs, however, from all class conflicts before it. Now, for the first time, all the people of the world are fully involved. More important still is this: The communist revolution consummates all previous class struggles. As each synthesis contains the truth of those theses and antitheses that precede it, the communist revolution contains the truth of all preceding revolutions of the oppressed against their oppressors.

This synthesis must, of course, play its role in dialectical history, again serving as thesis and giving rise to further negation and advance. But, because it is the sum of class conflicts, its negation cannot be another class conflict; its result cannot be the emergence of a new dominating class and a repeat of earlier conflicts. At this apocalyptic stage, the dialectic opens an entirely new phase of world history, in which the division into classes comes to an end.

This cannot happen straightaway. During the long transition to the classless society, the old class struggle continues. Strongholds of bourgeois class interests—the United States and some European countries—fight to keep the control of production and distribution in private hands. Even after socialist governments are established, rear guard actions are needed; shoots springing from the old roots need to be pruned off until the roots themselves are finally exterminated. During this period of struggle, class interests—those of the proletariat, of course—must govern. But the goal is a society in which there *are* no class interests—and in which, therefore, no class struggles can arise.

This will transpire only when the population of the entire globe has recognized its social solidarity. This is not a utopian dream. Indeed, global unity has been made necessary in the real world, unwittingly but inevitably, by the bourgoisie itself. Obliged by its own internal dynamic forces to be multinational, its negation must be equally so. Its hunger for exploitable labor, and its need for markets to sell what it produces, eventually sucks everyone who is not an exploiter into the ranks of the exploited. Professionals become wage earners and organize; small businesses and farms are absorbed by larger and larger bourgeois conglomerates. Industrial laborers and illiterate peasants alike become grist for the capitalists' international mill. Class conflict thus not only becomes universal but is *seen to be* universal. Everyone comes to realize that everyone's productivity is everyone's concern. Everyone recognizes the justice of sharing the common wealth.

29. The Bourgeois State

Until that time the world remains divided into nation-states that apportion territory and cooperate or quarrel in the exploitation of resources and markets. The quarrels—between the United States and Japan, or between Germany and England, for example —rise quickly and mend quickly. Selfish, petulant, sometimes vicious, the bourgeois states feed and bicker like spoiled children.

Nation-states are, in essence, products of class conflict and instruments of the dominant class. Legislatures that make their laws, police and courts that enforce them, executives who apply them—all represent the bourgeoisie. "The business of America," as President Calvin Coolidge proudly announced, "is business."

Officers of the bourgeois state often do their duty honorably; by their own lights they are fair and impartial. They cannot see themselves clearly, cannot penetrate the fog of advertising, patriotic blather, and spurious economic argument that conceals the exploitation of human labor on which their whole structure is founded. Bourgeois standards and values have been internalized; their conception of justice is warped, their vision myopic.

They will insist that before the bar of justice all are treated equally—yet they perfect systems of taxation that protect private wealth, and systems of law enforcement under which the rich are assured treatment that the poor cannot obtain. All get free public schooling—but the children of the bourgeoisie go to the better public schools, and only the children of those who can afford the high price of admission go to the best private schools. All have equal opportunity (they say) for goods, jobs, or entry into professions. This is only a veneer. In fact, entry into the professions is only possible through the professional schools, whose admissions criteria and examinations carefully screen out most of the proletarians. The very best jobs are saved for the sons and daughters of the rich. For persons in the right circles, with money and influence, the paths to advancement are smooth. In every way, hidden and open, with devices subtly adjusted to fit the changing circumstances or national mood, state institutions work in the service of the bourgeois class. Close examination reveals this class character to be pervasive. In the bourgeois state, as Anatole France remarked in a famous passage, "The law, in its majestic equality, forbids all men to sleep under bridges, to beg in the streets, and to steal bread—the rich as well as the poor."

Whether the laws are made for the bourgeoisie by "elected representatives" clothed in business suits, or by a junta of uniformed military chiefs, doesn't really matter. In either case, these are only forms by which we are misled. Whatever political forms the bourgeois state exhibits, its results will be essentially the same. They must be—because those economic results are the underlying reasons for the creation of those political forms.

Elected legislatures in bourgeois states illustrate this perfectly. The citizens vote for their representatives expecting the resultant laws to serve the electorate. It is remarkable that intelligent people can continue to delude themselves in a system so patently corrupt. Elections are absolutely permeated by class interest. Systems of registration and voting are organized so as to discourage or bar some segments of the population and encourage others, thus tainting the entire process.

In the electoral contest, the one absolutely essential weapon is money. If the candidate is very wealthy—a Rockefeller or a Kennedy—his political success is likely to come quickly and easily. With only moderate wealth, the chances are only moderate. If the candidate is poor, he must cater to those with money and influence. Some representatives are bought outright. Most, basically honest, are the *de facto* captives of bourgeois interests—the oil companies, airplane manufacturers, mine owners, or other industrialists of the constituency whose money keeps viable candidates afloat. Because elections recur with frequency, the prospect of future financial support is a constant lure; the power of capitalist money over political parties, over legislatures, over all elements of the state machine is perennially renewed. The electoral system of Western "democratic" states is a gigantic fraud. Yet the electorates of these states stubbornly hope that somehow, next time, a government really in the service of the people will be elected. Blind! They will not learn! There cannot be a people's government until the economic base on which all government rests belongs to the people. So long as production and distribution are privately controlled, we may cast our votes (as Lenin observed) every two years or four years to see who will misrepresent us next.

Is there no escape from this trap? Of course there is. We must rid ourselves, once and for all, of the bourgeois state; ultimately we must rid ourselves of states—all states, altogether. That will happen only after classes have been entirely done away with. When there are no more classes, when the bourgeoisie has disappeared and with it the exploited proletariat upon which it feeds, there will be no further need for the vilest instrument of oppression, the state.

30. The State as a Repressive Force

When the economic system is no longer split into exploiters and exploited, political institutions will no longer be needed for the work of exploitation. The state is essentially a repressive force. The modern state has the task of repressing the working classes so as to facilitate their exploitation. In the first stages of the revolution, with the abolition of the bourgeois state and its replacement by the rule of the proletariat, states will remain—but with a different function. They will be repressive still; that is unavoidable. But the object of the repression will then be (as it is now in some socialist states) the former exploiting class. That transitional condition must last only so long as other bourgeois states remain capable of destroying or undermining our revolution. The repressive institutions of statehood, armies and police, we retain for self-protection. So long as there are states—even proletarian states—the classless society remains to be achieved.

The schedule for its ultimate achievement cannot be known in advance, even though the general path of economic development toward it is understood. Some communists have erred seriously here, supposing that the phases of dialectical development could be charted on a calendar and anticipated as virtual certainties. This is mistaken and dangerous. Our entire view of world history, scientifically grounded, is thrown into doubt by speculative predictions very likely to miss the mark. Thoughtful communists will carefully avoid this pretension. We cannot say that at a given date one phase of the revolution will end, the next begin. We cannot say that by a given date the classless society will have been achieved. We are not political crackpots claiming powers of clairvoyance. Dialectical materialism is a science, whose results have been confirmed repeatedly, and whose study discloses the true laws of social development, giving solid grounds for general predictions about the direction of world history. We disavow those misguided zealots who claim to know what even the dialectic does not claim to reveal.

31.   The Abolition of Private Property

Much can be said about the future, however, though we do so with language that is unavoidably imprecise. We speak mainly about the first stages of a process that will have many stages. We also predict in general terms important long-term changes whose specific character cannot be described in detail. How these developments will transpire no one can confidently say. Great transformations, scientific and social, are in store. Each phase of history must develop its own institutions; the shapes and rules of the institutions of the classless society are necessarily hidden from the eyes of those who come before. Because we cannot foresee their shape, however, we must not suppose that they cannot be. The mills of the dialectic grind out ever new and surprising meal. Capitalists say that things must always be essentially as they have been, that there will always be rich and poor, exploitation and war. We are confident, on rational grounds, that this is not so. They are fools who say, in effect, "History has yielded much that is new and different—but it stops now." History does not stop. Nor need we (as Marx said in criticism of Hegel) see always its posterior only. We can discern the course, planning for the next great phase of human history.

A world without classes becomes possible when economic exploitation ends. Economic exploitation—the purchase of human labor as a commodity, and all that that entails—will end when the *social* character of human production is matched by a *social* system of appropriation. The fundamental contradiction of capitalism, as we have seen, is the clash between the way things are produced (cooperatively, intelligently) and the way things are distributed (anarchically, through a private market). The classless society will arise when these chaotic modes of appropriation have been eliminated—when, in a phrase, private property has been abolished. The abolition of private property is the threshold of the classless society.

We speak here of productive property, not the intimate possessions of daily life. No one will be deprived of his private effects. Those who suggest that toothbrushes and underwear must be shared under ideal communism are either stupid or scurrilous. Many things in the world are designed and suited only for the use of particular persons and can have—even in a fully communitarian world—no other status than that of private chattel.

Indeed, it is the bourgeois society that fails to meet even the most fundamental personal needs of many citizens—because satisfying those needs depends upon the power to purchase. Those who fail in the market economy may choose between seeking charity and doing without. But where appropriation is social, there can be no such destitution, no humiliating charity. One day we will all look back upon the cruelties of the capitalist world, puzzled that human beings could ever treat one another so heartlessly, ignore one another's sufferings so callously. Clothing, shelter, food should not be things people have merely opportunity to buy! Every human being—in a decent society—has a *right to them,* to their full enjoyment.

Capitalists give lip service to human dignity. But only a system that guarantees material well-being to every member respects that dignity in practice. The total wealth of the world is more than adequate to secure this guarantee, if distribution is just. The abolition of private property is the essential first step

in making distribution just. It will signal the end of those long
and dismal chapters of history during which the masses of
humankind could not know, from one year or one day to the next,
where their bread would come from. Communal control over all
productive wealth can insure the fair distribution of all goods on
the simplest principle: to each according to his needs.

Much of the wealth of the world will have to be redistributed;
present arrangements are grossly lopsided. But only those who
control production, who make profits at the expense of others,
need fear the abolition of private property. Their personal guilt
does not interest us; they are merely struggling to survive in a
competitive system, and we have no intention of punishing them.
On the contrary, when the systematic causes of mal-distribution
have been corrected, they will join us in brotherhood. The expro-
priators will be expropriated, as Marx wrote, but not vindictively.
The abolition of private property is not a punishment; it is the
foundation of social justice.

What will be expropriated? *Productive* property. What will be
abolished? The *private ownership* of production. It is an abomina-
tion when *land,* the ultimate source of material resources, is
owned by private persons to the exclusion of others, and the food
grown upon it is the private property of the landowner, no matter
who starves. It is wrong for *factories* to be privately owned, the
goods they produce to be the property of the owners, when those
goods are made cooperatively by workers whose labor has been
bought. We will abolish this private control of the productive
forces upon which life on a crowded planet depends. Precious
personal privacy we will respect and enhance. The private is the
exclusive; to specify private right is to delineate the spheres into
which none may intrude. There are such spheres, but production
is not among them. The social reality of modern production, the
planning and teamwork it entails, prove that it is not. Privacy in
its ownership is out of place, the vestige of an archaic and outmoded system.

The stock market will be done away with. No one will buy or
sell "shares" of "industrial securities." Capitalist shareholders
who feast luxuriously on the dividends of productive industry are
living proof of their own uselessness. They *do* nothing. Their
"ownership" is nothing but parasitism. The profits on which they
thrive are simply the product of the labor of others, labor in

which they do not share, and of whose pains they are totally ignorant. The pumping heart of the capitalist system will thus be cut out.

Who will then invest, and by investment make jobs, etc.? As if we need financiers to produce the real wealth of the world! Industrial growth, plant maintenance, planning, and transport— all will come then, as it comes now, from the physical and intellectual labor of working men and women. The organization of that work, and the distribution of the goods and services produced by it, require neither capitalists nor capital.

Capital, as the accumulation of the rewards of labor stored in gold blocks or bank accounts, can by an act of public will be forever eliminated. It is the manifestation of a deeply-rooted bourgeois frame of mind. We aim to uproot that way of seeing the world and of thinking about production. We aim to bring all mankind a new vision of how wealth comes to be, and what it is. By thus going to the very root of the matter, ours is a profoundly *radical* revolution.

32.   Vulgar Communism

Many schemes for collective ownership, proposed in the name of Marxism or socialism, are not radical at all. Their authors have not understood the truly revolutionary nature of the transformation in store. Learning that we intend to abolish the private ownership of property, some—both friends and enemies— have supposed that it will be replaced by the *joint ownership* of factories and land. Their error is that of generalizing the existing capitalist relations between people and things. Now a few persons privately own and enjoy; then (in the view of crude communists) everyone will own and enjoy. It is reasonable within a capitalist system to seek to extend the benefits of ownership—but our ultimate aim is to eliminate the relation of *ownership* itself.

So pervasive is the spirit of exploitation now that even decent people imagine no other relation to their material environment than possession. Goods are to be acquired, accumulated. Not only the forces of production but nature itself, lakes and forests, are bought and sold. Reformers with limited vision can imagine nothing better to replace ownership by a few than ownership by many.

Thus capitalism stupefies us. Through bourgeois acquisition we seek to reunite ourselves with a material environment from which our own institutions have alienated us. So blinded are we by the drive to *have* things, that we fail to dream of a social order in which nothing is had, nor needs to be had, but all is enjoyed by all, and incorporated into our active lives.

When Europeans first came to the new world, they immediately "staked their claims"—marked off the land for ownership, proclaimed possession. Native Americans were mystified. How can rivers and meadows be yours and not mine, theirs and not ours? The physical world upon which life depends is a great ecosystem that knows no artificial property divisions. Our material environment, natural and man-made, is our larger body, for all to use and enjoy. It is, for a short time, in our custody. By whatever is holy, the notion that parts of it can be treated like a capital investment is sacrilege.

The disease of ownership spreads from productive things to productive persons. Slavery is a natural extension of capitalist doctrine unfettered by principles of moderation. Slaves are property. In other forms as well, less blatant but more pervasive, humans are still treated like property. Marriage in bourgeois society has long supposed the virtual ownership of the wife by the husband. The payment of the dowery was made upon the signing of the wedding contract. And how does it happen, Marx asked, that bourgeois critics still complain that communism will introduce "the community of women"—the sexual use of women by men in common? Nothing has been further from our minds than organized debauchery, yet that is assumed to be our aim! Why? Because the capitalist critic begins with the tacit assumption that women are property. Hearing that we intend to collectivize property, he assumes, crudely but under that assumption naturally, that women too will be collectivized. This common criticism of communism reveals the underlying bourgeois attitude toward women—that they are commodities like all the rest of the world's goods, to be acquired, exchanged, and shared.

This crude collectivization of property Marx called *vulgar* communism, to distinguish it from the genuine kind. Vulgar communism is the program of Western "socialist" parties, only superficially appealing. It laments inequality, but its proposed remedy levels all downward, rather than raising all to a new material standard. It criticizes private capitalism, yet it proposes to institute what amounts to state capitalism. Its nationalization of industries and farms does no more than substitute the state for private owners, government for private bureaucracies. Vulgar Marxists, by presenting a state-oriented ideal, hinder rather than advance the coming of the classless society.

In a truly cooperative framework there is virtually no limit to human achievements and aspirations. In a capitalist framework, further corrupted by the concentration of all economic power in the hands of the state, the evils of private ownership are intensified. Under "socialist" leaders with totalitarian authority and half-baked understanding, crude communism may be the very worst of political systems, combining an exploitative frame of mind with irresistable force and universal scope.

Enemies of dialectical materialism often deliberately depict us as crude communists in order to frighten the masses. Others tilt their lances at the monsters of vulgar communism out of honest ignorance. But between vulgar communism and the genuine Marxist ideal lies all the difference in the world.

33.   Material Abundance

It is fitting to conclude this account of communism by noting three features that will characterize the new communist society.

First, *material abundance.* In a world rationally governed, and scientifically advanced beyond the dreams of the twentieth century, there will be enough of everything for everyone. Those stifled by the bourgeois frame of mind think this claim "utopian." They cannot envision a world without acquisitiveness and greed. People will forever compete for their livelihoods in a dog-eat-dog world, they say. But humans are not dogs. We have a potential for goodness and grace that is beyond the grasp of bourgeois cynicism. Greed is the psychological corollary of a system in which success depends upon accumulation. Capitalism thrives upon insecurity and fear, enforcing the imperative to acquire. So long as production and distribution are based on the sale of human labor, decent human beings will be obliged to struggle against one another, the winners climbing upon the losers' backs.

It need not be so. It is well within the power of humankind to change completely our ways of dealing with the material world, and by so doing to put an end forever to the extremes of wealth and poverty. It is within our power—not on some future day, but *right now,* yesterday, last year—to end all starvation and the abject miseries of extreme want. A just distribution of the world's present resources and current production would result in moderate well-being for all. The claim that "the poor will always be with us" is either a ghastly misunderstanding or a cruel deception, readily exposed when the entire economic system is revolutionized.

Given only the existing wealth of the world this is true. When the incredible waste of war and military production ends, as it must when states are no more, the usable wealth of the world will be far greater than it now is. When workers and peasants no longer need to protect themselves against insecurity in old age by having many children, and birth-control technology becomes universally available, birthrates will drop sharply, as they have already in the rich nations. Global population will stabilize; humanity will for the first time be able to plan for the nourishment and housing of a known human population.

All this, given only what we know now. Soon we will know vastly more. Technological powers grow speedily, and the *rate* of that growth grows even faster. Scientific materialism reinforces respect for the role of basic scientific research in improving man's condition. The real wonders of physics, biology, and high-powered computerization are just opening to us. The exploration of the oceans and of space has barely begun. With knowledge and tools not yet dreamt of, we humans will produce actual wealth—in usable goods and services, not capital!—many times greater than that now produced. Not very long from now, we will look back upon these years of the late twentieth century as an economically crude epoch during which a primitive humankind scratched out a living from an abused environment.

Humanity is destined to create, through communal effort, a world of genuine plenty, in which material goods of every kind are available to satisfy the healthy desires of every human being.

"To each according to his needs" will then be not at all utopian
—but the minimal requirement of fairness.

34. Self-Realization

Second, *human realization.* In the world revolutionized, all human
beings, for the first time, will have the opportunity to bring their
creative capacities to fruit. The spiritual and psychological satisfactions of genuine communism will be even more treasured than
its material benefits.

Human *alienation,* inherent in the capitalist system, is nothing mysterious. To be alien is to be foreign, estranged, separated
as most people are now, even in their own city and their own work
place, from what is properly their own. We saw earlier that workers are alienated from the *process* of their work, which becomes
tedious, frustrating, and mechanical. They are alienated also
from the *products* of their work, which, however useful or intricate, belong not to them but to others—their employers. All are
alienated from their *fellow human beings* with whom they are forced
to compete for wages and for the opportunity to prostitute themselves successfully. Unemployment is the lever wedged between
working comrades who must scrabble for their livelihoods.

Above all, workers under capitalism, whether artisans or
clerks, physicians or laborers, salaried managers or farmers, are
alienated from *themselves,* from their own essence as creative human beings. Man as maker, *homo faber,* is the most beautiful
realization of our species. The richest of human experiences, the
sweetest of its satisfactions, come in work. We esteem ourselves
most as persons with creative potential, with developed skills or
native talents. Human strength lies chiefly in what we can do,
make, accomplish. By forcing the sale and purchase of these
capacities, capitalism alienates us all from the essence of our
species.

Communism will eliminate all these forms of dehumanizing
alienation. In a world rationally organized, no pleasures will be
greater or more enduring than those of work. The place of work
will no longer be a prison from which the five o'clock whistle

signals escape, but a field for achievement and growth. The very contrast between work and play will lose its meaning—and good riddance! Why should the application of our productive energies be anything less than joyful? Why should the exploration of all the possibilities of our making and contributing be anything less than a satisfaction and an enlargement of ourselves?

"But if there is no paycheck to buy our labor," the critic asks, "what incentive will there be for us to work? If we all get what we need whether we work or not, why should we work at all?" That question reveals the bourgeois frame of mind, in which work is despised. A society in which pleasure comes only with release from effort is surely sick. Common experience confirms that sickness. Although we may for a short while enjoy the rest of sheer idleness, everyone soon realizes that true pleasures are those flowing from some creative, self-enlarging activity. In home workshops we make or repair, not to sell but to use. In sports we strive to better the performance of our team and our selves—not for salaries but because achievement is fun and satisfying. We read, travel, build, collect—doing happily what the nature of our species impels. Now we do all this only at the margins of our lives, while their centers are often dull and sometimes hateful. The communist revolution will transform these pleasures of creativity from honey on the bread of affliction into the hearty meal and substance of our lives.

We will work—and not for pay!—because when production is humanely organized and undertaken for purposes we choose for ourselves, we will enjoy the activities themselves. We will take pleasure in work—as a few fortunate people do even today—and choose no other way to spend the greater part of our time. It is not the stick of human want that will then beat men into creativity, but the carrot of self-realization that will entice them. We will find ourselves in our work, and resent those who keep us from making our contributions as we now resent those who keep us from our rest.

The forms work will then take cannot now be precisely described. But alienation arising out of the capitalist system will surely be no more. Universal material prosperity will make competition for livelihood needless, ending the alienation of workers from each other; the abolition of private ownership will erase the alienation between worker and product; halting the sale of labor will eliminate alienation between worker and work place. And finally, the encouragement of each member's unique contribution to society will overcome the alienation of humans from themselves.

We will produce and contribute because, loving one another, no cooperative activity will please us more. Not because of threat, but by nature and from our hearts, we will affirm: from each according to his ability.

35. Self-Government

Third, *cooperative self-government.* Who will govern us when classes are no more? No one. We will govern ourselves. The critic's condescending alarm flows only from ignorance.

Will communist society in its highest stages be democratic? Yes, if democracy means genuine self-rule and the absence of forced obedience to others. But if by democracy is meant a form of state organization with elected legislatures, police, and the like, the classless society will have none of it. Such institutions parade as the instruments of self-government while in fact they are the instruments of repression disguised. The bourgeois mind finds it hard to grasp our straightforward assertion: *We will have no state.* Not a state organized this way or that, with these trappings or those, but no state at all! States, as we have explained, are the political instruments of particular economic classes. Their reason for being is the repression of one economic class by another. When classes are no more, states will be no more. Then and only then will self-government become a reality, and not just a slogan.

"Then you are anarchists!" our critic cries. "But everyone knows that anarchy is totally impractical. Its history shows, furthermore that its advocates are often unscrupulous and violent." We are accused of advancing an unworkable, utopian ideal—and then told that it isn't really humane but vicious!

If anarchy seeks the ultimate elimination of the state, we are anarchists, of course, proudly. But the picture commonly conjured up by that name—infuriated leaders and unthinking crowds destroying all in their path—is very far from our intention. Some who have called themselves anarchists have been violent and irresponsible, regrettably, but that has nothing to do with us. They are not Marxists, as their conduct proves. Blind efforts to destroy the state immediately, without regard for historical process, are futile. Marxism is a rational system if it is anything at all; our aim is peaceful and productive *order*. The promotion of disorder is indeed irresponsible, and it certainly is not our purpose.

But human affairs *can* be conducted without the restrictive supervision of states as we now know them. The state as the monopolist of violence, the user of armies and prisons and police, is an institution decent human beings can live very well without. The anarchy we envisage is not a pipe dream. Vastly differing kinds of political organization have been experienced by humanity, each the natural reflection of the economic order of its time. When city-states were universal, great empires seemed no more than pipe dreams. When great empires were the natural order, secular nation-states seemed no more than pipe dreams. When states were monarchies, republicanism was a terror; when states became republics, monarchy was a horror. Secular nation-states have long been the reflection of a capitalist economy. But this too will pass. Small minds, without vision or dialectical understanding, cry "pipe dream" whenever great change is contemplated. Even as transformation begins, they continue to deride it—until they are swallowed by it.

Everyone has experienced fair and rational organization while doing day-to-day business. We do not need regulation imposed upon us from above. When we are wholesomely motivated and have reasonable confidence in our fellows, we do not need protection from one another. We do not normally fight one another. When material support is adequate and the spirit of the group is healthy, we are all anarchists—delighted and tranquil anarchists. To call for repressive force in such circumstances would be paranoid. We resort to that call only when conditions are so threatening as to require arms for self-protection. Repressive organizing forces are necessary in some unhappy circumstances, to be sure, but not in all.

Imagine present circumstances profoundly changed. Imagine the production and distribution of all goods and services so arranged as to eliminate the alienation described earlier and to assure material property for all. Would aggressive armies be needed then? Imagine human beings developing from childhood to maturity in a spirit of cooperative endeavor. Imagine all adults practicing their conviction that their own satisfactions come from contributing to the common weal, helping others, and building for all. Imagine that all receive what they need and never dream of getting rich by buying cheap and selling dear. Imagine a community of healthy people seeking, above all, opportunities for themselves, their children, and their fellow humans to realize better their own potentialities. Will police and prisons be needed then?

We think human character is strong enough, and flexible enough, and, yes, good enough (though admittedly not saintly) to give rise to new generations not motivated by greed or the lust for power. There will be flaws and frictions, surely. Mankind must organize, plan, relate reciprocally in effective ways. Of course goods must be manufactured efficiently and distributed fairly. Decisions will have to be made to act, in concert, for this end or for that. There will be rules, naturally arising out of common concerns and lubricating common activities. There will be order —certainly! But, dialectical conflict having shifted from the clash of classes to tensions between humanity and the system of nature itself, the order of the globe will be more profound than any we now know. That rational order need not be, will not be, imposed. The day of rulers exercising power over us will have passed. The eagles and the lions of nation-states will be no more than painful reminders of an earlier, primitive time. Order will be international—or, to be more accurate, planetary; perhaps it will even be galactic. Its symbols will be the tools of those who work with and for one another—the sickle of the farmer, and the hammer of the builder.

With the overthrow of the capitalist system already under way, the end of the bourgeois state is not far off. Over the decades that follow its replacement, as we grow into the forms of the new communist order, the socialist states that serve as transitional repositories of the people's power will also wither away. In the highest stages of communist society, when at last human society has been fully revolutionized, there will be no need for *archos,* for rule. Then we will enjoy a true and productive *an-archy,* the absence of all law imposed from without. Fully developed humankind, having at last understood and applied the principles of dialectical transformation, will govern itself.

Readings

(Other defenses of communism, chronologically arranged)

Nineteenth Century

Date of Origin

(1844)   **Karl Marx,** *Economic and Philosophic Manuscripts.* Edited by Dirk J. Stenik, Translated by Martin Milligan. New York: International Publishing, 1844.

(1848)   **Karl Marx and Friedrich Engels,** *Manifesto of the Communist Party.* San Francisco: China Books and Periodicals, 1964.

(1865)   **Karl Marx,** *Value, Price and Profit.* Edited by Eleanor Aveling, Translated by Edward Aveling. Chicago: C. H. Kerr, 1865.

(1882)   **Friedrich Engels,** *Dialectics of Nature.* New York: International Publishers, 1940.

(1884)   **Friederich Engels,** *The Origin of the Family, Private Property and the State.* New York: International Publishers, 1972.

(1887)   **Karl Marx,** *Capital,* volume 1. New York: Modern Library, 1936.

(1898)   **Georgi V. Plekhanov,** *The Role of the Individual in History.* London: Lawrence & Wishart, 1950.

(1899)   **Ferdinand Lassalle,** *The Workingman's Programme.* Translated by W. H. Babbit. In *German Classics of the 19th & 20th Centuries,* vol. 10, New York: AMS Press, 1914.

(1899)   **Eduard Bernstein,** *Evolutionary Socialism.* New York: Schoken Books, 1961.

Twentieth Century, before World War II

(1914)   **Vladimir I. Lenin,** *The Teachings of Karl Marx.* New York: International Publishers, 1964.

(1916)   **Vladimir I. Lenin,** *Imperialism: The Highest Stage of Capitalism.* New York: International Publishers, 1969.

(1917)   **Vladimir I. Lenin,** *State and Revolution.* New York: International Publishers, 1932.

(1928)   *The Programme of the Communist International.* New York: Workers Library, 1936.

(1929)   **Leon Trotsky,** *The Permanent Revolution.* New York: Path Press, 1969.

(1935)   **Rosa Luxemburg,** *Leninism or Marxism,* in *Russian Revolution & Leninism or Marxism.* Ann Arbor, Mich.: University of Michigan Press, 1961.

(1936)   **Thomas A. Jackson,** *Dialectics: The Logic of Marxism.* New York: Burt Franklin, 1971.

(1938)   **J. B. S. Haldane,** *The Marxist Philosophy and the Sciences.* New York: Arno Press, 1939.

(1940)   **Joseph Stalin,** *Dialectical and Historical Materialism.* New York: International Publishers, 1940.

Twentieth Century, after World War II

(1945)   **Vernon Venable,** *Human Nature: The Marxian View.* Magnolia, Mass.: Peter Smith, 1945.

(1949)   **Mao Tse-tung,** *On People's Democratic Dictatorship.* New Haven, Conn.: Far Eastern Publications, 1949.

(1952)   **John D. Bernal,** *Marx and Science.* London: Lawrence and Wishart, 1952.

(1952)   **Mao Tse-tung,** *On Contradiction.* Peking: Foreign Languages Press, 1953.

(1952)   **Mao Tse-tung,** *On Practice: On the Relation between Knowing and Doing.* Peking: Foreign Languages Press, 1953.

(1965)   **Ernesto (Che) Guevara,** *Socialism and Man.* New York: Path Press, 1965.

(1966)   **Paul A. Baran and Paul M. Sweezy,** *Monopoly Capital.* New York: Monthly Review Press, 1968.

(1967)   **Gajo Petrovic,** *Marx in the Mid-Twentieth Century.* Garden City, N. Y.: Anchor Books, 1967.

(1969)   **Leszek Kolakowski,** *Marxism and Beyond: On Historical Understanding and Individual Responsibility.* London: Pall Mall Press, 1969.

(1969)   **Herbert Marcuse,** *An Essay on Liberation.* Boston: Beacon Press, 1969.

(1970)   **Jurgen Habermas,** *Toward a Rational Society: Student Protest, Science and Politics.* Boston: Beacon Press, 1971.

(1974)   **Mihailo Markovic,** *From Affluence to Praxis.* Ann Arbor, Mich.: University of Michigan Press, 1974.

(1975)   **Dick Roberts,** *Capitalism in Crisis.* New York: Path Press, 1975.

INDEX

(P in front of page numbers stands for Preface)

gold, men of, 125
Golf Links, The, 203
grades, 146
Great Britain (*see also* England),
6, 10, 16, 24, 93, 108, 156,
163, 205, 209
Greece, ancient (*see also*
philosophy, Greek), 147, 155,
175, 176, 180

happiness, 77, 78
Hartford, 210
Harvard University, 147
Hayek, Frederick, 104
health, 168
regulations, 42
Hegel, Georg, 130, 176–180,
184, 225
Heraclitus, 175, 176
heroism, 18, 165, 166
heterogeneity, 79–81
hierarchy, 25, 26, 64, 81, 108,
111, 112, 118–120, 151, 154,
156, 215
historical materialism, 183–185
history, 11, 131, 143, 154, 155,
158–163, 163, 167, 171–175,
177, 191, 193, 224, 226
dialectical, 177, 185, 220
dialectical laws of, 212
human, 181, 184, 185, 190,
193, 196
of democracy, 142
world, 180, 188
Hitler, Adolf, 134, 135, 215
Holland, 6, 209
Homo faber, 231
Homo sapiens, 120
homogeneity, 79–81
Hong Kong, 96
honors, 146
housing, 50
Hudson River, 46
human nature, 85

humanity, 148
humility, 166
hypocrisy, 86, 142

idealism, 184
ideals, P10, 118
ideology, 186, 211
idiots, 149
idolatry, 183
ignorance, 137, 143–147
illiteracy (*see also* literacy), 26, 76
immorality, 121, 160, 197, 216
imperialism, 172, 208–211, 219
increasing misery, law of,
205–207
India, 43, 209
individuality, 65
industry, 43–46, 186, 189
inefficiency, 100
inequality, 32, 47, 111, 120, 121,
126, 148, 150
of wealth, 140, 141
inequity, 16
inflation, 16, 47, 53, 54, 97, 127,
143, 201
injustice, 15, 25, 63
Inland Steel Corporation, 45
insane, the, 149
intelligence, 50, 121, 139
International Business Machines
Corporation, 204, 207
International Telephone and
Telegraph Corporation, 204
Internationalization, 209
investment, 83, 195, 196, 202,
204–206, 210, 227, 228
invisible hand, 39, 58, 90
Iran, 96
iron, men of, 125
irrationality, 17, 39, 135–139,
142, 147
Israel, 6, 96
Italy, 96, 135, 163, 165

ABOUT THE AUTHOR

Carl Cohen is a professor of philosophy at the Residential College of the University of Michigan. He is editor of *Communism, Fascism, and Democracy* and the author of *Civil Disobedience* and *Democracy.* He received his A.B. from the University of Miami (Fla.), his M.A. from the University of Illinois, and his Ph.D. from the University of California, Los Angeles.

Professor Cohen has served as Chairman of the Academic Senate of the University of Michigan, and as a member of the National Board of Directors of the American Civil Liberties Union. He has received a number of awards for outstanding teaching, and has held visiting appointments at the Hebrew University (Israel), the University of Otago (New Zealand), and the University of Illinois; he was Fulbright Lecturer at several Peruvian universities, and was Mellon Distinguished Visiting Professor at Davidson College, N.C. He has been consultant to Federal agencies and private foundations and hospitals, and lectures widely on the philosophical issues underlying contemporary conflicts.

Carl Cohen has been a frequent contributor to *The Nation,* as well as to *Commentary, Ethics,* and many law reviews and medical journals in which he has defended civil liberties and explored their foundations. His essays on freedom of speech, on privacy, on civil disobedience, and on affirmative action have provoked considerable controversy. In bioethics, his writings on human experimentation, on recombinant DNA technology, and on birth control have been much anthologized. Currently he is at work on a novel, is writing the Introduction to Volume XV of *The Middle Works* of John Dewey, and is preparing the third edition of *Communism, Fascism, and Democracy* (Random House).